READING PROBLEMS
Consultation and Remediation

The Guilford School Practitioner Series

EDITORS

STEPHEN N. ELLIOTT, Ph.D.
University of Wisconsin—Madison

JOSEPH C. WITT, Ph.D.
Louisiana State University, Baton Rouge

Academic Skills Problems: Direct Assessment and Intervention
EDWARD S. SHAPIRO

Curriculum-Based Measurement: Assessing Special Children
MARK R. SHINN (Ed.)

Suicide Intervention in the Schools
SCOTT POLAND

Problems in Written Expression: Assessment and Remediation
SHARON BRADLEY-JOHNSON and JUDI LUCAS-LESIAK

Individual and Group Counseling in Schools
STEWART EHLY and RICHARD DUSTIN

School-Home Notes: Promoting Children's Classroom Success
MARY LOU KELLEY

Childhood Depression: School-Based Intervention
KEVIN D. STARK

Assessment for Early Intervention: Best Practices for Professionals
STEPHEN J. BAGNATO and JOHN T. NEISWORTH

The Clinical Child Interview
JAN N. HUGHES and DAVID B. BAKER

Working with Families in Crisis: School-Based Intervention
WILLIAM STEELE and MELVIN RAIDER

Practitioner's Guide to Dynamic Assessment
CAROL S. LIDZ

Reading Problems: Consultation and Remediation
P. G. AARON and R. MALATESHA JOSHI

Crisis Intervention in the Schools
GAYLE D. PITCHER and A. SCOTT POLAND

READING PROBLEMS
Consultation and Remediation

P. G. AARON
Indiana State University

R. MALATESHA JOSHI
Oklahoma State University

THE GUILFORD PRESS
New York   London

© 1992 The Guilford Press
A Division of Guilford Publications, Inc.
72 Spring Street, New York, NY 10012

Printed in the United States of America

This book is printed on acid-free paper.

Last digit is print number: 9   8   7   6   5   4   3   2   1

Library of Congress Cataloging-in-Publication Data

Aaron, P. G.
    Reading problems : consultation and remediation / P. G. Aaron,
R. Malatesha Joshi.
        p.   cm. — (The Guilford school practitioner series)
    Includes bibliographical references and index.
    ISBN 0-89862-365-0   ISBN 0-89862-244-1 (pbk.)
    1. Reading disability.   2. Reading—United States—Remedial
teaching—Aids and devices.   3. Reading, Psychology of.   I. Joshi,
R. Malatesha.   II. Title.   III. Series.
LB1050.5.A19   1992
372.4'3—dc20   92-3124
                                                                       CIP

Preface

Imagine your advice being sought by the parents of a 6-year-old boy regarding their son's promotion to the first grade. The boy's kindergarten teacher thinks that he is not quite ready for the first grade because he does not even know the alphabet. The parents disagree with the teacher; they think he is a bright boy and expect him to do well in the first grade. Traditional assessment procedures may not be of much help in decision making because the situation is complicated by two facts: the boy has not been exposed to formal reading instruction, which excludes the use of reading tests; he could, as the parents think, be quite intelligent but still have reading disability, which could diminish the value of administering an IQ test.

Consider another situation. A school corporation seeks your assistance in identifying those children in their schools who have reading disabilities. IQ test scores cannot be used for this purpose because the State has mandated that IQ tests should not be employed in making decisions regarding placement of children in special classes.

These are but two examples of dilemmas the school psychologist and reading specialist face in the course of their professional practice. At first sight, these problems might appear to be formidable and beyond resolution. Fortunately, they are not. Research in the psychology of reading and reading instruction is sufficiently advanced that these questions can be answered with a reasonable degree of objectivity. This book is intended to bring together information available on the psychology of reading, reading disabilities, and instructional practices and to enable the school psychology consultant and reading specialist to resolve problems like those discussed above.

This book is written for the school psychologist and the reading specialist from a consultation perspective. The current trend in school psychology practice is to move away from an exclusive emphasis on testing to that of consulting. The techniques that have been developed in school psychology consultation originate from a mental health perspective. These principles and techniques have to be adapted when they are applied to reading instruction and reading disabilities. Basic principles of consultation as they are applied to these aspects of reading are presented in Chapter 1.

There is a noticeable gulf between the educational backgrounds of the school psychologist and the classroom teacher. This often results in divergent perspectives about educational problems and their solutions. With a view toward narrowing this gap and aligning the two perspectives, a brief history of reading instruction in the United States is presented in Chapter 2. This information will also help the consultant evaluate the historical significance of educational fads which, from time to time, attain wide but fleeting popularity.

To be valid and reliable, consultation practices should be founded on scientific knowledge. The psychology of the reading process, reading instruction, and the nature of reading disabilities are discussed from a scientific perspective in Chapter 3. The diagnostic procedure presented in Chapter 4 departs from the conventional method of assessment commonly practiced today. The advantage of the present approach is that it has been designed with instructional practices in mind.

Chapters 5 and 6 deal with intervention strategies. Instructional approaches and methods that can be used for improving word recognition skills and those for improving vocabulary and comprehension are presented separately. A cafeteria-style presentation of diverse but tested methods for reading remediation, along with detailed descriptions, is provided. In Chapter 7, we present a comprehensive discussion of the different ways minicomputers can be utilized as instructional aids; a brief survey of software programs designed to assist reading instruction is also provided.

The Appendices contain samples of informal tests that can be used in the assessment procedure, an evaluation of basal reader series published by several companies, as well as reviews of standardized reading tests. Appendix V also contains questions on dyslexia that parents and teachers usually ask and suggested responses.

This book has been reviewed by many experts in its manuscript stage. Their comments and suggestions have greatly enhanced the quality of the book and have broadened its scope. We are much indebted to them. We particularly wish to thank our colleagues at Indian State University: David Memory, reading educator and Associate Dean, School of Education; Bill Barratt, Professor, Department of Counseling; and Cathy Baker, Academic Coordinator. A special thanks to Stephen Elliott, the series editor, who made several useful recommendations, and to the editorial staff of The Guilford Press, for their perceptive suggestions, for catching the spelling and grammar glitches in the manuscript, and for finally putting it all together.

P. G. AARON
R. M. JOSHI

Foreword

Of all the possible difficulties one may experience in life, reading problems may be one of the most silent yet pervasive handicapping conditions in our society. Depending on various estimates of incidence, it may be projected with some confidence that at least one child in every classroom in the United States has significant problems in learning to read.

School psychologists increasingly are being asked to serve as learning consultants as they move away from their historical role as psychometrist toward that of an educational consultant. In the role as a consultant, the school psychologist not only needs to be aware of how one might identify these children but also needs to be familiar with traditional and emerging intervention procedures; whether or not these children may qualify for special services outside the classroom. In fact, recent trends suggest that direct intervention within a child's classroom setting is increasingly the norm as school psychologists work more closely with the classroom teacher in establishing, monitoring and validating successful intervention programs.

The authors of this book are eminently qualified to provide school psychologists with the most current and emerging perspectives on how to consult with teachers, parents, and other concerned educational specialists in identifying and establishing intervention programs for these children. Critical in the success of their efforts are excellent chapters covering not only the history of thought regarding reading disabilities but comprehensive chapters that focus on both the psychological processes involved in reading and how one identifies these children through formal and informal means.

Consistent with the consultative approach advocated by these authors, the main focus of this essential volume is on intervention practices that span the complex processes associated with reading. Unique to this volume, and in contrast to other more dated sources, are thorough discussions of the role and uses of computers in reading. Computer simulation, assisted and maintained instruction, and selected software are all discussed in considerable detail. Further, valuable appendices are found in this volume that provide relevant information on basal readers, reading tests, and tests of phonological awareness. Finally, the authors demonstrate their sensitivity to the many questions parents have about reading disabilities by providing a very useful question and answer guide to dyslexia, a term often used in describing reading disabled children but often misunderstood by professionals and parents alike.

Having authored a book on reading disabilities nearly a decade ago, I can attest that the authors of this book have done an exceptional job in integrating the many exciting advances that have occurred in the research literature over the past decade with a consultative approach to educational intervention. As a school psychologist, this is the one book I feel that I would need to guide me in more effectively working with teachers and parents in their efforts to enhance the probability of success of children who experience reading problems. This book is a superb contribution and will serve as an essential resource for school psychologists for many years to come.

GEORGE W. HYND
University of Georgia

Contents

1

Basic Principles of Psychological Consultation as Applied to Reading Problems

INTRODUCTION

Over the past 20 years or so, a slow but perceptible change has been taking place in the role of school psychologists, from providing only testing services to active participation in problem solving. Such problem-solving activity is undertaken in collaboration with school personnel and has come to be considered a form of consultation. The large number of articles published on consultation and the many books written on this topic within the last few years indicate that the practice of school psychology is moving in this direction rapidly. According to Gutkin & Curtis (1990), approximately 20% to 30% of the school psychologist's time is being spent in activities related to consultation. Many school psychologists not only perceive consultation to be an integral part of their professional responsibility but also prefer to redefine their primary function as consultation rather than assessment. For instance, a survey of 758 school psychologists by Meacham and Peckham (1978) found that school psychologists reported consultation to be their most

1

preferred role with assessment as a secondary responsibility. Smith and Lyon (1985) assessed the changes that took place between 1981 and 1984 and reported that there was a significant increase in both the actual amount of time spent in consultation and the amount of time desired for consultation.

The metamorphosis of the school psychologist from psychometrician to consultant, however, is neither total nor complete; some surveys show that many school psychologists still spend almost all their time in testing activities (Siegel & Cole, 1990). It is for this reason some authorities wish to emphasize the consultative role of the school psychologist and question the wisdom of utilizing the knowledge and skills of the school psychologist primarily for testing purposes. For example, in his book *School Psychology at a Turning Point,* Phillips (1990) poses this rhetorical question: "Will school psychology be an occupation that continues to play a role limited largely to assessment and determination of special education eligibility . . . or will school psychology become a speciality and profession that reaches for new roles, that raises the academic standards of training programs and the practical competence of its members?" (p. 252). The answer to this question is obvious; psychologists would prefer to be involved in educational decision making and be considered as problem solvers rather than mere diagnosticians.

The efforts to broaden the responsibilities of school psychologists and the actual events that have altered their role do not imply, however, that school psychologists should relinquish their psychometric obligations altogether. The need for psychometric data will persist in the field of education as long as teaching and learning strive to be scientific, and special education placement decisions mandated by legislative bodies are made on the basis of test data. But the future appears to move in a direction where standardized testing will play a diminished role and the consultative skills and knowledge of the school psychologist will be utilized in a progressively wider range of educational decision-making responsibilities. In view of the recent disenchantment with the value of standardized tests in remedial education, the transformation of the school psychologist from psychometrician to consultant, even though slow, is almost certain to occur.

To successfully fulfill their obligation as consultants, future school psychologists must possess two sets of skills: consultative skills and expert knowledge of the psychological principles of teaching and learning. This book represents an effort to bring together an understanding of the skills essential for successful educational consultation and a knowledge of the psychological principles that govern learning and instruction, with particular reference to reading.

BASIC PRINCIPLES OF PSYCHOLOGICAL CONSULTATION IN SCHOOLS

It is generally considered that Gerald Caplan is the pioneer who introduced the term *consultation* into the mental health field in 1970 and defined its parameters. As a psychiatrist, Caplan provided expert advice to classroom teachers who sought this service to enable them to deal with psychological problems seen in their students. Under such a circumstance, the consultant (i.e., the psychiatrist) helps clients (i.e., children) indirectly through the consultee (i.e., the teacher). Because of the indirect nature of service delivery, one consultant can treat several clients; the consultant's expertise is, therefore, more efficiently utilized than it would be if the psychiatrist were to treat one child at a time, directly. Because Caplan envisoned consultation as a system of mental health services delivery, he delineated the concept along psychodynamic lines. Since then, principles of behavioral psychology, organizational psychology, humanistic psychology, and educational psychology have been incorporated into consultation processes in an effort to solve a wide variety of psychological problems. Consequently, at present the term *consultation* describes problem-solving activities that utilize a variety of psychological procedures to address different types of problems in diverse settings. Broadening the scope of consultation has led to the emergence of different consultation models. As can be expected, these changes have made it difficult to define psychological consultation with precision.

Although models of psychological consultation differ from each other, they all share certain features because they have evolved from the mental health model and are patterned after it. According to Gutkin and Curtis (1990), models of consultation in the field of psychology include most of the following characteristics: the consultant–consultee relationship is collaborative and equal; service delivery to the client is indirect; the focus of consultation is the consultee rather than the client; the consultee has the right to reject the consultant's suggestions; the consultation process is initiated voluntarily by the consultee; the consultee is actively involved in the consultation process; the goals of consultation are remedial and preventive in nature; and the consultant–consultee communications are confidential.

A survey of the literature on psychological consultation by Dougherty (1990) showed that despite a lack of consensus in definitions of the different forms of consultation, some agreement could be discerned among them. Dougherty identified a set of characteristics which are common to all forms of psychological consultation; the following is a slightly modified version of his list:

1. Consultation is collaborative in that the consultant and the consultee both contribute toward the solution of the problem.
2. The relationship between the consultant and the consultee is one of equality.
3. The consultant provides indirect service to the client.
4. The consultee is under no obligation to implement the consultant's recommentations.
5. Either the consultee or the client may be given priority over the other at a given time.
6. A consultant can be either separate from or part of the system in which consultation occurs.
7. Participation in consultation is voluntary for all parties involved.
8. The consultant–consultee relationship is temporary.
9. Consultation is marked by three stages: entry, intervention, and termination.

DEFINITION OF SCHOOL CONSULTATION

In this section we present a few selected definitions of psychological consultation. It can be seen that with some minor modifications, these definitions apply to school consultation also.

Stressing its collaborative nature, Siegel and Cole (1990) define consultation as "a process through which psychologists and educators work coordinately to resolve educational problems from positions of mutual respect for one another as professionals" (p. 9). According to Idol, Whitcomb, and Nevin (1987), "Consultation is an interactive process that enables people with diverse expertise to generate creative solutions to mutually defined problems. The outcome is enhanced, altered, and produces solutions that are different from those that the individual team members would produce independently" (p. 1). Conoley and Conoley (1982) define consultation as "a voluntary, nonsupervisory relationship between professionals from differing fields established to aid one in his or her professional functioning" (p. 1). Brown, Pryzwansky, and Schulte (1987) have adopted a broader perspective and define consultation as a "voluntary problem-solving process that can be initiated and terminated by either the consultant or consultee . . . the goals of the process are twofold: enhancing services to third parties and improving the ability of consultees to function in areas of concern to them" (p. 8). After noting that there is no single definition which has gained universal support, Gutkin and Curtis (1990) adapted the one proposed by Medway (1979): "Consultation is a process of collaborative problem solving between a mental health specialist (the consultant), and one or more persons (the consultees) who are responsible for providing some form of psychological assistance to another (the client)" (p. 578). If the term "school psychologist" is substituted for the term "mental health specialist," this definition can be used to describe school consultation.

Because schools are complex organizations dealing with different types of problems, some flexibility must be allowed in applying these definitions to school consultation. For example, even though the classroom or special education teacher is often the consultee, a school principal, college professor, or parents could also be consultees. Similarly, even though the student with some problem is often the client, a school system can also be the client, for example, when the psychologist is consulted about setting up a computer-assisted instruction program; or a school board could become the client when it wishes to consult with the psychologist about implementing a remedial reading program. An institution of higher education is the client when it consults about setting up a learning skills program. Consultation in school psychology would, therefore, include all four patterns suggested by Caplan (1970), namely, client-centered case consultation, consultee-centered case consultation, program-centered administrative consultation, and consultee-centered administrative consultation. Also it is not always necessary that consultation occur between individuals from differing fields, as stated in some mental health consultation definitions. For instance, a school counselor with a counseling psychology background may consult with the school psychologist and, under such a condition, the consultee and the consultant may not be considered to be from "differing fields."

Notwithstanding the differences among these definitions, a core of characteristics can be extracted from them and used for defining school consultation. Such characteristics would include the following: consultation is collaborative in nature; it deals with professional problems and takes place among professionals; the relationship between the professionals is egalitarian; the consultant (i.e., school psychologist) may not always deliver services directly to the client (i.e., the student) but usually works through the consultee, who often happens to be the teacher.

Because consultation occurs under a variety of circumstances and involves diverse parties trying to solve different kinds of problems, it is unreasonable to expect that all these requirements would be fulfilled to the letter by all forms of school consultation. For instance, even though ideally consultation is expected to take place between professionals, one survey (Martin & Meyers, 1980) found that client-centered consultation predominates among school psychologists; less frequent is the consultee-centered form, and least common is organizational consultation. As will be seen later, instructional consultation, particularly in regard to reading instruction, remediation, and diagnosis, will necessitate that some of these requirements be relaxed.

BASIC PRINCIPLES OF CONSULTATION
IN READING

Consultation in reading shares with psychological consultation the core characteristics described below.

1. The focus of consultation is remedial or preventive when individual students are concerned; when the system is the client, setting up a new instructional program or the improvement of an existing program may often be the goal. Two examples of these two "systems of consultation" would be when the psychologist is consulted by a school wishing to install a computer-assisted program, and when the school psychologist's expertise is sought for modifying an existing reading readiness assessment program in the kindergarten.

2. When consultation involves individual students, the focus of consultation may be shifted to the client (i.e., student) even though the ultimate goal is to enable the teacher to acquire the diagnositc and remedial skills that can be subsequently applied to other students with reading problems. The communication between the consultant and the consultee has to be open and honest, and the ultimate objective should be one that is mutually shared. When reading improvement is the mutual goal of consultation, it aligns the consultee onto the side of the consultant; they become a single team with a common goal.

3. The consultee (i.e., the teacher) is involved actively in the consultation process. When the teacher perceives a program to be imposed by external agents, he or she may resist it. Factors such as perceived loss of status and incompetence regarding the technology of diagnosis and remediation of reading problems can also generate resistance on the part of the consultee. Additional factors responsible for resistance are anxiety produced by the perception of the consultant as a "supervisor," incongruence in the expected outcome of consultation between the consultant and the consultee, and reluctance on the part of the consultee to change the traditional ecology of the classroom structure (Piersal & Gutkin, 1983).

One way to avoid resistance is to keep in sight the collaborative nature of consultation. Teachers have special knowledge and skills, particularly in the area of reading instruction, which the school psychologist may not have. Teachers also have more information about the client on whose behalf the consultation process is initiated. Active utilization of the consultee's knowledge, skills, and information makes him/her an active partner in the consultation process. The consultant's enthusiastic acknowledgement of the teacher's contribution is one way to ensure such full participation.

4. The consultee has the right to accept and implement the consul-

tant's recommendations or to reject them. Forced compliance is rarely successful in any human endeavor, particularly with regard to educational practice. As Gutkin and Curtis (1990) state:

> Once the door to the classroom is closed, there is little that any of the educational specialists can do to insure the occurrence of any event that the teacher does not want to occur. . . . Attempting to force a consultee to accept a consultant's suggestions typically results in a situation where either the consultee refuses to act on the recommendations, or the recommendations are carried out by the consultee in such a way as to ensure their failure (p. 579).

5. The consultant should be in possession of expert knowledge even though the relationship between the consultant and the consultee is one of collaboration. Clearly, the psychologist must have expertise in the area of reading; otherwise, he/she would not be sought as a reading consultant in the first place. Because the most common role consultants take on is that of expert or technical advisor, the need for the consultant to have specialized knowledge is frequently stressed by authorities in the field of psychological consultation. Under such a circumstance, the consultee needs some knowledge, advice, or service that the consultant can provide. Hansen, Himes, and Meier (1990) note that when the consultant assumes the role of an active participant in the consultation process, decisions are made based on the consultant's expertise. Nevertheless, the primary responsibility of seeking solutions to problems rests with the consultee. Hansen et al., cite evidence to show that attribution of expertise to consultants is positively related to consultation outcome; however, they note that problems arise when too much emphasis is placed on the consultant as expert. Gutkin and Curtis (1990) observe that knowledge in content area does enhance the consultant's effectiveness and that expert status is critical for the school psychologist's credibility with parents and teachers. However, this does not mean that the psychologist should assume a domineering role and flaunt his/her expertise, disregarding the skills and knowledge brought by the teacher into the consulting situation. In this context, Gutkin and Curtis stress the need for maintaining a collaborative problem-solving approach during consultation. As Idol-Maestas, Nevin, and Paolucci-Whitcomb (1984) put it, "Parity is demonstrated as the mediator's skills and knowledge are blended with the different skills and knowledge that the consultant shares" (p. 9). The psychologist should recognize the fact that the teacher also possesses expertise and should actively utilize it in problem-solving efforts. Thus, the relationship between consultant and consultee is egalitarian even though consultation services in reading disability diagnosis and remedial instruction require the consultant to have specialized training and knowledge. (The objective of this book is to help the school psychologist to acquire that amount of expert knowledge in

the area of reading which may be necessary to make him/her an effective consultant. Several books deal with school psychology consultation procedures in detail; therefore, consultation techniques are not dealt with in great detail in this book.)

6. Consultation involves the *indirect* delivery of services to the client. From the outset it was believed that this feature would enable the mental health specialist to serve many clients simultaneously rather than assisting one at a time. Therefore, the skills of the specialist could be utilized more effectively than would be in the case of direct delivery of services. The involvement of three parties—the consultant, the consultee, and the client—is, therefore, considered a common characteristic of all forms of psychological consultation. Implied in the tripartite consultation model is the assumption that the consultant does not deal directly with the client but works through the consultee. Within the school psychology setting, these three parties, viz., the consultant, the consultee, and the client, often, but not always, correspond to the school psychologist, the classrom teacher, and the student, respectively. Occasionally, the consultee can be the school principal or a school board, and the client can be a group of teachers or a school system itself. There also are occasions when a parent is the consultee and the child, the client. Such situations are often likely to be encountered by psychologists in private practice. The tripartite format of service delivery can be contrasted with the dyadic format in which the psychologist deals directly with clients (for example, to test and counsel students). Under the traditional dyadic system the psychologist generally functions as a diagnostician and therapist, dealing directly with the client.

Can consultation in the area of reading disability strictly adhere to the expectation that the consultant deal only with the consultee and not with the client? Reynolds, Gutkin, Elliott, and Witt (1984) have addressed this question and concluded that effectiveness, cost, and acceptability are the three criteria to consider in answering this question. Brown et al. (1987) suggest that choosing between direct and indirect service delivery should depend upon which intervention will best meet clients' needs. As noted earlier, the trend within school psychology is to provide services through the indirect mode of delivery. While this may be possible under most circumstances, there are occasions when the psychologist may have to deal directly with the client. For example, while the consultant may help the special education teacher acquire skills needed for developing curriculum-based assessement instruments to diagnose reading disabilities, the learning problems of a particular student may require that his IQ be determined. As the only qualified professional available to administer intelligence tests, the psychologist would have to deal directly with that student. Furthermore, the psychologist may have to determine whether the reading disability is attributable to extrinsic factors, including family dynamics, or to cognitive factors intrinsic to the student. This would require that the psychologist interview both student and parents.

7. Participation in consultation should be entirely voluntary, but schools sometimes do not follow this policy. The school as a system shares many characteristics with other organizations and corporations. For example, there is a power structure in the school system, and the execution of power follows a hierarchical pattern. Consequently, the teacher may not always have absolute freedom in making decisions regarding educational matters. Often the school system has a policy requiring teachers to consult with the psychologist whenever they encounter children with reading problems. Pipes (1981) calls this "mandated consultation" and considers this approach to be less effective than when consultation is purely voluntary. As noted earlier, mandated consultation is thought to increase a consultee's resistance to a consultant's idea. Under such circumstance, the consultee becomes defensive and may associate the consultant with the authority, unable to see him/her as a collaborator. Since consultation in schools usually is mandated by state and federal agencies, the psychologist will have to make special efforts to establish rapport with the teacher and identify with the teacher as a collaborator rather than with the administration.

8. The relationship between the consultant and the consultee is temporary. This, of course, applies to school psychologists in private practice but may not be relevant to those in the employ of a school system or school corporation. When the school psychologist is on staff, he/she is likely to come in contact with the teachers repeatedly during the course of an academic year, and the professional relationship can extend into many years. An emerging trend is for schools to employ in-house psychologists, who are likely to have enduring relationships with consultees.

9. Consultation is marked by three stages: *entry, intervention,* and *termination.* The entry stage of consultation may be spread over several sessions, starting with informal encounters between the consultant and the consultee, and include formal interviews when problems are identified and a program of action is planned. Before getting into the professional aspects of consultation, it is highly desirable that the psychologist establish rapport with the consultee under informal circumstances. The informal encounter between the consultant and the consultee usually consists of one or two meetings during which time the problem is defined clearly and a mode of action planned. Witt and Elliott (1983) suggested that the interview be used as a means of achieving the following objectives:

- definition of the problem;
- identification of the problem, its nature, intensity, and duration;
- identification of the conditions under which problems occur;

- identification of the desired performance level;
- identification of the student's strengths;
- identification of the assessment procedures;
- identification of the consultee's likes and dislikes, and the method of teaching used;
- planning a collaborative mode of action; and
- planning a program for evaluating the outcome.

It is desirable that the reading consultant follow the basic principles that govern nondirective counseling transactions when obtaining information from the consultee during the interview. As Rosenfield (1987) put it, the consultant should not adopt an "inquisitional mode" in eliciting information from the consultee. The consultant should also encourage the consultee to ask questions. Because the interview is a two-way process, it offers an opportunity also for the consultee to appraise the consultant. The questions raised and other transactions carried out should, therefore, reflect the consultant's expertise in the area of reading, reading disabilities, and remedial instruction.

Implementing the planned reading program is the primary responsibility of the consultee even though the psychologist may, under certain circumstances, administer some tests to the student, conduct interviews with the student and parents, and even observe the student's behavior in the classroom.

Termination of consultation provides an opportunity to evaluate the success of the consultation process as well as the impact of the intervention program on the reading performance of the clients. Termination of the consultation program consists of assessing progress made by the client, an exit meeting between the consultant and the consultee, and completion of a written report by the consultant. The consultant's report differs from the traditional psychological report in that the consultation report contains not only information regarding the nature of the problem but also a description of the intervention plan, its effectiveness in enhancing the reading achievement of the client, and an overall evaluation of the consultation process.

MODELS OF CONSULTATION

Even though a majority of the characteristics presented above are shared by all forms of psychological consultations, the procedures adopted in implementing a preventive or remedial plan can differ according to the nature of the problem to be solved and the setting in which problem resolution is to be carried out. Thus, consultation can be sought for solving mental and physical health problems, behavioral problems, organizational problems, or academic problems; the procedure adopted to deal with these matters might be psychotherapeutic, behavioral, or educational; and the setting could be a mental health clinic, an educational institution, or a corporation. One way to impose a semblance of order upon the plethora of these variables is to view the consultation process in terms of three major dimensions: the consultant's target population, the goals of consultation, and treatment procedures to be established. The target population ideally would be the consultee (classroom teacher, teachers, administrators, or parents), or it could be the client, or an organization. The goals of consultation could be preventive, remedial, or organizational–developmental (Kratochwill, VanSomeren, & Sheridan, 1989). Treatment could involve mental health procedures (psychotherapies, including psychoanalysis and counseling); behavioral methods; ecological strategies such as adjustments in the social climate of the classroom, home, or the instructional environment (Jason, Ferone, & Anderegg, 1979); or instructional programs which match teaching techniques with instructional needs of clients (Rosenfield, 1987). This general picture of consultation procedure is also applicable to reading consultation and is shown in Fig. 1.1.

It should be noted that often it is not possible to delineate the three dimensions unambiguously, nor can clear-cut distinctions be drawn among the four treatment methods. Since consultants consider problem

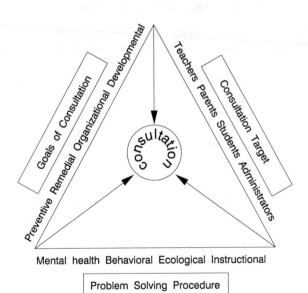

FIGURE 1.1. A three dimensional model of consultation.

resolution to be the most important goal, they are likely to adopt an ecclectic approach.

The diverse nature of problems and their respective treatments have resulted in the evolution of different models of consultation. Traditionally, psychological consultation has been concerned with emotional and behavioral problems, and utilized psychodynamic and behavioral principles to deal with them. Consultation based on these principles is placed within either the *mental health model* or the *behavioral model*, respectively. The *ecological model* is primarily concerned with the conditions and environment in which learning takes place. The *instructional model* was recently introduced to differentiate consultation for learning and instruction problems from that concerned with behavioral and emotional issues. The instructional model relies heavily on procedures adopted from cognitive psychology and information processing techniques for resolving educational problems. While it would appear that reading consultation could be placed in its entirety within the instructional model, strategies unique to the other three models can also be useful in dealing with problems related to reading improvement and reading disabilities.

In the following section, brief descriptions of the four models (the mental health, behavioral, ecological, and instructional models) as they relate to reading disabilities are presented.

The Mental Health Model

This model is concerned with the "delivery of psychological services in the schools that attempt to promote the mental health of children" (Meyers, 1981, p. 39). According to Alpert (1981), the goal of mental health consultation is to extend teacher knowledge about mental health and to provide skills in the prevention and remediation of related problems. Some authors (e.g., Brown et al., 1987) recognize two subcategories of the mental health model: client-centered and consultee-centered consultation. In client-centered consultation, the focus is on the client's problem even though the consultant's efforts to resolve the difficulty can be channelled through the consultee; in consultee-centered consultation, the consultee is helped to develop psychotherapeutic skills necessary to deal with a variety of mental health problems without reference to any particular client. These perspectives can be broadened to accommodate consultation in reading instruction to the extent difficulties in learning to read can be attributed to problems associated with the emotional health of the learner (or the teacher).

As noted earlier, consultation in psychology evolved from community mental health treatment programs. Caplan developed his definition of consultation with mental health services in mind. The consultation procedures that emerged from the mental health model were greatly influenced by psychodynamic concepts. Consultation envisaged within this model, therefore, addresses psychological problems from a psychoanalytic perspective and seeks to eradicate the cause of the problem at its source. Traditionally, such causes have included unconscious motives, intrapsychic conflicts, and excessive reliance on defense mechanisms. The scope of the model, however, can be considerably expanded beyond the traditional psychoanalytic boundaries by incorporating into the consultation process concepts such as teacher expectation, student expectation, self-concept, locus of control, learned helplessness, feelings of inferiority, and interpersonal conflict.

The Mental Health Model and Reading Disabilities

True to its name, the mental health consultation model is concerned mainly with the emotional well-being of the client; the reading problems of the student are only peripherally important and only to the extent their etiology can be attributed to unhealthy emotional conditions. Efforts to trace reading disability to emotional problems have a long history. Psychoanalytically inclined writers have attempted to explain reading disability in psychodynamic terms and attribute reading problems to inner conflicts arising from unhealthy parent–child relationships. For instance, Fenichel (1945) noted that neurotic difficulties in reading are usually due to oral–sadistic conflicts; Buxbaum (1964) considered learning difficulty to be due to a disturbed ego function arising from a partial symbiotic relationship between mother and child. Berger and Kennedy (1975) proposed that children who are overprotected tend to retain a status of dependency and infantilism and consequently fail to make progress in acquiring skills needed for independent reading. These authors reported that children who fail to do well at school have mothers who have a striking need to denigrate their children and to keep their offspring in a state of ignorance. These children appear to adapt to their mothers' perceptions of them in order to ensure and preserve the interpersonal relationship.

Bettelheim and Zelan (1982) have addressed the problem of reading difficulty in children from a purely psychoanalytic perspective and claim that "careful attention to the unconscious processes at work in these [reading disabled] children and application of therapeutic and educational methods based on psychoanalytic thinking permitted practically all of them to overcome the severe handicaps from which they had suffered" (p. vii). More specifically, these authors claim that some children may actively resist learning to read because of anxiety stemming from inner conflicts. These authors have addressed two observable behaviors in children with reading difficulties and offered a psychoanalytic interpretation of these behaviors. These are errors of mis-reading and errors of reversals in oral reading. According to Bettelheim and Zelan, misreadings result primarily from the impact of quite specific unconscious or preconscious processes. To that extent, misreadings are subjectively meaningful and often serve important purposes in respect to inner psychic processes, of which they are an expression. Further, misreading often signals a reader's conflict between his conscious at-tempt to read what is printed and a subconscious need to give a different word as response. For instance, a child who reads *Tigger* as "tiger" is caught up in a conflict between the fear of a tiger and a desire to suppress that fear; this conflict interferes with accurate reading. Sim-ilarly, the boy who reads the word *detective* as "defective" is caught in a conflict between the desire to read the word correctly and an un-conscious feeling of boredom caused by insipid books he had to read in the classroom. Reading aloud *lemon* as "melon" might be due to the child's dislike for the sour taste of lemon and a liking for the sweetness of the melon; and the child "struggling to separate past and present . . . [expresses] this desire by reading *saw* as *was*" (p. 183). Accord-ing to these writers, such errors should be treated with sympathy, or be-nign neglect, and the teacher should look for the inner meanings these errors imply.

In the current climate of scientific psychology, some of these claims would appear to be farfetched and excessively speculative because these explanations can neither be proved nor disproved, thereby excluding them from the body of science. Explanations about the etiology of reading errors and the nature of reversals from the perspective of cognitive psychology are more readily acceptable to science and are presented later in this book.

Even though the reading disability consultant may not find psy-choanalytic concepts very palatable, he/she cannot avoid considering family dynamics and emotional and interpersonal factors as potential contributors to reading difficulties. Admitting that attempts to identify the relationship between reading disability and emotional problems had not been very successful, Harris and Sipay (1990) propose several psy-chological factors that may be associated with reading disabilities. These include hostility, inappropriate identification, anxiety, depression, and excessive reliance on defense mechanisms.

According to Harris and Sipay, the child who identifies reading with the teacher or parent toward whom he/she feels intense hostility may transfer this hostility toward reading. This is more likely to occur when the teacher and child come from different ethnic or social backgrounds. A child with a sibling who is an avid reader and is praised by the parents overtly for such an accomplishment may associate reading with the sibling, develop rivalry and, therefore, reject reading altogether. A child who identifies himself with a parent who expresses contempt for book learning also is likely to model after such a parent. This phenomenon, widely recognized as an important determinant of children's reading skill, can also be explained in terms of social learning theory. While consulting with parents, the psychologist should be sensitive to the significance of family environment as a contributing factor to children's reading achievement and the importance of parents as role models. Undoubtedly, the atmosphere that prevails in the family has much impact on the way the child learns and behaves. For this reason, when the consultant suspects that the family atmosphere is the chief source of the learning problem, he/she may encourage the entire family to be involved in remedial efforts. Even if this is not always possible, the school psychologist should be aware of the fact that the progress of the child in learning to read involves the cooperative effort of the entire family and that the child cannot be successfully treated in isolation.

Singer and Pittman (1968) and Kaye (1982) consider a distorted social expectation to be one of the factors that contributes to the failure of some children learning to read. These authors believe that children who manifest reading dysfunction are more sensitive than children who become adequate readers to the hypocrisy of the society in that they perceive little relationship between educational achievement and economic attainment.

Psychologists who subscribe to the psychoanalytic view-point, as well as those who do not, have noted that excessive anxiety has a reciprocal effect on children's reading performance and can impede the normal reading processes by causing children to divide their attention between the reading task and their concern with how well they are reading (e.g., Willig, Harnisch, Hill, & Maehr, 1983; Wigfield & Asher, 1984). Poor readers must work hard to read correctly; errors committed during oral reading aggravate tension and anxiety, and this, in turn, can further disrupt the reading process. Because all attention is invested in reading correctly, these children fail to comprehend the text's meaning. Eventually, they avoid reading at all costs, and this results in poor readers falling even further behind. According to Willig et al. (1983), minority children from upwardly mobile families are more likely to show signs of anxiety than children who are trapped at the lower end of the socioeconomic spectrum.

If the child shows signs of anxiety and tension during reading, it may be suggested to the consultee (teacher) that the child not be pressed hard to read aloud in front of the class. Forcing a child to do so can irrevocably ruin his/her interest in reading. Even though reading disability and emotional disturbance have been reported to coexist in children, it is not easy to separate cause from effect (Bricklin & Gallicon, 1987). Information regarding family conditions and the child's educational history may be useful in reaching tentative conclusions as to which is the cause and which is the effect.

Understandably, children who are depressed will not be interested in reading, and prolonged depression can lead to a permanent state of reading retardation. Harris and Sipay (1990) suggest that a diagnosis of depression requires that the child display a sad or irritable mood, or loss of interest or pleasure in activities that usually elicit such responses, for at least 2 weeks. These should be accompanied by additional symptoms such as a change in eating habits and sleep patterns.

Begab (1967), in his discussion of childhood learning disabilities and family stress, points out that psychodynamic factors can induce parents to adopt many defense mechanisms and prevent them from providing appropriate information about their children's problems; defense mechanisms may also render parents nonreceptive to recommendations made by a psychologist and thus prevent them from implementing them faithfully. According to Begab, denial, projection, helplessness, and hopelessness are common among parents of children with reading problems. Denial and projection are particularly unhelpful defense mechanisms in regard to learning to read. Parents who rely excessively on defense mechanisms may deny that their child is a poor reader but claim that he/she is merely learning-disabled or dyslexic; they may project the reading problem on to the teacher, the method of teaching, the textbooks used, and a host of other things.

Not only parents, but reading-disabled children themselves, may resort to concealing their failure by using various defense mechanisms. Smith (1989), in an article on the behaviors of learning-disabled children who try to evade their problems, describes several "masks" these children wear. Included in this list of defense mechanisms are the mask of helplessness ("I do not know," "I can't do it," "I can't read two letters together"); the mask of invisibility (the student tries to get through school by assuming a low profile, by self-effacement); the mask of victim (indicated by frequent use of statements such as "the teacher does not like me" or "I can't help it"); the mask of indifference (the student assumes an "I don't care" attitude and behaves as though school is unimportant); the mask of contempt (the student blames everything and everybody—the school is no good, teachers are no good, textbooks are stupid); and the mask of frailty (marked by statements such as "I am dumb," "I am not able to remember anything"). According to Smith, by helping children understand the nature of their disability and the defense mechanisms they are using, and by assisting them to reach a comfort level and thereby gain self-confidence, these masks can be removed.

Noting that family dynamics can contribute importantly to reading disabilities, Abrams and Kaslow (1977) described several intervention strategies. As noted earlier, an association between emotional problems and reading difficulties does not necessarily imply a cause–effect relationship. It is equally likely that reading difficulties could cause many of the emotional prolems, or that they both could be triggered by an unknown third factor. Even though emotional distress can contribute to reading difficulties, psychological problems are unlikely to be resolved by using traditional psychoanalytic techniques. Behavioral therapies such as counterconditioning, systematic desensitization, and modeling have been shown to be more effective tools in dealing with psychological problems than psychoanalytic strategies. We now turn our attention to the behavioral model, which encompasses several of these behavioral therapies.

The Behavioral Model

As the consultation procedure was broadened to deal with different kinds of psychological problems, and as it became evident that environmental factors are as strongly associated with behavior problems as intrapsychic factors are, principles of behavioral psychology were incorporated into the consultation process. As a result, the behavioral model of consultation emerged.

According to Dougherty (1990), behavioral consultation is characterized by four principles: (1) use of indirect service delivery models, (2) implementation and assessment of treatment procedures based on behavioral principles, (3) diversity of intervention goals, ranging from problem solving to enhancing competence of the client, and (4) a clientele which includes individuals, groups, and organizations. According to Bergan (1977), behavioral consultation stresses the importance of problem identification without value judgment, quantification of the skills or their absence in the consultant as well as the client, and the evaluation of the consultation process as well as the treatment outcome.

The behavioral model of consultation and the mental health model differ from each other in the intervention techniques they utilize but not in the kinds of problems they address. Behavioral change can also be more easily evaluated than change in psychodynamic processes.

The Behavioral Model and Reading Disabilities

The behavioral model of consultation makes use of the principles of behavioral psychology. Consequently, the problem-solving techniques used in this form of consultation are derived from the belief that undesirable behavior is learned and, therefore, it can be unlearned. Conversely, desirable behavior can be learned. Behavior is sustained by reinforcers, and to extinguish undesirable behavior, the reinforcer sustaining the undesirable behavior must be identified and eliminated; at the same time, a desirable behavior should be substituted and reinforced. In addition to the principles derived from Pavlovian and Skinnerian forms of conditioning, the behavioral approach also incorporates principles derived from social learning theory and, more recently, cognitive–behavioral therapies.

Behavior modification techniques have been used by many investigators attempting to improve the reading skills of children. Hauserman and McIntire (1969) noted success with elementary schoolchildren by using reinforcers in conjunction with fading techniques. Pikulsky (1971) found the use of tangible reinforcers to be effective in improving word recognition skills in beginning disadvantaged readers. Glavach and Stoner (1970) reported that by using behavioral techniques, they obtained successful results in improving the reading skills of reading-disabled ninth-grade children. According to one report (Heitzman, 1970), migrant children who have not been accustomed to reinforcement in the past showed improvement when they were frequently reinforced for their reading performance. Reinforcers found to be effective were tokens that could be exchanged for tangible rewards, free time, praise, encouragement, and positive feedback on progress. Reinforcing entire groups of children was also effective.

As a matter of course, most teachers use verbal reinforcers such as praise and other positive feedback in their day-to-day teaching. It appears, however, that reinforcers are highly task-specific and, therefore, the behavior that is to be promoted has to be carefully chosen and closely monitored. In one study, Deaton (1975) found that poor readers from fourth grade who were reinforced for accuracy improved in both accuracy and on-task behavior, but those who were reinforced for on-task behavior improved in that aspect but failed to improve in accuracy. It is also suggested that teachers refrain from reinforcing certain forms of errors committed by children when they read aloud by ignoring such errors. When an error in oral reading is corrected, the teacher should provide *corrective feedback*. Such feedback can be immediate or delayed (i.e., right after a word is misread or after the sentence is read); it can be partial or complete (i.e., the misread letter or syllable is corrected or the misread word is corrected). Experts are divided as to the effectiveness of corrective feedback for reading instruction. Those who favor the use of corrective feedback believe that it helps children to improve their word-recognition skills as well as their own self-correcting behavior. Critics believe that when a poor reader is corrected repeatedly for oral reading errors, it may divert his/her attention from comprehension to decoding, increase anxiety, prevent the poor reader from using self-correcting strategies, and eventually make him/her dependent upon the teacher for such feedback.

So, what is the answer to the issue of corrective feedback during oral reading? After reviewing the pros and cons of corrective feedback, Harris and Sipay (1990) conclude that this is not an either/or proposition, but the appropriateness of corrective feedback varies from student to student and with the instructional situation. They recommend that the teacher ignore nondisruptive errors as well as an occasional disruptive error. Disruptive errors are those which alter the meaning of the sentence whereas nondisruptive errors are those which leave the meaning of the sentence more or less intact. When the child makes a disruptive error while reading aloud, allow about 5 seconds for self-correction, and if this does not happen, take corrective action. It is worth remembering that accurate and quick word recognition is a fundamental skill that lays the foundation for proficient reading. Children who fail to acquire word recognition skill in primary grades have the unenviable prospect of remaining as disabled readers. It is clear, therefore, that behavioral principles cannot be applied across the board without careful thought concerning which behavior is to be reinforced, diminished, or extinguished. It is also evident that recommendations in this regard require that the consultant possess expert knowledge of reading.

Modeling and observational learning are important components of social learning theory. Reading teachers in elementary schools frequently model reading behavior which they hope will be imitated by the students. Occasionally, they also use good readers from the classroom as models. In addition to increasing children's awareness of the prosodic features of reading, models also help increase children's interest in reading. Teachers also use modeling to promote comprehension skills in students. For instance, they may simulate angry or exuberant intonation to convey the mental state of a story's hero. According to Harris and Sipay (1990), internal mental processes can also be modeled. For instance, as he/she reads, the teacher may point out main ideas in the passage by changing his/her voice and stress patterns, may express occasional doubt about the views of the author, and also offer critical comments. Making internal thought processes in a skilled reader's mind explicit through overt statements is labeled as "thinking aloud." The expectation is that a student who is repeatedly exposed to such "thinking aloud" demonstrations will emulate the model's behavior and adopt similar thought processes when he/she reads. Different steps that can be used by the teacher for modeling thinking while reading are provided by Nist and Kirby (1986) and by Herman (1988).

Cognitive behavior modification has been sometimes claimed to be effective in treating the impulsive behavior of children with Attention Deficit Hyperactive Disorder (ADH syndrome; Kirby & Grimley, 1988). It would, therefore, be natural to expect that if the reading difficulties of some children are the result of their impulsive nature, cognitive behavior modification might be effective for improving reading skills. Derry and Murphy (1986) have provided useful hints for designing a system to train children with learning disability based on the principles of cognitive behavior modification. Although impulsivity may lead to reading errors, there is no compelling evidence suggesting that impulsive behavior leads to reading disability per se. Support for the view that cognitive styles such as impulsivity can be altered, and that by doing so children classified as impulsive can be made to be reflective, is also equivocal (e.g., Whalen, Henker, & Hinshaw, 1985).

Computer-assisted instruction utilizes behavioral principles such as response learning, immediate feedback, and reinforcement of responses. Computers can also be programmed to present the reading material in graded steps and thus "shape" the behavior of the learner. Some computer programs are designed in such a way as to facilitate errorless learning. Thus, the computer can be a versatile tool in reading programs. One of the common criticisms against computer-assisted reading instruction, however, is that once the initial fascination wears off, students easily get bored with such lessons. However, several programs have tried to avoid this problem by presenting the material in a game-like format, thus making computer-assisted instruction interesting. As a matter of fact, a large number of computer programs available today teach vocabulary and comprehension skills through a game-like format. Computers with speech synthesizing capability can be useful in promoting decoding skills. Research in the development of software that can be used in promoting decoding skills is underway and these software programs are likely to become available in the near future. The use of computers in reading disability programs is described in Chapter 6.

To a large extent, behavioral techniques are motivational devices that can sustain and promote cognitive skills, once they are acquired. Without motivation to read, few children make satisfactory progress in learning to read; if interested in reading, even children with reading disabilities make progress, albeit at a slow rate. For this reason, extreme care should be taken to see that word recognition drills and other exercises do not become a chore and drudgery, thus making children lose interest in reading. Identifying effective ways to promote the interest of children in reading should be a fundamental goal of the consultation process.

The Ecological Model

Consultation procedures presented under the ecological model have also been variously described as "ecological consultation" and "ecological approach" (Jason, Ferone, & Anderegg, 1979) and have been usually implemented within a behavioral setting. Since procedures described under the ecological model can also be implemented without regard to principles of behavioral psychology, we have assigned it an independent status. The ecological model of consultation is concerned with the environmental and sociological factors that prevail in the classroom, the school, and home, and their impact on an individual's performance. Examples of the factors which affect children's performance are class size, ability grouping, placement in remedial classes, mainstreaming, and parents as role models for children's reading habits. Relatively unimportant features such as seating arrangement of children and the degree of freedom children have to move around in the classroom can also be considered ecological factors that affect reading performance. The influence of some ecological factors on children's reading achievement have been well studied, particularly by educators.

Ecological factors can also affect teachers' behavior as much as they do children's reading. For instance, some teachers may be effective with small groups of students, whereas others may prefer to teach children in a large class; and some teachers may work well with gifted students, whereas others may have special skills in teaching low-ability students. It is also documented that teachers tend to spend less time interacting with students who are placed in low-ability groups than with students who are not so identified (Johnston & Allington, 1991). This is not a deliberate policy followed by teachers, but they are often unaware of their own behavior. Thus, ecological factors, although different from instructional factors, can influence the ultimate outcome of the teaching–learning process. The school psychology consultant, therefore, cannot afford to overlook ecological factors even though reading problems cannot be solved by attending exclusively to such factors.

The Ecological Model and Reading Disabilities

Under the heading "educational factors" Poostay and Aaron (1982) identify 10 environmental parameters that contribute to reading problems in children. These are "ecological in character." Included in this list are: insufficient time scheduled for reading instruction, crowded classrooms that hinder the teacher who tries to adjust her instruction to meet individual needs, materials that are too difficult for students, an overemphasis on certain skills at the expense of others, inadequate time set aside for practicing skills, a disorganized classroom, insufficient quantities of materials, inadequate materials, and attempts to push a child to complete a minimum number of books during the year. The consultant has to look at these factors as potential contributors to reading problems in children, particularly when consultation involves the consideration of educational practices such as *ability group-*

ing and placement in remedial classes, peer tutoring, and *cooperative learning.* We will briefly describe the advantages and disadvantages of these practices.

Ability Grouping and Remedial Classes. The desirability of grouping students on the basis of their reading ability is a widely discussed issue in reading literature. Classifying students according to their ability level can be practiced within the classroom or among classrooms of the same grade. It is also possible to group students across grades which results in "nongraded" classrooms, as far as reading is concerned. Placing students of similar ability in a single classroom, regardless of their age, has one advantage, namely, it makes the teacher's task somewhat easy because she/he can target her/his teaching at a single ability level. In contrast, if several groups of children of different ability levels are housed in the same classroom, this puts much demand on the teacher's time and resources. An advantage of nongraded classrooms is that children do not "flunk out" because they move on when they have attained the goals set for a particular level. Placement in nongraded levels, however, requires accurate assessment of children's reading skills and careful programming of the class sessions.

When viewed from the perspective of the student with reading difficulties, the advantages of homogeneous grouping do not appear to be substantial. According to Harris and Sipay (1980), when achievement in homogeneous classes was compared with that in ungrouped schools, only slight differences were found. They conclude that the evidence about homogeneous grouping's effect is mixed and inconclusive with regard to achievement. However, the low self-esteem of students placed in lower groups is well documented. It should also be noted that children placed in lower groups seldom move up regardless of the intensity and length of remedial teaching they receive, a possible outcome of self-fulfilling prophecy. When compared to successful learners, children who are placed in remedial classes or those identified as reading-disabled or low-ability students are found to be unreflective, less positive about reading and writing, less persistent in the face of failure, and engage in less reading and writing (Johnston & Allington, 1991). As for the accomplishment of remedial programs, including those operating on a "pull out" basis, the verdict is no better. A study by Allington and McGill–Franzen (1989) shows that children in these programs receive less reading instruction than their normally achieving peers. This is because more time is allocated to seatwork, filling in of worksheets, and other mechanical activities. Research also shows that teachers' instructional behavior during remedial sessions is much influenced by the ecology of the setting. Johnston and Allington (1991) cite a number of research studies which show that there is often little teacher involvement beyond monitoring on-task behavior and providing feedback as to whether the child is right or wrong. These investigators add that "the teacher moves about monitoring these activities and checking responses but rarely uses instructional strategies such as explaining, modelling, or prompting. Each child receives but a few moments of teacher attention and that attention is most commonly feedback concerning the accuracy of responses" (p. 994). These teacher–pupil interactions are described by Cazden (1988) as "abrupt, perfunctory, and ritualized praise" (p. 20). Johnston and Allington (1991) add that in remedial interventions with teacher aides, the situation is even more dismal.

These observations show that the consultant has to have a clear knowledge about the ecological factors that prevail in any particular remedial or reading disability program. Making a diagnosis and recommending certain remedial instructional procedures may not be sufficient to improve the child's reading performance unless these "hidden" factors are also taken into acount. Teachers themselves may not be aware of their own behavvior, and the consultant can perform an important service by drawing their attention to these important ecological factors.

One solution to these problems in remedial classes, suggested by Johnston and Allington (1991), is to change the instructional setting from an *ego-involving situation* to that of a *task-involving situation*. An ego-involving situation is governed by notions such as "capacity," "competition," and "norm"; a task-involving situation is characterized by factors such as "interest," "cooperation," and "criterion." In ego-involving situations, students who perceive themselves as having low ability are unlikely to ask for assistance because they see help-seeking as an evidence of their own weakness. In contrast, the same students freely seek assistance in task-involving situations because they view help-seeking as a demonstration of their effort to learn.

There also exist some potential alternative to ability grouping. These are *peer tutoring* and *cooperative learning*. In contrast to ability grouping, peer tutoring and cooperative learning are said to be more successful in helping poor readers.

Peer Tutoring. In order to be successful, peer tutoring should be carefully planned and the tutors properly trained. Care also should be taken to see that the "tutors" do not spend too much time tutoring lest their own learning suffers. It is suggested that tutors be selected by children themselves rather than appointed by the teacher. Tutors are more likely to be accepted by group members when selected by them than when appointed by the teacher. Of course, the teacher will have to provide the necessary guidance in the selection of competent tutors. There can be more than one tutor in every group and the position can be rotated. Teachers who have used peer tutoring are supportive of such practice and report that poor readers accept this help with good grace and benefit from it.

Cooperative Learning. This ecological arrangement involves heterogeneous ability groups with four or five pupils working together on "team tasks" (Harris & Sipay, 1990). Unlike peer tutoring, in cooperative learning, each member in a group is individually responsible for his/her assignment; at the same time, the group is collectively responsible for its performance as a team. Students within a group can consult with fellow members and receive help from them. Indeed, they are encouraged to do so. Teachers may assign separate grades for individuals and groups. One of the benefits of cooperative learning is that peer pressure to achieve works as an excellent motivating factor. The teacher has to carefully select members of the groups so that differing ability levels are well balanced within each group. This form of grouping can also be used as a device to split "cliques" in the classroom and thus maintain discipline. Cooperative learning, when used as a supplement to regular classroom instruction, can provide a lively diversion. Teachers who use cooperative learning are enthusiastic about it. Research also shows that children exposed to cooperative learning show higher achievement than those taught only through traditional methods (Stevens, 1987). Both peer tutoring and cooperative learning are procedures that are supplementary to regular classroom instruction.

The Instructional Model

The instructional model is also sometimes referred to as the Education and Training model (Hansen et al., 1990). When the consultant's role is primarily that of an advisor, educator, or trainer, the consultation process can be placed within the instructional model. *Staff development* or *in-service training* assistance also fit within this model. In the instructional consultation model, either the classroom teacher or the special education teacher is invariably the consultee; the client can be an individual or a group of individuals such as children in a reading disability class, or it can be an organization such as a community college. Instructional consultation can, therefore, take place at several levels. Even though the most frequently encountered consultees by the school psychologist are teachers, it is not unusual that a parent, a school board, or an educational institution can be the client.

The objective of instructional consultation is to educate, teach, train, or instruct the consultees so that they can be effective in their interaction with clients. According to Rosenfield (1987),

> The focus of instructional consultation is on the quality and nature of the interaction, which usually is an instructional mismatch between an often vul-

nerable learner, inadequate instruction, and a muddled conception of the task. It is the goal of the collaborative consultation process to analyze the mismatch and facilitate a more productive interaction. (p. 10)

While we agree that there might be a mismatch between the student's learning style and the teacher's method of instruction, this definition appears to hold "inadequate instruction and a muddled conception of the task" to be solely responsible for all forms of reading disability and, therefore, places the entire onus of the client's reading disability on the teacher. This, however, need not always be the case. There are several instances, particularly in reading, wherein the child has a specific disability and in spite of the teacher's best efforts, no single method of instruction would readily produce the expected results. Therefore, we would define instructional consultation broadly as efforts to improve diagnostic, prescriptive, and teaching skills of the consultee to enhance the client's academic achievement. Instructional consultation is concerned with the technology of education.

The instructional model of consultation adheres to the basic tenets of collaborative consultation. According to Rosenfield (1987), instructional consultation may work at four levels: (1) direct service to the client through assessment, interviewing, or observation; (2) indirect service to the client through the consultee, usually the teacher (but the consultant remains responsible for most of the data-gathering and remedial processes); (3) service to the consultee which eventually will result in changes for the pupils; and (4) service to the system which leads to changes in the organization of its instructional program. Of these four possibilities, the second level in which the consultant delivers services both to the consultee and the client appears to be the one that is most often encountered in school systems. This is generally true of consultation in reading disabilities.

Instructional consultation, as applied to reading, draws heavily from principles of cognitive psychology and information processing techniques and focuses on the improvement of students' learning skills. In contrast, behavioral consultation, in spite of the fact that it has recently been expanded to include cognitive behavioral techniques, continues to focus more on prelearning and postlearning behavior of children and less on their learning skills per se. Thus, principles derived from cognitive psychology remain as a major guiding factor in implementing the instructional procedures, even though behavioral principles can be utilized to support a cognitively oriented instructional program. For example, a teacher may use the phonics method to teach children word recognition skills, but may rely on shaping technique with different reinforcers to sustain those skills. It should be noted, however, that the phonics method is the major tool of instruction, whereas shaping and the application of reinforcers play only supporting roles.

Periodic assessment of the client and evaluation of the effectiveness of instructional procedures adopted are important components of instructional consultation. Unlike the traditional psychometric assessment that is carried out for classification and eligibility purposes, instructional consultation is conducted with an express objective to improve the quality of instructional decision making. Thus, assessment is expected to lead to instructional recommendations that can be implemented in the classroom. For this reason, it is often suggested that students be assessed in terms of educational criteria established in the classroom and not with reference to external norms. To accomplish this goal, test items are usually taken from the curriculum to which the student is exposed. This method of evaluation is referred to as *curriculum based assessment*. There are, however, occasions when assessment is carried out to see if the student has mastered some of the fundamental principles of reading, writing, or math. Under these circumstances, the teacher may use standardized tests. For instance, when assessing the decoding skills of a student, it is desirable to use a standardized test because when words taken from the textbook are used, it may be difficult to determine if the student uses decoding skill or sight vocabulary to recognize the words. The assessment and evaluation procedures relevant for reading disability instruction are discussed in Chapter 4. The assessment itself may be carried out by the consultant or he/she may have it done by the consultee.

There have been a few attempts to evaluate the effectiveness of consultation procedures carried out under the different models and to compare the perceptions of classroom and special education teachers as to the relative benefits of these consultation procedures (e.g., Curtis & Zins, 1981; Babcock & Pryzwansky, 1983; Jason & Ferone, 1978; Fedner, Bianchi, & Duffey, 1979; Conoley & Conoley, 1982). In general, these studies indicate that teachers prefer instructional consultation procedures of a collaborative nature and value the special information and expertise consultants can provide them.

Instructional consultation requires that the consultant be knowledgeable in two fields: psychology and education. According to Anserello and Sweet (1990):

> Historically, more effort has been directed toward psychological content, but educational content is equally important. School psychologists who maintain current knowledge of materials and methods of instruction for specific content areas (e.g., reading, math, or language arts curriculum) will find the classroom teacher more cooperative when it comes to designing and implementing plans for intervention. For instance, a psychologist who is able to speak knowledgeably about commonly used basal reading programs gains a significant amount of credibility when consulting with the classroom teacher about a student's reading difficulties. (p. 180)

Reflecting a similar opinion, Rosenfield (1987) observed that teachers and many school psychologists themselves often will not consider a psychologist an appropriate professional to solve instructional problems, because many school psychologists have received relatively little or no training in this area. This certainly is true of the psychology of reading, reading disability, and reading instruction—areas in which many school psychologists have had little or no training. The expectation that the instructional consultant should have expertise in the field is not alien to the philosophy of consultation. For instance, Schein (1978) several years ago, recognized "expert" role to be one of the consultant's four roles. The other three were facilitative, process, and content roles. A major objective of this book is to provide technical information in the areas of the psychology of reading, reading disabilities, and corrective instruction which can be helpful in building expert knowledge essential to fulfil the expert role in consultation.

The Instructional Model and Reading Disabilities

As noted earlier, the instructional model of consultation relies heavily on principles of cognitive psychology and information processing, and on data obtained from educational and psychological research. The consultant shares this information with the consultee who, in turn, can use it in assessing the reading performance of children, in understanding the nature of reading disabilities, and in designing instructional programs for children with reading disabilities. Evaluating the effectiveness of the consultation program is also an integral part of the instructional model of consultation. These procedures constitute the subject matter of this book and are presented in the following chapters.

Academic disciplines use different theories to explain different phenomena, and frequently this results in disagreements regarding explanations of problems observed and the proposed solutions. The fields of reading instruction and reading disability are no exception. Often a method or an idea is claimed to be outmoded and then jettisoned, only to be reclaimed many years later and promoted with a great deal of passion. In the field of education, the pendulum swings more often than it does in other fields. A knowledge of where we come from, where we are, and where we are heading is, therefore, essential to the consultant wishing to avoid past mistakes and current fads. Because those who do not remember the past are condemned to repeat it, Chapter 2 provides a brief history of reading instruction and research in reading disabilities.

2

History of Reading Instruction and Reading Disability Research in the United States

INTRODUCTION

An understanding of the history of reading instruction and reading disability is an area of expert knowledge that can be helpful to the psychologist–consultant. It will enable the psychologist to view reading instruction in the proper perspective and help him/her steer away from old methods tried in the past and found wanting, and avoid being caught up in new but unproven fads. A historical overview is also a convenient means of introducing different methods of teaching reading as well as the specialized terminology unique to this field.

This chapter traces the history of two aspects of reading: reading instruction and reading disability research. Whereas reading instruction in this country has a history of almost three centuries, research in the reading process and reading disability is almost entirely limited to the present century. Nevertheless, an enormous amount of data pertaining to the reading process and reading disability has accumulated within this short period because the research is multifaceted and contributors include cognitive and experimental psychologists, reading specialists, and individuals interested in reading disabilities. This brief review will focus only on major historical trends.

HISTORY OF READING INSTRUCTION

A fairly accurate history of culture and thought in the United States can be reconstructed by examining the textbooks used in American schools since formal reading instruction began some 300 years ago. According to Nila Banton Smith, who has written a fascinating book on the history of reading instruction in the United States (first published in 1934 and republished in 1965 and 1986), clearly identifiable changes in teaching methods have taken place in this country, and these relate to certain cultural shifts. A slightly modified version of Smith's scheme of these developments, along with their associated chronology, is presented in Table 2.1.

TABLE 2.1. Changes in the Emphasis of Reading Instruction in the United States During the Past Three Centuries

Period	Emphasis on
Before 1776	Religion
1776–1820	Nationalism
1820–1880	Intelligent citizenship
1880–1910	Reading as cultural asset
1910–1925	Science and quantification
1925–1935	Research and application
1935–1965	International competition
1965–Present	Reading competency

Period Prior to 1776: Emphasis on Religion

According to Smith (1965), the first reading material used in American schools was the *Hornbook*. It appears that the *Hornbook* was not manufactured in this country but was imported from England. According to

Mitford (1966), the *Hornbook* resembled a tiny ping-pong paddle with a sheet of paper pasted on one side containing the ABCs, some simple syllables, and the Lord's Prayer. The single leaf of paper was protected from wet, dirty fingers by a thin, translucent sheet of horn, hence the name "hornbook." The material in the *Hornbook* was used for teaching reading as well as catechism.

There was also another reader, simply referred to as the *ABC,* which went a little further than the *Hornbook.* As the name of this early book indicates, the first step in reading instruction was to teach the names of alphabet letters. The fact that the ABC method of teaching reading survived almost until the middle of the 19th century shows that for a long time very little attention was paid to teaching methods—it was the subject matter taught that was important. Enterprising individuals, however, invented unusual devices to implement the ABC method; for example, one such ingenious device was using gingerbread that was shaped in the form of the letters of the alphabet. The use of gingerbread in teaching reading had an advantage over other methods as the following old English poem shows:

> A hornbook gives of Ginger-bread,
> And that the child may learn the better,
> As he can name, he eats the letter
> Proceeding thus with vast delight
> He spells, and gnaws from left to right.
> (SMITH, 1965, p. 7)

Even though the *ABC* book's primary aim was reading instruction, Smith believes that the use of this book was not widespread in America because after mastering the *Hornbook,* the child could move directly on to the *Primer* which contained both the ABCs and some religious selections. The *Primer* was originally produced in England under the name *Protestant Tutor;* in the United States it was first published in Boston in 1685. It was called the *Primer* not because it was the first book used for teaching reading but because it was considered to be primary, or vital, for learning to lead a spiritual life.

By the turn of the 18th century, the *Primer* met with competition in the form of the *Speller,* which was designed for teaching students how to read any passage in the Bible. The title of the book also indicates that reading and spelling were taught simultaneously. In spite of the advanced selections it had, the *Speller* was designed to teach reading through the ABC method. Once the child had learned the names of the letters by rote, forward and backward, syllables were introduced. The ABC method, however, had its detractors in European countries, if not in America.

Period from 1776 to 1820: Emphasis on Nationalism

By the end of the 18th century, the country had gone through a great political change and the primers of this period reflect this fact. Religious and moralistic reading materials slowly were replaced by others intended to stir up patriotic fervor and promote a sense of nationalism. The portrait of King George III was renamed "John Hancock" (although the picture itself was not changed!); and the verse which, before independence, stated

> The royal oak, it was the tree
> that saved his Royal Majastie.

now read as follows:

> The royal oak, it was the tree
> that saved us our libertie.
> (SMITH, p. 1965, p. 63)

In 1807, Noah Webster produced the first set of readers by an American author, a series of three graded books. First was the *American Spelling Book;* the next level was a treatise on grammar; the most advanced book contained lessons on the history and geography of the United States. The content of these textbooks, therefore, reflects the pupil's steady progression from a stage in which he/she was "learning to read" to a state of "reading to learn." Other readers published by different educators also became available at this time, and some of these books contained exercises and rules for correct pronunciation and enunciation. The reason for emphasizing these skills was "to diffuse a uniformity and purity of language in America, to destroy the provincial prejudices that originate in trifling differences in dialect" (Smith, 1965, p. 38). In spite of these changes in reading material, teaching methods remained essentially the same as in earlier periods: spelling, along with the memorization of letter names, remained the chief method of reading instruction.

Period from 1820 to 1880: Emphasis on Citizenship

Inspection of books used in the classroom from 1820 through 1880 indicates that acquisition of general knowledge and principles of good citizenship were emphasized during this period. This era is also noteworthy for one other important event: for the first time in American education, serious attention was given to the method of reading instruction, which would become a controversial, emotionally charged issue. This marked the beginning of the still ongoing "Reading War," as a recent issue of *Newsweek* called it. Because the origins of many contemporary teaching methods such as *analytic phonics, synthetic phonics, whole word method, language experience method,* and *whole language method* can be traced to the 19th century, it is worth examining this period in some detail.

The ABC method and the books that promoted it came under criticism when educators began to realize that recitation of the alphabet and the rote memorization of a handful of words were not sufficient to master the increased amount of material that had to be read and understood. As a result, new methods of reading instruction were devised and promoted. One alternative to the ABC method was advanced by Prof. Thomas Gallaudet from Connecticut. In this program, about 50 words were first introduced, and children learned to associate each written word with its pronunciation without analysis of the names or sounds of constituent letters. Next, the letters in the words were attended to. Even though this method appears to be a "Whole word" method, it was not a pure whole word method because at some point during the course of instruction, letters were introduced. This approach, strictly speaking, is the analytic phonics method even though a clear-cut distinction between the whole word method and the analytic phonics method cannot be drawn unless the whole word method excludes the introduction of letters altogether.

By far the most ardent advocate of the whole word, "look-and-say" method during this period was Horace Mann (1796–1859) who, after being elected to the Massachussets State Legislature, became the Secretary of the Board of Education. Mann had personally observed German classrooms in which the instructional procedures were based on Pestalozzian philosophy. Comparing this to the American ABC method ("abecedarian," as Mann derisively called it) in which "children blundered through sentences, spelling each word and pronouncing it before passing to the next, imitating sounds . . . [like] a parrot or an idiot" (Mitford, 1966, p. 77), he advocated introducing a set of words first, and then the letters of the alphabet because "I do not see indeed, why a child should not learn to read as easily as he learns to talk, if taught in a similar manner" (Mitford, 1966, p. 80). This argument is similar to the one advanced today by advocates of the whole language approach even though the *whole language* (discussed later) is distinct from the *whole word method.* As we will see later, the claim that children can learn to read the same way they learn to talk is debatable.

In spite of his power and influence, Mann, however, failed to persuade many Massachussets teachers to his way of teaching because the teachers thought that Mann did not understand the difference between letter *names* and letter *sounds*. Furthermore, teachers who had tried his system testified that even though children had learned a word previously in one context, they were unable to recognize it later in another context.

One of the positive outcomes of this conflict was that attention was drawn to a distinction between introducing letter names and introducing letter sounds as a first step in teaching reading. Furthermore, virtually all educators appear to have been convinced that the ABC method not only involved tedious drill but confused children because the names and sounds of letters do not always match. Subsequently, the ABC method of introducing the names of letters had been abandoned and replaced by the *phonic method* in which letter sounds were introduced.

Even as the phonics versus whole word method controversy was raging, an approach which emphasized meaning began to emerge. In 1881, George Farnham, a superintendent of schools in New York, brought out a small manual for teachers titled *The Sentence Method of Teaching Reading,* which argued that pupils should develop the ability to look directly through the written expression to the meaning. The *sentence method,* which emphasizes meaning, differs from the *whole word method* in certain respects. Whereas the whole word method may introduce letter analysis after several words are introduced, the sentence method would postpone letter analysis indefinitely and even never pay attention to letters. The sentence method works in the following way. First, the teacher repeats a story until the children become thoroughly familiar with it. Then the written form of the story is presented, and each sentence is analyzed into words. The greatest champion of this "meaning approach" to reading during the 19th century was Francis Parker who in his book, *Talks on Teaching* (1883), stated that "Reading may be defined as the act of the mind in getting thought by means of written or printed words arranged in sentences . . . The mere pronunciation of words, however correctly and readily done, is not reading" (Mitford, 1966, p. 106). Hardly any educator would disagree with Parker's definition of reading. In fact, this view is almost identical to the one advocated today by the *whole language* method enthusiasts. The disagreement, however, was—as it is now—over how to teach the child to get meaning from the printed page. Some educators argue that in order to know the meaning of a word, the child should first be able to recognize the word and that word recognition skill can be developed only by teaching the child how to decode. This argument makes a distinction between *learning to read* and *reading to learn.* Others believe that the explicit teaching of decoding skill is not necessary, even when the child is learning to read. Parker's definition ignores the distinction between beginning and skilled reading.

The most widely used books during this period were the McGuffey readers. The McGuffey readers were a series of graded books, first published in 1836 and continuously printed until 1907. The materials in these books became progressively more complex and were designed to fit each grade in the elementary school. In the beginning grades, much emphasis was given to repetition and drill, and very few new words were introduced in each lesson. As a result, sentences were choppy and stilted with little narrative interest. For example, in an early lesson two-letter words were introduced with the aid of these sentences: "Do we go? Do we go up? We do go up." The limited number, the simplicity, and the repetitiveness of these words suggest that meaning was not the primary goal. The texts intended for upper grades, however, contained more selections from literature. The McGuffey reader is considered the fore-runner of the modern day *basal readers* which, understandably, came under heavy criticism in the 1960s for their repetitive, somewhat meaningless lessons emphasizing drill.

Period from 1880 to 1910: Emphasis on Culture

According to Smith (1965), in the early 1880s the nation had reached a state of tranquillity and security and had the time and inclination for music, art, and literature. As culture began to exert its influence, schools were blamed for not teaching children what to read and how to appreciate what they read even though they were taught how to read. Charles Eliot who, during the closing years of the 19th century, was the president of Harvard University, even went to the extent of stating that he would like to see such texts as the McGuffey reader excluded from schools, with real literature substituted in their place. In order to satisfy this hunger for culture, books containing selections from literature were produced. It was also during this time that professional books about how to teach reading made their first appearance.

Literary materials are eminently suitable for promoting meaning as the goal of reading instruction; understandably the *sentence* and *story methods* found vigorous support during this period. The teaching controversy, however, was far from being settled, and in spite of the emphasis on meaning and literature, some educators remained sceptical about the effectiveness of the whole word and sentence methods.

Convinced that the nature of the English orthography (spelling pattern) is a major impediment to reading acquisition, many reformers have, over the years, attempted to impose some "regularity" on English spelling. The rationale for these efforts is that in the English language, the relationship between a letter and its sound is not one-to-one and is, therefore, unpredictable; if only one letter could be made to represent one sound, the spelling reformers reason, the phonics method of teaching would be quite successful. One such reformer was Shearer, who in 1894 published *The Shearer System* (Smith, 1965). His system, with extensive use of diacritical marks, made a one letter–one sound relationship possible. Another system called the *Scientific Alphabet* was introduced in 1902. This system, in addition to using diacritical markings, reduced the number of characters needed in representing sounds by respelling words and omitting silent letters. The *Initial Teaching Alphabet (ita)* represents a similar effort of recent vintage. First introduced during the mid-19th century by Isaac Pitman in England, it has received favorable reports from England.

The Shearer system, Scientific Alphabet, as well as *ita,* however, have failed to capture the interest of American educators. This may be because educators, from teaching experience, might have realized that the inconsistent nature of the English orthography is not the *only* reason why some children find learning to read very difficult. Orthography of the English language is *morphophonemic:* spellings facilitate pronunciation as well as the extraction of meaning. However, in reading, getting the meaning of the word is more important than pronouncing it; consequently, precedence is given to meaning over pronunciation. Consider the following sentence: "We rode along the rode to the lake and rode across it." Is it not easier to read when it is written as "We *rode* along the *road* to the lake and *rowed* across it"? It is sometimes claimed (e.g., Chomsky & Halle, 1968) that when the fact that the English alphabet consists of only 26 characters is taken into account, the English orthography is optimally efficient for reading. This may be a reason why the augmented alphabets such as the Scientific Alphabet and *ita* were not found to be useful.

It would be a mistake to expect that a reading war beginning nearly half a century ago would have abated, with meaning-based strategies (e.g., whole word, sentence, and story methods) triumphant. Far from it. The continuation of the controversy is evident from the pro-phonics remarks made by James Hughes in his book *Teaching to Read,* published in 1909. Hughes, who was an inspector of schools in Toronto, recommended a combination of synthetic and analytic phonics to instruct beginning readers. Most of what he wrote is relevant today, and his comments are similar to those of current critics of the whole language method. To impress upon the reader the fact that the *whole language* versus *phonics* debate is not new but has almost a hundred years' history behind it, a few excerpts from Hughes's book are quoted.

Oral language being natural, is learned without conscious effort. Visible language, being artificial, has to be learned by a conscious effort. (p. 41)

Word recognition is the only possible basis of reading . . . the best method of teaching word recognition is the one which makes the child most independent of the teacher. (p. 9)

The phonic method is the only method that fulfils these [conditions] completely. . . . (p. 58)

Hughes did not stop with these theoretical propositions, but went on to give step-by-step instructions for implementing his method in meaningful and interesting ways. He also suggested games to make phonics instruction enjoyable and meaningful. For instance, he suggested that each pupil may be made to impersonate a letter by having it written on a flash card and pinned on his/her shirt. The pupils stand in a row and the teacher may slowly utter the sounds of the letters (not the names of the letters) J—U—M—P in the word "jump" and ask the four children who represent the letters to step forward. The rest of the class can now be asked to read the newly formed word. An obvious variation of this game is when the teacher says the word and the four children who wear the corresponding letters step forward and face the class. The class then sounds out the letter sounds. After a few words have been learned this way, simple sentences can be formed, written and read.

In addition to the ongoing reading methods controversy, the period between 1880 and 1910 is notable also for three other important events: publication of professional books on reading, the beginning of research efforts that compared the effectiveness of different teaching procedures, and the recognition of the existence of reading disability. An important book published during this period was *The Psychology and Pedagogy of Reading* by Edmund Huey (1908/1968). This book, in addition to presenting an impartial discussion of teaching methods, also provides a scientific treatment of the psychology of reading. The book contains information still relevant today. Several other professional books on reading were also published during this period or soon after.

According to Smith (1965), between 1884 and 1910, 34 research studies were published in the United States and England. Even though most of these studies investigated eye movements, visual perception, and reading speed, a handful of reading surveys were also published. One of the earliest "experimental" studies, conducted by Josephine Bowden (1911), examined the effectiveness of the meaning-oriented teaching method. Because it was claimed that reading should be learned as speaking is learned, she taught five kindergarten children by using the "natural way." Under this method, children made up stories or described their experiences; the teacher wrote these on the chalkboard which the children read and copied. After 8 weeks of instruction it was found that children, indeed, learned to recognize most of the words with which they were familiar. However, they misread many words that were similar in appearance (e.g., *coast*—"coat"; *fed*—"red"). Surprisingly, they read equally well whether the familiar words were correctly positioned or turned upside down. Bowden concluded that children could not learn to develop a system for recognizing words on their own and that only early introduction of phonics could supply this skill.

Period from 1910 to 1935: Emphasis on Assessment and Research

Prior to 1900, reading assessment was primarily qualitative in nature, accomplished by observing the oral reading performance of the pupils. Even though oral reading might provide a rough estimate of the pupil's word-recognition skills, it is not very useful in assessing reading comprehension. Starting at about 1910, and during the period that immediately followed, tests designed to assess comprehension and other reading related skills, such as spelling, were developed. These instruments were not only helpful in evaluating the reading ability of children but were also instrumental in facilitating reading research by making a comparison of the effectiveness of different methods of reading instruction possible. Furthermore, the fact that these tests were standardized enabled researchers to carry out assessment of reading performance on children with a fair degree of objectivity unknown till then. More importantly, these tests were designed with the ultimate goal of devising specific methods of instruction aimed at improving reading.

The speed with which reading achievement tests were developed and utilized can be appreciated by noting the different tests used by Arthur Gates in his 1922 study on the relationship between intelligence and reading–spelling achievement. The list of tests includes *Holley's Sentence Vocabulary Test, Burgess Reading Test, Brown's Reading Test, Curtis Silent Reading Test, Monroe's Silent Reading Test, Thorndike–McCall Reading Test, Gray's Reading Test,* and *Stanford–Binet Intelligence Test.*

The recognition that some children experienced a considerable amount of difficulty in learning to read, and the shocking realization that a large number of soldiers in the US Army could not read well enough to follow printed instructions necessary for operating machinery and handling arms, brought the realization that there was an enormous variability in the reading skill of children and adolescents and that reading difficulties should be reliably diagnosed and treated. This gave impetus to the development of remedial reading programs. The publication of *Deficiencies in Reading Ability: Their Diagnosis and Treatment* by C. T. Gray in 1922 is an outcome of such efforts.

The term "remedial reading" was first used by Uhl in 1916 and came to be widely used in the early 1920s. In comparison with the development of standardized tests in the diagnosis of reading difficulties, remediation techniques lagged behind. According to Smith (1965), three types of remedial procedures were used: (1) alphabet–spelling method, used primarily by workers in the medical profession, (2) phonics and kinesthetic methods, used primarily by clinicians, and (3) exercises to improve oral reading, silent reading, and word recognition, used primarily by teachers. Grace Fernald, originator of the Visual-Auditory-Kinesthetic Teaching (VAKT) method of reading published her work about this time (1921).

An innovation introduced during this period was *Experience Charts.* These were developed on the basis of children's own experiences. Students were invited to tell about their experiences such as a visit to a farm or a hospital, which the teacher wrote on the chalkboard. The children then read the sentences which they had dictated. Subsequently, they might copy these in their workbooks. It is believed that these materials were more interesting and meaningful to children than the information presented in textbooks. The Experience Chart was similar to the material Bowden (1911) used in her study and is a forerunner of today's *Language Experience* method.

Textbooks of this period began to make use of highly controlled lists of vocabulary. These were selected from standardized works such as Thorndike's *The Teacher's Word Book* (1921). Because the major goal of these books was to introduce a basic vocabulary, they came to be referred to as *basal readers.* In spite of the popularity of the meaning-based methods of teaching beginning reading during the 1920s and 1930s, authors of basal readers made provisions in their textbooks for the teaching of phonics. Many of the basal series also came with teachers' manuals and supplementary workbooks for students. Today, the package is much larger and may include primers, readers, teachers' editions, workbooks, drill and practice sheets, pretests, posttests, and classroom libraries. Basal readers have had tremendous influence on reading instruction in the United States, and today about 90% of the schools use these series published by eight or nine major companies. Over the years, the content of basal readers has changed to reflect shifts in educational philosophy and psychology (Chall & Squire, 1991). For about three decades, starting with the late 1920s, the whole word method and controlled vocabulary predominated; in the 1960s and the subsequent two decades, texts focused on phonics instruction. In the late 1980s, the content reflects the influence of "literature-based instruction" with more literary selections included. Even though modern-day basal readers published by different companies share similar educational philosophies, differences do exist among them. Because a knowledge of the basal readers is vital for reading consultation, the salient features of readers published by different companies are presented in Appendix I.

Period from 1935 to 1965: Emphasis on Meeting International Competition

The three decades covered in this segment witnessed the Second World War and the flight of the Russian Sputnik. Both drew attention to the need for an educated populace and a high quality education in general. Recruitment efforts during the Second World War, like those during the First World War, revealed that a large number of young high school graduates were not skilled readers. What was found to be true of soldiers was also found to be true of many college students. This is evident from the fact that the National Society for the Study of Education chose to devote their 1948 yearbook to *Reading in the High School and College*. Interest in high school and college reading, while not new, greatly increased. According to Smith (1965), the number of published studies as well as dissertation topics about reading in high school and college outnumbered studies of reading at all other levels.

The critical attitude about education in general, and reading in particular, reached a fever pitch with the publication of the book, *Why Johnny Can't Read* (Flesch, 1955). Flesch unreservedly asserted that Johnny could not read because he did not have phonics skills; the author's solution to this grave problem was to teach beginning reading through systematic phonics instruction. Even though this book was considered in academic circles as polemic and an oversimplification, it was instrumental in drawing public attention not only to the importance of reading, but also to how it is taught in the schools.

An important publication that followed *Why Johnny Can't Read* was Jean Chall's *Learning to Read: The Great Debate*, published in 1967. Chall evaluated nearly 50 years of research in reading instruction and compared the effectiveness of methods that emphasized code (i.e., phonics) against those focused on meaning. She cautiously concluded that

> It would seem, at our present state of knowledge, that a code emphasis—one that combines control of words on spelling regularity, some direct teaching of letter–sound correspondences, as well as the use of writing, tracing, or typing—produces better results with unselected groups of beginners than a meaning emphasis (p. 178–179)

Chall, however, did not minimize the importance of meaning in beginning reading instruction. She also warned educators not to overemphasize decoding *drill* at the expense of meaning and interest, and advised moderation in the use of different methods of teaching. Chall's conclusions have however, been challenged by some who allege that she included in her analysis studies that did not use proper statistical procedures and the required experimental controls (Carbo, 1988).

During the 1964–65 academic year, the U.S. Office of Education supported 27 studies that assessed the effectiveness of instructional techniques in the first grade and followed the children through the second year. Bond and Dykstra (1967) summarized the results of the first-year studies and concluded that word study skills must be emphasized and taught systematically regardless of which approach to initial reading instruction was utilized. Combinations of programs, such as a basal program with supplementary phonics materials, often were found to be superior to single approaches. They also pointed out that no one approach is so distinctly better in all situations and respects than the others. Also, they suggested, because pupils experience difficulty in each of the programs utilized, improvement of reading instruction depends on the training of better reading teachers rather than on individual methods and materials. Reflecting on the results of the first year and the follow-up studies, Dykstra (1974) later wrote:

> We can summarize the results of 60 years of research dealing with beginning reading instruction by stating that early systematic instruction in phonics provides the child with the skills necessary to become an independent reader at an earlier age than is likely if phonics instruction is delayed and less systematic. (p. 397)

A "new" method of reading instruction, claimed to be distinct from the phonics method although similar to it, was introduced at this time. Named the *linguistic method,* it focused on the sound patterns of word families, rather than those of the individual alphabet letters. Based on the assumption that a child can learn to read once he recognizes the correspondence between oral language cues and written language symbols, it first introduces words which have consistent spelling-to-pronunciation relationships. The focus of initial instruction is not on meaning but on enhancing the decoding skill of the child. For this reason, words with a short vowel sound (such as "mad" and "mat") are introduced first. After this letter–sound association is mastered, the long vowel sound is introduced (e.g., "made" and "mate"). This highly controlled vocabulary can result in sentences such as "Dan can fan a tan man," a ready target for criticism from "meaning enthusiasts." The two books based on the lingistic method were *Let's Read: A Linguistic Approach* by Bloomfield and Barnhart (1961), and *Linguistics and Reading* by Fries (1963). One of the basal reader series which encourages a controlled step-by-step phonics mastery and presents only one new variable at a time (but still moves quickly through the phonics program) is *Lippincott Basic Reading* series (Walcutt & McCracken, 1981.) The Merrill reading series (Wilson & Rudolph, 1986) also has a linguistic program for K–3 which attempts to improve word-recognition skills through exercises in word and spelling patterns, i.e., similar-sounding words and similar-looking spellings.

Period from 1965 to the Present: Emphasis on Reading Competency

The present scene is once again a period of intense concern over education, particularly about reading and reading instruction. Two areas are receiving much attention: method of instruction in early grades and means of promoting comprehension in later grades. The present day basal readers reflect these two concerns.

The relative effectiveness of the various methods of reading instruction continues to be a research topic, and the writings of a number of researchers indicate support for instruction in phonics. Chall updated her book, *Learning to Read: The Great Debate* (1983), and came to essentially the same conclusion she had reached in 1967 that phonics instruction is a valuable component of beginning instruction. Another widely distributed publication is the book, *Becoming a Nation of Readers*, by Anderson, Hiebert, Scott, and Wilkinson (1985), which stated that "the issue is no longer, as it was several decades ago, whether children should be taught phonics. The issues now are specific ones of just how it should be done" (p. 36). A bulletin released in 1988 by the U.S. Department of Education entitled, "What We Know About Phonics" states that children should complete their study of phonics by the end of the second grade. In her recent book, Adams (1990) recognizes the importance of phonics: "evidence suggests strongly that something about phonics instruction is of genuine and lasting value" (p. 7).

Even though these publications create an impression that the code versus meaning issue has been settled, it still remains unresolved. There are several reasons for the persistence of this issue. One of them is that the distinction between phonics and nonphonics is not absolute but one of emphasis even though antagonists perceive these approaches as all-or-none positions. A second reason is that despite a phonics emphasis in many classrooms for the past 20 years, the United States ranks a dismal 49th in literacy out of the 159 members of the United Nations; in contrast, the country that ranks first, New Zealand, utilizes what appears to be a whole language approach (WL) even though some phonics is also taught (Carbo, 1988). Whole language (more fully described in Chapter 5) is an educational philosophy which emphasizes meaning and literature in the teaching of reading, and frowns upon the teaching of skills in isolation. However, there is no compelling reason to assume a causal connection between the methods of teaching and the difference in literacy rates between the United States and New Zealand, as advocates of WL would lead us to believe. Two additional reasons, both invalid, are advanced by WL supporters as to why systematic phonics instruction should be discouraged. First, it is asked, why do children who are good at learning to speak find learning to read difficult? The answer given by proponents of WL is that children grow up in an environment in which people use language meaningfully and naturally, but reading is made difficult and unnatural by phonics instruction which takes the language apart into words, syllables, and sounds (Goodman, 1986). Second, it is argued that since words written in orthographies such as Chinese which cannot be phonologically analyzed can still be read and understood, it follows that phonics skill is not a requirement for learning to read (Smith, 1979). There are good reasons to reject these two arguments, which are presented in Chapter 5. Our view in this matter is that phonics should be taught to beginning readers; our argument is that it should and can be taught in meaningful, interesting ways. What we want to stress here is that phonics skills are necessary for word recognition and that they have to be explicitly taught because these skills do not spontaneously emerge in children who are potential candidates for reading disability when they are merely exposed to printed stories. Phonics instruction should, however, not become drudgery and carried to excess. In this respect, WL has rendered a useful service by reacting vehemently against the mechanical teaching of reading. As Waterman (1991) puts it, WL represents not an action, but a reaction.

Another aspect of reading disability and reading instruction that has received much attention in recent years is reading comprehension. Specific topics that have been investigated in this regard are metacognition, the role of schemas, cognitive styles, learning styles, and the development of specific strategies that improve reading comprehension. These will be discussed in some detail in upcoming chapters.

THE STUDY OF READING DISABILITIES

A historical survey of the studies of children who experience difficulty in learning to read indicates that in some children the difficulty exists as an isolated problem, whereas in others it occurs in conjunction with other cognitive deficits. The former group of children have IQs in the average or above-average range, whereas the latter group has below average IQs. Children whose deficit is limited to the written form of language are considered to have Specific Reading Disability or Developmental Dyslexia, whereas children whose learning difficulty involves written language in addition to other cognitive skills are considered to have Nonspecific Reading Disability. Failure to separate these two groups of poor readers has caused a good deal of confusion in the field of learning disabilities. In the following section, the history of the investigation of these two forms of reading disabilities is presented under separate headings.

Specific Reading Disability

Historically, three major approaches have been utilized to investigate the nature of Specific Reading Disability (SRD). These can be loosely classified as neuropsychological, biological–genetic, and psychological.

Neuropsychological Studies

Inspection of educational journals published during the late 19th and early 20th centuries reveals that few articles make reference to reading disability in children. A quarter of a century later, however, the situation was vastly different. Although it is too simplistic an idea to consider a single event to have provided the impetus needed for launching studies of reading disabilities, the use of terms "congenital word-blindness" and "congenital dyslexia" by some educators led Pelosi (1977) to believe that the starting point for the study of reading disability may well have been the 1896 publication of "A Case of Congenital Word Blindness" by Pringle Morgan.

During the later part of the 19th century, reports of isolated instances of sudden but circumscribed loss of reading ability as a consequence of neurological impairment in literate adults began to appear in medical journals. The first accounts of such reading ability loss, along with postmortem findings, were provided in 1891 and 1892 by Dejerine, a French neurologist (Geschwind, 1974). Dejerine not only demonstrated that reading ability could be lost discretely with other mental abilities well preserved, but he also provided a plausible neuro-anatomical explanation for such a circumscribed loss. Because the symptoms seen in Dejerine's patients closely resemble those seen in children with developmental reading disability, it is worth describing his findings in some detail. One of the patients described by Dejerine (1892) was a very intelligent 68-year-old man who, on waking up one morning, was startled to find that he could no longer read a single word. He could see objects well, and his speech was totally unaffected. In fact, there was no hint whatsoever that he was ill. Upon the death of the patient 4 years later, an autopsy revealed that, in addition to damage in parts of the left visual cortex, the splenium of the corpus callosum (through which fibers from the visual cortex reach the angular gyrus) was also damaged (see Fig. 2.1). Dejerine concluded that at the time of the onset of the disability, the angular gyrus (which he thought stored the visual representations of words) was unaffected and this was why the patient could write spontaneously. Since his right visual cortex was intact, he could see objects, relate their representations to the language area of the left hemisphere, and name the objects. The visual representations of printed

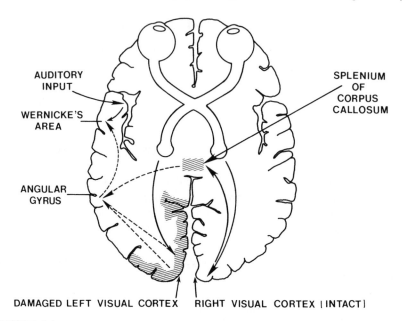

AUDITORY INPUT

WERNICKE'S AREA

SPLENIUM OF CORPUS CALLOSUM

ANGULAR GYRUS

DAMAGED LEFT VISUAL CORTEX   RIGHT VISUAL CORTEX (INTACT)

FIGURE 2.1. Anatomy of an acquired reading disorder.

words, however, could not be named in a similar fashion because the fibers connecting the right visual cortex and the angular gyrus were disrupted.

In 1895, James Hinshelwood, an ophthalmologist from Glasgow, published a similar report in which he described a 58-year-old teacher of French and German who suddenly lost his ability to read printed and written materials. Hinshelwood called this condition "word-blindness." The following year (1896) Pringle Morgan, another physician from England, published a report of a healthy 14-year-old boy in whom he observed a set of symptoms similar to the ones described by Dejerine and Hinshelwood in adult patients. The boy had failed to learn how to read in spite of many years of schooling, and Morgan called this condition "congenital word-blindness," the first known report of developmental dyslexia in English. Morgan, who was familiar with Hinshelwood's paper, was quick to observe the similarities between the traumatic and congenital forms of word-blindness. The boy, according to Morgan, was bright and intelligent; he could read and write all the letters of the alphabet even though he had great difficulty in reading even common monosyllabic words. His spelling was poor and while writing he committed errors by substituting word suffixes (winding—"winder") and by transposing letters. At times he could not write his own name correctly (Percy—"Precy"). His oral language was good, and the teacher who taught him for some years thought that he would have been the smartest lad in the school had the instruction been entirely oral. He experienced no difficulty in math and correctly solved problems such as $(a + x) (a - x) = a^2 - x^2$. Since the health history revealed no illness or injury, Morgan considered the etiology of the reading disability to be congenital and attributed it to defective development of the left angular gyrus.

Hinshelwood (1907) himself soon published detailed accounts of four cases of congenital word-blindness. He not only used the term "congenital word-blindness" but also coined the term "congenital dyslexia." In the United States, two reports of developmental reading disability were published in 1906 in the *Journal of the American Medical Association* and the *Journal of American Medical Science* by Clairborne and Jackson. However, by 1905, a sufficient number of cases had already accumulated to enable Thomas to provide a summary based on nearly 100 instances of the condition recorded at "special schools" in England. Thomas's publication foreshadowed many of the current descriptions of developmental dyslexia. He noted that congenital word-blindness was more frequent than had been suspected. It often had a family history, and in many instances more than one member of the family was affected; it occurred three times more frequently in boys than in girls; and the condition was usually associated with a good visual memory, intelligence, and skill in arithmetic calculations.

Even though some educators used neurologically oriented terms such as "congenital word-blindness" to refer to specific reading disability (e.g., Lord, 1925; Dearborn, 1925), these terms slowly fell into disuse. Eventually, as Harris and Sipay (1980) point out, two opposing tendencies came into existence regarding the etiology of reading disability. Physicians postulated a basic constitutional condition; educational psychologists, on the other hand, impressed by the wide range of psychological, emotional, sociological, linguistic, and educational handicaps that could be seen in poor readers, favored a pluralistic theory of causation.

A new explanation of SRD, more neuropsychological in nature than any hitherto proposed, was advanced in this country in the mid-1920s. The author of this new theory was Samuel Orton, a neuropsychiatrist with extensive firsthand experience in dealing with children having educational problems. Even though Orton used the term "word-blindness" in his early writings (1925), later on he objected to the term, since there was no "blindness" in the ordinary sense of the term nor, indeed, was there even blindness for words. Ironically, the very term Orton chose to replace it—"strephosymbolia" (literally, twisted symbols)—was later subjected to similar misinterpretation by those who took mirror-reversed writing and reading to be the most salient feature of developmental dyslexia. Orton, however, coined the term to highlight a deficit in the *sequential processing of visual language* and a striking tendency in children with reading disability to distort the order of letters recalled while reading and spelling. He made special mention of the fact that "reversals are not an outstanding feature" of specific reading disability (1937, p. 93) and frequently used the phrase "specific reading disability" in place of strephosymbolia.

To replace Hinshelwood's angular gyrus hypothesis, Orton proposed his own. In his clinical experience, Orton had observed a high incidence of left-handedness among dyslexic children and members of their families. He also noticed that children with dyslexia could read mirror-reversed words at least as well as conventional print. On the basis of the neuropsychological information available to him at that time, Orton considered the control mechanisms for speech, reading, and writing to be concentrated in one hemisphere of the brain and thought that this specialization had an intimate relationship to the development of unilateral manual skills. He further believed that normal reading is strictly a unilateral operation in the sense that in a majority of people, engrams necessary to recognize words are located in the left hemisphere. In normal readers, any registration of word images that reaches the right hemisphere is suppressed or "elided." If, however, engrams persist in the nondominant right hemisphere, they cause confusion in word recognition and recall, since these engrams have an "orientation opposite to the ones in the dominant hemisphere." The existence of two sets of representations, the engram and its mirror image, is one of the causes of reading disability. Orton suggested that incomplete dominance which often manifests itself in the form of mixed handedness, eyedness, and so forth is indicative of such a diffuse cerebral condition.

A literal version of Orton's hypothesis is not accepted by many authorities today, because there is no reason to believe that engrams present in the opposite cerebral hemispheres are mirror images. Moreover, numerous studies have failed to establish a significant link between "mixed dominance" and reading disability. Nevertheless, many of Orton's insightful observations in connection with SRD are worth mentioning. First of all, like Hinshelwood some years before, Orton (1937) emphasized the purity of the symptoms of SRD. He noted that many children show no deficit other than reading, spelling, and written language and that the most searching examinations revealed no deviations in brain function. In this context, he mentioned that the auditory development of these children was usually quite normal and the spoken language of reading-disabled children could be normal or even superior. Their visual–motor coordination could be excellent. Strephosymbolics were found to be no less bright than normal readers and, in fact, some of them ranked high in intelligence. Orton emphasized the distinction between children with SRD and children in whom reading disability was seen in conjunction with depressed intellectual ability, even though both groups of children were poor readers.

A considerable portion of Orton's book was devoted to the diagnosis and treatment of SRD. He did not offer a blanket prescription but recommended capitalizing on poor readers' auditory competence by teaching them the phonetic equivalents of printed letters and combining them with the kinesthetic approach. In general, he favored a phonics approach and stressed the importance of developing word attack, blending, and written spelling skills.

The tremendous influence Orton had on the study of developmental dyslexia is exemplified by the establishment of the Orton Dyslexia Society, an organization which holds international and regional meetings and provides a forum for physicians, psychologists, educators, and dyslexics themselves to meet and share their knowledge in this rapidly developing field of research.

As noted earlier, a literal version of Orton's hypothesis is not accepted by many contemporary researchers, but an operational version of the hypothesis in a modified form holds much promise for our understanding of developmental dyslexia. This version is based on the observation that the two hemispheres differ in the *strategies* they utilize, with the left cerebral hemisphere processing information sequentially and the right hemisphere processing information in a simultaneous fashion. Reading involves a well balanced blend of the two strategies; skilled reading depends on the rapid processing of familiar printed words as wholes in addition to the phonological analysis of uncommon and unfamiliar words (Pennington, Lefly, Van Orden, Bookman, & Smith, 1987; Van Orden, 1987). An excessive dependence on one strategy and underutilization of the other are likely to impede the reading process. This proposition, also known as the Imbalance Hypothesis (Aaron, 1978), attributes developmental dyslexia to an overdependence on the simultaneous strategy and an associated underutilization of the sequential strategy. This "imbalance hypothesis" has received experimental support from studies that have used cognitive approaches (Aaron, 1989; Kershner, 1977) as well as from neuropsychological investigations (Witelson, 1977). Recently, Kirby and Robinson (1987) studied 105 reading-disabled children by administering a battery of tests and concluded that these children employed simultaneous processing in reading tasks that normally require successive operations.

In recent years, several investigators have attempted to diagnose and classify the different types of reading disabilities by using neuropsychological tests (e.g., Mattis, French, & Rapin, 1975; Petrauskas & Rourke, 1979). Such attempts are based on the expectation that children with reading disabilities have neurological deficits which can be identified with the aid of such tests. As noted earlier, this expectation is based on the "deficit model" of reading disabilities. These studies have produced conflicting results. In addition to the lack of strong empirical support for a neurologically based etiology of reading disabilities, neuropsychological test batteries are time-consuming to administer and offer little help in providing treatment guidelines. For these reasons, the use of neuropsychological batteries in reading consultation is not further discussed in this book. Studies that have utilized sophisticated visualization techniques (such as CAT scan) also have failed to reach firm conclusions regarding the neurological basis of dyslexia because they are marked by numerous methodological and design problems (Hynd & Clikeman, 1989).

In addition to studies that investigated children, information obtained from neurological patients who once were literate but have lost the ability to read as a result of brain damage have also been utilized in the study of developmental dyslexia. This neuropsychological approach utilizes detailed neurolinguistic case studies and investigates very thoroughly the reading performance of these patients. The impetus for this type of research came from the seminal work of Marshall and Newcombe (1966, 1973) who identified two different forms of reading failure and labled them as *deep dyslexia* and *surface dyslexia*. *Deep dyslexia* is characterized by the following features that become apparent when the patient tries to read isolated words: presence of semantic paralexic errors (*act* → play, *close* → shut, *tall* → long); visual errors (*stock* → struck, *saucer* → sausage, *crocus* → crocodile); derivational errors (*wise* → wisdom, *truth* → true, *strange* → stranger); a hierarchy of word-reading difficulties, with more nouns correctly read than adjectives, which are, in turn, read better than verbs; function-word reading more erratic than that of content words; and an almost total inability to read aloud pronounceable nonwords such as *nol* and *wux* (Marshal & Newcombe, 1980). In contrast, patients who are classified as *surface dyslexics* are thought not to be able to recognize words on the basis of their meaning, but tend to sound them out by applying literal spelling-to-sound rules. Comprehension appears to depend upon the oral response. Thus, the word *sale* is read as "Sally," and when asked what it means, the patient says it is the name of a woman. As data from more surface dyslexic patients have accumulated, however, it has become apparent that a great deal of variation is observable in the performance of these subjects (Patterson, Marshall, & Coltheart, 1985) and additional subtypes have been postulated to accommodate these differences.

One of the major goals of the investigators who have analyzed reading disturbances from a cognitive neuropsychological perspective is to develop a theory and model of the normal reading process. For example, errors committed by adult dyslexic patients suggest that the deep dyslexic is poor in grapheme–phoneme conversion skills (decoding) but is able to comprehend the written word much better than pronounce it; where-as the surface dyslexic is able to convert print into sound, but is unable to comprehend the written word correctly. It is suggested, therefore, that phonological conversion of print and the comprehension of the printed word are two separate skills which may be affected independently. Experimental and genetic studies also support this interpretation, thus justifying the separation of SRD from NSRD.

Biological–Genetic Studies

As noted earlier, it has been recognized from the beginning of the present century that certain variables were associated with SRD to a degree more than chance would warrant. These include sex ratio, genetic tendency, and handedness. In a series of three articles, Geschwind and Galaburda (1985a, 1985b, 1985c) have presented a unified hypothesis about the biological mechanisms which lead to the unusual lateralization of cerebral functions and, at the same time, would account for these associated features. These authors have proposed that lateralization of brain functions is influenced by neurochemicals such as sex hormones present in the maternal uterine environment, as well as fetal tissue sensitivity. Neuroanatomical studies show that in other animals and in humans, the left cerebral hemisphere matures later than the right hemisphere, a fact that leaves the left hemisphere immature for a longer period than the right hemisphere. Geschwind and Galaburda propose that because testosterone has a retarding effect on neural tissue, it will have greater retarding effect on the development of the immature left than the right hemisphere. It is further hypothesized that the underdevelopment of the left cerebral hemisphere results in a compensatory overdevelopment of the contralateral right hemisphere, which can lead to an atypical form of cerebral dominance. Such a retardation of the left hemisphere, therefore, will usually show diminished left hemispheric skills and a corresponding augmentation of right-hemisphere skills. Because males are likely to have above-average amounts of fetal testosterone, atypical cerebral lateralization is likely to be seen in more males than females. Testosterone also affects mechanisms involved in the development of immunity. The Geschwind–Galaburda hypothesis can, therefore, account for facts such as higher incidence of reading diability in males than in females, a higher than chance association between reading disability and left-handedness, immune system disorders such as allergies, and superior visuo–spatial abilities.

Even though investigations of the genetic nature of dyslexia have been reported since the 1950s, the earlier studies were essentially surveys. Reliable conclusions had to wait until better analytic tools became available. The Colorado Family Reading Study, which began in the mid-

1970s, is noteworthy for its utilization of sophisticated statistical procedures and experimental design. Since that time, several reports of this project have been published which indicate substantial heritability of dyslexia (see Pennington, 1990). Recent reports further suggest a significant heritability for spelling, word reading, and WISC-R digit span, but not for reading comprehension. In word reading, the contribution of phonological coding to the heritability of reading was about .93, whereas the contribution of orthographic coding was essentially zero. The mode of genetic transmission, whether autosomal dominant, autosomal recessive, or co-dominant, however, is still undetermined.

Psychological Studies

Ever since SRD was recognized as a developmental disorder, various psychological hypotheses have been proposed to account for it. These psychological explanations can be broadly classified into two categories: visual and phonological.

The view that visual memory may play a causal role in reading disability has a long history. Even Hinshelwood attributed developmental reading disability to a deficit in visual word-form memory. A number of studies undertaken within the last 50 years have investigated the relationship between SRD and different aspects of visual memory. Vellutino (1979), who has reviewed these studies, concluded that there is insufficient evidence to attribute dyslexia to a weakness in visual memory. This conclusion is based on the findings that even though dyslexic children have poor visual memory for verbal materials, they have normal memory for nonverbal visual stimuli. The fact that a linguistic component has emerged as part of visual memory in some studies supports the possibility that visual memory for words may be partially linguistic in nature. Memory for the written spelling, also known as *orthographic memory,* therefore, may not be exclusively visual in nature but may have visual memory as only one of its components.

The visual component of orthographic memory involves three types of information about the written word: spatial redundancy, sequential redundancy, and high-frequency spelling patterns. Spatial redundancy refers to the fact that certain letters occur more often in certain positions in the word than others (e.g., the letter "e" occurs in the terminal position of words such as *cute* and *mate* which have a laxed vowel sound). Sequential redundancy refers to the frequency with which some letters follow other letters in words (e.g., the letter "q" is almost always followed by "u"; the letter "h" is more often preceded by "t" than "a"). Consistent spelling patterns occur as digraphs, trigraphs, and four-letter units with a high degree of freqency (e.g., "ed," "ing," and "tion"). Reading teachers sometimes refer to these units as "word patterns" or "word families."

Knowledge of this orthographic information is likely to prevent an individual from spelling *cute* as "cut," *question* as "qestion," and *attention* as "attension." Other units of spelling patterns are "onset" and "rimes." An *onset* is the letter string pattern in a word that precedes a vowel; the remainder of the word is the *rime*. For example, *str* is the onset of words such as *strip, string, strap,* etc. Training children in word patterns is recommended as a means of improving word recognition skills (cf. Henry, 1990). Berninger (1990) has stressed that it is important for school psychologists to take into account orthographic skills while assessing and planning interventions for disabled readers.

As noted earlier, orthographic memory is not a pure form of visual memory but is partially dependent on the phonological and semantic features of the written word (Aaron, Wills, & Wleklinski, in press). This may be why unpronounceable letter combinations are not seen in the written language. Orthographic memory could also be a product of reading experience (cf. Stanovich & West, 1989) rather than an intrinsic skill. It would appear, therefore, that poor visual memory is not likely to be a cause of reading disabilities. The implication of these studies for the consultant is that (a) poor spelling skill should not be interpreted as poor visual memory, and (b) classifying children with reading disabilities into "auditory dyslexics" and "visual dyslexics" (e.g., Johnson & Myklebust, 1967; Gjessing & Karlsen, 1989) is a questionable procedure.

In contrast to the ambiguity that surrounds the importance of visual and orthographic memories in reading disabilities, phonological skills have emerged as strong correlates of reading skill. One such phonological skill is *phonological awareness,* which is an ability to recognize sound segments in the spoken word. Phonological awareness is considered a prerequisite for the development of a knowledge of letter–sound correspondence. As early as 1974, Liberman, Shankweiler, Fischer, and Carter found that only 17% of kindergartners showed evidence of phoneme awareness. Many studies of English-speaking children indicate a close association between phoneme awareness and success in learning to read (see Blachman, 1984, for a review) and that a measure of phonological awareness is the best single predictor of reading achievement in young children (Stanovich, Cunningham, & Cramer, 1984). This has also been found to be true for Swedish (Lundberg, 1988), French (Bertelson, 1987), Spanish (de Manrique & Gramigna, 1984), and Italian (Cossu, Shankweiler, Liberman, Tola, & Katz, 1988) languages. The importance of phonological awareness for reading has also been demonstrated by studies which have shown that training in phonological awareness improves the reading skills of very young children (Bradley & Bryant, 1983).

Related psychological factors that have received considerable attention are short-term memory and the speed with which words are retrieved from the memory store. Investigators study deficits in these areas by assessing the reader's ability to repeat a series of digits or by measuring the time it takes to name pictures rapidly (Denckla & Rudel, 1976; Rudel, 1985). The poor performance of many dyslexic children in these tasks was taken to mean that SRD may be due to a poor short-term memory capacity and an associated deficit in word-retrieval skill. Recent studies, however, suggest that performance of digit recall tasks may be determined by a speed factor rather than a capacity factor. This interpretation receives support from the observation that English–Welsh bilinguals tend to recall more digits in English than in Welsh (Ellis & Hennely, 1980). This is attributed to the fact that digits in Welsh take longer to utter than digits in English. As will be seen later, slow processing of information as indicated by a below-average digit span is one of the symptoms of SRD.

Nonspecific Reading Disability

Sporadic reports of children who could decode written words with surprising facility but could not comprehend what they had read have appeared in educational literature since the early part of the present century (e.g., Bronner, 1917). Recognition of the existence of some children who could read aloud fluently but not understand what they had read, together with the knowledge that there are children with normal intelligence who cannot decode printed language, led to a distinction between the two types of poor readers (Monroe, 1932). An almost pure condition of Nonspecific Reading Disability, in which a striking discrepancy between decoding skill and comprehension is seen, has been reported by Silberberg and Silberberg (1967) who used the term "hyperlexia" to describe word-decoding ability that is out of proportion to comprehension ability.

By 1982, sufficient information about hyperlexic children had accumulated for Healy (1982) to raise the question: "Is there an identifiable syndrome of hyperlexia?" (p. 323) and to answer it in the affirmative. Reviewing research undertaken prior to 1989, Aaron (1989) concluded that hyperlexia is a syndrome manifested by three symptoms: (1) spontaneous reading of words before age 5, (2) impaired comprehension of both listening and reading tasks, and (3) exceptional word recognition (decoding) skill compared to other cognitive or linguistic abilities. Although rare, hyperlexia is associated with an extreme comprehension deficit and therefore, is, of interest to the reading consultant. A detailed description of a hyperlexic child is provided by Aaron, Franz, & Manges (1990).

By far the largest number of poor readers seen in schools have a combination of poor comprehension and decoding skills. These children are sometimes referred to as "garden variety" poor readers (Gough &

Tunmer, 1986). Contemporary research, therefore, suggests that there are three kinds of poor readers: those with deficient decoding skills but normal comprehension, those with adequate decoding skills but poor comprehension, and those with deficits in both areas.

Research indicates that a failure to comprehend well what is read can be caused by poor metacognitive skills, certain types of cognitive styles, and by poor word knowledge and vocabulary. Because cognitive style and metacognition will be discussed fully in Chapter 4, we will limit our discussion here to word knowledge and vocabulary.

Word Knowledge and Vocabulary

It should come as no surprise that vocabulary size is a major correlate of comprehension skill. A study of reading comprehension in 15 countries shows that the correlation between vocabulary and reading comprehension ranges from .66 to .75 (Thorndike, 1973). The role played by vocabulary in reading is so important that one investigator (Manuel Sebo, personal communication) refers to it as the "John Effect" after the Gospel according to St. John (*John 1:1*): "In the beginning was the word." An intriguing fact, however, is that vocabulary and reading comprehension have a reciprocal relationship. That is, just as vocabulary determines how well an individual can read, reading experience also influences vocabulary development. This finding has important implications not only for remedial instruction but also for policy decisions regarding mainstreaming.

Although estimates of children's vocabulary vary considerably, a figure of 40,000 words appears reasonable for an average high school student. The fact that spoken language is limited both in the variety and quality of words used leads to the conclusion that beyond a certain level, acquisition of vocabulary depends on reading experience. There is evidence to show that children differ a great deal in reading experience. Nagy and Anderson (1984), for example, estimated that, as regards in-school reading, the least motivated children in the middle grades might read 100,000 words a year while average children at this level might read almost 1,000,000 words. An avid middle-grade child might read even as many as 10,000,000 words a year. Thus, good readers read more and develop large vocabularies which, in turn, enhance their comprehension skill; poor readers read less and, consequently, stagnate as far as vocabulary growth is concerned, falling further and further behind in reading skills compared to their peers. This phenomenon, originally noted by Walberg and Tsai (1983) has come to be known as the "Matthew Effect." This designation refers to the biblical passage in the Book of Matthew (*Matt.* 25:29): "For unto every one that hath shall be given, but from him that hath not shall be taken away even that which he hath." The Matthew Effect has been demonstrated in the English (Stanovich, 1986) and Dutch (van den Bos, 1989) languages. The implication for remedial instruction is obvious: pull-out programs which remove children from regular classrooms, in order to provide highly restricted, specialized drills, can deprive them of reading experience and thereby set the Matthew Effect in motion.

It should be noted that simply increasing the reader's vocabulary size does not by itself automatically guarantee a corresponding improvement of sentence and text comprehension. Sentences and texts require that the reader go beyond the information present in the printed page.

Studies investigating reading disabilities have generated a vast amount of data. This information, along with knowledge gained from studies of normal readers, has considerably enhanced our understanding of reading dynamics. The psychology of the reading process is the subject matter of the next chapter.

3

The Psychology of Reading

INTRODUCTION

More than half the children evaluated by the School Psychologist are referred for poor academic performance. Many of these children are diagnosed as having learning disabilities based on their performance on standardized reading tests. As a result, statements made with reference to reading disabilities are also applicable to most learning problems. Learning difficulties of many high school and college students also originate from poor reading skills. A knowledge of the psychological processes behind reading, therefore, is necessary for the School Psychologist in educational decision making under these varied settings and conditions.

In this chapter, we provide an overview of the psychological processes that underlie reading. A knowledge of what happens when we read is essential to understanding why an individual cannot learn to read. Recommendations for diagnosis and remedial instruction presented later in this book are based on the descriptions of the psychology of reading delineated in this chapter. An appreciation of the psychology of the reading process is, therefore, essential for implementing the recommended diagnostic and remedial procedures and for effective consultation.

An understanding of the reading process would be enormously facilitated if we could break it down into smaller elements and study them closely, rather than investigating this complex activity wholistically. Therefore, the first step in examining reading is to ask whether it is comprised of simpler, constituent processes.

Components of Reading

The diagnostic and treatment approaches presented in this book are based on the premise that even though reading is a complex skill, it is made up of certain identifiable components. A component can be defined as an elementary information process that operates upon internal representations of objects and symbols (Sternberg, 1985). Whether a process is elementary enough to be a "component" depends upon its independence (Carr, Brown, Vavrus, & Evans (1990) and the desired level of theorizing chosen by the researcher. While some researchers identify the components of reading at a comparatively general, "basic" level (e.g., Leong, 1988), others prefer a fine-grained analysis (e.g., Frederiksen, 1982). Because of this, the number of reading subprocesses reported by researchers varies. For our purpose, reading is approached at a basic level and is considered to be made up of two major components: the ability to pronounce the written word, either overtly or covertly (also referred to as *decoding* in this book), and the ability to comprehend words and text. Findings of experimental, neuropsychological, genetic, and developmental studies indicate that these two components are more or less insulated from each other and, therefore, modular and independent. Some of these studies are briefly reviewed in the following pages. A logical expectation of the two-component view of reading is that during development, each component could be affected independently, leaving the other intact and thus causing different types of reading disabilities.

In an experimental investigation, Jackson and McClelland (1979) studied undergraduate students and found that comprehension ability and reaction time in a letter-matching task accounted for nearly all of the variance seen in reading ability. Investigations by Hunt, Lunneborg, and Lewis (1975) and by Palmer, McCleod, Hunt, and Davidson (1985) also found that comprehension and speed of decoding print are the two most important components of reading. After reviewing a number of research studies, Levy and Carr (1990) also concluded that word recognition and comprehension skills are dissociable. They use the term "word recognition" to indicate phonological processing which plays an important role in decoding.

Neuropsychological patients who have lost their ability to read and are labeled either as "deep dyslexics" or as "surface dyslexics" were described in Chapter 2. The reading disorders of these two groups of patients indicate that some patients can comprehend words far better than they can pronounce them, whereas other patients can pronounce words far better than they can understand them. These acquired disorders of reading, therefore, demonstrate the independence of phonological decoding and comprehension of the written language from one another.

Genetic studies also support the notion that comprehension and pronunciation skills are independent. DeFries, Fulker, and La Buda (1987), in a study of twins with reading disabilities, found a significant heritability for word recognition, spelling, and WISC-R digit span but not for reading comprehension. Olson and his associates (cited in Pennington & Smith, 1988), who studied the same population of MZ and DZ twins, found significant heritability for nonword reading (which is a measure of decoding) but not for comprehension. Commenting on these studies, Pennington and Smith (1988) concluded that in SRD, single-word reading, spelling, and digit span, but not reading comprehension, are genetically influenced.

Reports of developmental studies are in agreement with the above studies and show that comprehension and the ability to pronounce the written word are the most important variables of reading achievement. Frith and Snowling (1983) have shown that children with dyslexia comprehend much better than they can read aloud, and some autistic children with hyperlexic symptoms decode print with considerable skill but do not comprehend what they have read. A study by Aaron, Franz, and Manges (1990) in which children with three different kinds of reading disabilities were investigated, also found a similar separation between decoding and comprehension skills.

Our choice of two components is motivated by empirical as well as pragmatic considerations. The empirical consideration is that the two-component view is in agreement with the findings of studies discussed above; the practical consideration is that the proposed model of reading based on this two-component assumption leads to relatively simple diagnostic procedures that can be carried out quickly and easily without the need for elaborate instruments and a multitude of tests.

The first component, the ability to pronounce the written word, is also referred to as *decoding skill, phonological encoding skill,* and *grapheme–*

phoneme conversion skill. It is an operation that is specific to the written form of language. The second component, comprehension, is used in this book as a generic term to encompass both reading and listening comprehension. (The decision not to make a distinction between reading and listening comprehension is based on empirical evidence which will be presented in Chapter 4.) Skilled reading requires that the integrity of decoding and comprehension be preserved. Inefficient operation of either one of these components can, therefore, disrupt the reading process and result in reading disabilities. Furthermore, because these two components are independent of each other, weakness in different components can lead to different kinds of reading disabilities.

In addition to these two skills, reading involves sensory, perceptual, and motor processes. Nevertheless, because most reading disabilities arise from deficits in decoding or comprehension, in our discussion more attention will be given to these two skills than to sensory and perceptual processes. It is possible that orthographic skill also plays a role in word recognition. However, as noted in the previous chapter, it is uncertain whether orthographic memory is a pure form of visual memory independent of phonological and semantic memory structures.

Since decoding and comprehension are influenced by factors such as information stored in the reader's long-term memory (LTM), the reader's background knowledge, and his/her ability to make inferences, reading is an *interactive process.* In spite of this fact, we will describe the reading process *as though* it is carried out sequentially in a series of discrete stages. Such an approach makes the elucidation of the reading process relatively easy. Reading will be examined from the perspective of four substages: sensory encoding, word recognition, sentence comprehension, and passage comprehension. Finally, we will also discuss the role played by metacognition. Each one of these aspects is a potential locus of reading difficulty.

THE SENSORY ENCODING STAGE

Eye Movements

It has been known for almost a century that when we read, our eyes do not move smoothly and continuously over the printed line, but make a series of moves interspersed with stops. The moves are referred to as *saccades* and the stops as *fixations.* Each saccade lasts approximately 15 to 35 milliseconds (msec) depending on how far the eyes travel, and the average fixation duration is about 250 msec, even though factors such as familiarity and ambiguity of the printed word can influence the fixation duration (Rayner & Pollastek, 1989). The average fixation duration of 250 msec fits neatly in with the observation that proficient readers can read about 250 words per minute. This means that approximately four words can be processed per second. Generally speaking, a single word is focused on and processed during a single fixation, even though two adjacent words can be processed if the second word is short and is predictable from context (Just & Carpenter 1987). Examples of these include "function words" such as *and, the, on,* etc. At times, function words are even skipped altogether. During saccades, the neural system inhibits visual input; information is taken in only during fixations. Without this neural phenomenon, the printed line and, indeed, the entire visual world would appear to us as a big blur.

The Iconic Store

During the initial stage of reading, specifically during fixations, the photic stimulus is transduced into neural impulses, and the mapping of the visual stimulus onto the sensory system is accomplished. Experimental studies suggest that the visual stimulus which is transformed into sensory input is retained in a temporary store called *icon.* The iconic store is thought to have a very short duration but a relatively "large" capacity. Studies by Sperling (1960) indicate iconic duration to be about 100 msec and the iconic capacity to be about 12 letters. The capacity of the icon is considered "large" because it exceeds that of the short-term memory (STM) which ranges from 7 to 9 items. Interestingly, the extremely short duration of the icon falls well within the average period of the eye fixation, and the iconic capacity of about 12 items is sufficient to process most written words in the English language. Eye movement studies show that every letter in the written word is sampled and that readers notice specific letter information in the words they read (Rayner & Bertera, 1979; Zola, 1984). This is not to say that every letter in a written word is processed serially one by one, but it appears that letters in the word are the basic units of analysis and that all the letters in a word are processed simultaneously, in parallel.

Even though the psychological reality of the iconic store is questioned by some, it is apparent from eye movement studies that whatever the nature of the store is, the initial visual input has to be cleared from the temporary store in less than a quarter of a second to make room for the subsequent input. If this does not happen, the first visual input could linger on and interfere with subsequent input. In order to avoid such a logjam, the reader may have to slow down the movement of his/her eyes to allow time for the icon to be cleared, which would retard the rate of reading. For this reason, the iconic process of poor readers has been investigated to see whether this might be a source of reading disabilities. Studies that examined this question are equivocal in their findings, and there is no convincing evidence to show that poor iconic functioning or any problem associated with visual perception plays a causal role in reading disabilities. As a matter of fact, a number of studies show that the dyslexic reader's visual memory for nonverbal material is as good as, or even better than, that of normal readers (Aaron, Bommarito, & Baker 1984; Fisher & Frankfurter, 1977). As Daneman (1991) points out, good and poor readers do not differ in visual perception processes, but the differences between these readers become apparent only when some verbal or linguistic coding operation is involved.

Furthermore, if sensory and perceptual factors play a causal role, the visual problem need not be limited to written language alone; it should result in impaired vision for all stimuli. In addition, as will be seen later, reading disabilities constitute syndromes comprising many symptoms, including poor spelling. Thus, the reading problem is not limited to the input aspect of information processing but also involves output processes such as spelling which cannot be explained by deficiencies of the visual input system. This conclusion also follows from the findings of many studies demonstrating that remedial methods such as speed reading and eye movement and perceptual training are of little value in improving reading skill. The implication for the consultant is that visual perception training, eye-movement training, and speed reading cannot be recommended as procedures for improving reading skill.

After mapping of the visual stimulus onto sensory input is accomplished, the word can then be recognized.

THE WORD RECOGNITION STAGE

Studies that have had computers track eye movements during reading suggest that, generally speaking, the word fixated on is recognized before the eyes move and fixate on the next word. The traditional view is that a written word is recognized when the sensory input corresponding to the word makes contact with the representation of the word stored in the long-term memory. The written word is most likely represented in terms of its features such as pronunciation, spelling pattern, and meaning. These are referred to as the *phonological, orthographic,* and *semantic* properties of the word, respectively. Thus, recognition of a word includes retrieving not only its pronunciation, but also accessing its semantic properties. In the case of writing, the orthographic features of the word may also be retrieved. The notion that all these properties are realized as soon as the reader encounters a word within a sentence rather than later, when the phrase or sentence has been completed, is referred to as the *immediacy hypothesis* (Just & Carpenter, 1987). The rejection of a "wait-and-see" strategy of comprehension is based on the observation that when readers encounter a misspelled word or an uncommon word, fixation time is longer than with correctly spelled common words. For example, eye-movement studies show that readers fixate longer on the word *sable* than on the word *table* before proceeding to fixate on the next word in the sentence. Such observations are taken as evidence that the eyes do not move until a word is recognized. If the eyes had moved and some difficulty was encountered with word recognition, they move back to refixate on the word. Such a regressive movement indicates that a reader is keeping track of the word recognition process and, if it fails, is able to take adequate measures to correct the situation. Regressive movements, therefore, cannot be considered a *cause* of reading disability but, rather, as evidence of the reader's corrective actions. This is an important point to keep in mind because some "specialists" attribute reading disabilities to faulty eye movements and prescribe eye-training exercises to improve reading skill.

Even though the immediacy hypothesis is true generally speaking, changes in this way of processing occur when the reader encounters ambiguous statements and anaphoric references (Rayner & Pollatsek, 1989). For example, realization of the full import of the word *what* in the sentence "What Johnny wants to do is to read all day and all night" may not be accomplished immediately upon its first encounter but will have to wait until the entire sentence is processed. It is also possible that upon the reader's first encounter with a word, its several potential meanings are aroused, and the appropriate meaning confirmed only by the sentence context. It is also reported that when the reader encounters an ambiguous word with more than one meaning (e.g., *rose* = "flower," or past tense of "rise") all the meanings of the word are temporarily but simultaneously activated and a final selection is made on the basis of semantic and syntactic contexts. In spite of these exceptions, it appears that the properties of a majority of words are realized before the eyes move and make the next fixation. Word recognition, therefore, is an important first step in reading.

We now return to the crucial question: How is a word recognized in terms of its phonological, orthographic, and semantic properties? Considering the fact that a skilled adult reader may know as many as 150,000 words (Aitchison, 1987), the ability to recognize and pronounce a written word in less than 250 msecs is an astounding feat. It is argued that to accomplish such a quick retrieval, information regarding the phonological, semantic, and orthographic features of words have to be organized and arranged in the brain in some systematic fashion. Psychologists and psycholinguists often use structural metaphors such as "dictionary" and "library" to describe such an organization of information. In fact, this putative organization of word knowledge is given the name *mental lexicon*. It should be noted that the mental lexicon is a hypothetical construct only and that such models do not describe psychological entities in an absolute sense but tend to explain them in terms of phenomena familiar to us. That is why analogies such as "library," "dictionary," and "network" are often used for describing the mental lexicon. A model reflects our inability to understand a phenomenon in its true form.

In spite of the hypothetical nature of models, certain characteristics of the mental lexicon are known. For instance, the mental lexicon for words is not organized on an alphabetic basis like a dictionary. This can be easily demonstrated by asking someone to recall the names of calendar months, first in chronological sequence from January and then in alphabetical order, from April through September. The fact that the second task takes much longer than the first should not be surprising. But how can the difference between recall times be explained? One reasonable explanation is that names of months are stored in chronological rather than in alphabetical order. This explanation is based on the assumption that reaction time (RT) reflects the organization of the mental lexicon and, therefore, if two words are recalled in quick succession, they are close to each other in the lexicon. In fact, psychologists who study the mental lexicon use RT as a major dependent variable to make inferences regarding characteristics of the mental lexicon. It has to be noted, however, that with some practice, it is possible to recite rather quickly the names of the months in alphabetic order. This shows that we can create lexical files in our long-term memory on the basis of new formats, if we want to. What is obvious, however, is that the format in which information is filed in the lexicon has much influence on recall. In other words, if the pattern of input does not match the order in which the output is required, or if the input is unsystematic and disorganized, recall will be difficult or poor. The organizational format of the poor reader's lexicon can, therefore, be one source of learning problems. A knowledge of the nature of the mental lexicon can, therefore, provide us with useful information regarding the nature of reading disabilities.

To understand the nature of the mental lexicon, we raise three questions and try to answer them without losing sight of the fact that the "mental lexicon" is only a theoretical construct. The three questions are: How many lexicons are there? How is their information organized? How is a written word recognized? These are not trivial questions because they may contain answers to the puzzle of reading disabilities and potential clues for remedial instruction. Answers to the three questions come from observations and experiments. This research draws upon evidence showing our ability to pronounce words we have never seen before, patterns behind slips of the tongue, and clinical symptoms such as the selective inability of some neurological patients to pronounce grammar words and word suffixes. Thus experimental data come from normal subjects as well as neurological patients who have lost their ability to read.

Researchers have used the following three techniques to collect data:

lexical decision tasks, semantic decision tasks, and *priming tasks.* In the lexical decision task, the subject is presented with a string of letters (e.g., "bromp") and is asked whether it is a word or a "nonword." In the semantic decision task, the subject is presented with a word (e.g., "chicken") and is asked whether it is a member of certain category (e.g., *animal*) or not. In the priming task, the target word is preceded by another word which may or may not be related to the target word and the RT for pronouncing the target word is measured. In all of these experiments, RT is the dependent variable, the assumption being that the larger the difference in RT between two words, the further away from each other they are represented in the mental lexicon. For instance, in a semantic decision task, if the RT for the question, "Is a robin a bird?" is shorter than it is for the question, "Is a chicken a bird?" it is inferred that *robin* is closer to *bird* than *chicken* is to *bird.* By asking many such "bird-related" questions, one can construct an organizational hierarchy for the concept of *bird* in the mental lexicon. In the priming task, if the RT for *nurse* is shorter when preceded by *doctor* than when preceded by *milk,* it is assumed that the words *nurse* and *doctor* are represented closer to each other in the lexicon than *nurse* and *milk.*

We will now attempt to answer the three questions we raised regarding the mental lexicon.

How Many Lexicons Are There?

On the basis of word recognition studies, cognitive psychologists have concluded that there ought to be at least three lexicons which play a role in word recognition processes. These are: *phonological rules lexicon, word pronunciation lexicon,* and *semantic lexicon.* Another property of the written word which is sometimes considered to play a role in word recognition is its spelling pattern. The possibility of a fourth—*orthographic lexicon*—is, therefore, entertained by some researchers.

The Phonological Rules Lexicon

The phonological rules lexicon is envisaged as a holding place that contains the rules needed to pronounce and spell words correctly. Several studies suggest that the phonological lexicon is independent of the word pronunciation and semantic lexicons. In a previous section we saw that two outstanding symptoms of deep dyslexia are an inability to read aloud nonwords and an impaired ability to read grammar words even though the patients could demonstrate better comprehension of words. It is assumed that because nonwords are not listed in the semantic lexicon, pronunciation of such words can be accomplished only by applying the spelling–pronunciation rules located in the phonological lexicon. Similarly, because grammar words do not refer to objects, actions, or properties, and do not have meaning, they cannot be pronounced on the basis of meaning. Thus, it appears that deep dyslexia is caused by an impairment of the phonological rules lexicon, not by any problem in the semantic lexicon. Taken together, deep dyslexia and surface dyslexia suggest that the phonological and semantic lexicons are indepentent of each other. Developmental reading disorders such as dyslexia and hyperlexia also suggest that the semantic lexicon and phonological rules lexicon have independent histories of development.

Experimental studies also provide support for postulating a lexicon containing phonological rules independent of the semantic lexicon. In lexical decision tasks, normal subjects say "yes" faster to common nouns such as *cat* and *house* than "no" to pronounceable nonwords such as *neet* and *cleer*. This difference in RT is explained by postulating that two different lexicons are tapped in such tasks, the semantic lexicon and the phonological rules lexicon. In this lexical decision task, both lexicons produce a "yes" response to real words, whereas for pronounceable nonwords the semantic lexicon produces a "no" response but the phonological rules lexicon produces a "yes" response. This conflict increases RT.

The Word Pronunciation Lexicon

Unlike the phonological rules lexicon in which rules for pronouncing words are represented, the word pronunciation lexicon is thought to contain a representational list of word-specific pronunciations. Thus, while the phonological rules lexicon helps in "assembling" the pronunciation of words, the pronunciation lexicon enables the reader to "address and retrieve" appropriate pronunciations of words wholistically, as single units. The operational basis of the rules lexicon can be viewed as algorithmic, and that of the pronunciation lexicon as associative. The fact that we can pronounce exception words (e.g., *have, sew, pint*) which will lead to mispronunciation if spelling–pronunciation rules are applied, is sometimes cited as a reason for postulating a lexicon in which whole-word pronunciations are listed.

The neuropsychological literature also provides support for the belief that the phonological rules lexicon is independent from the word pronunciation lexicon. The observation that there are neurological patients who could pronounce written real words rather well but could not pronounce nonwords is cited as evidence for this conclusion (cf. Funnell, 1983; Lytton & Brust, 1989). These patients apparently can pronounce words by using an associative process but are unable to pronounce words by applying pronunciation rules to words because of an impaired phonological rules lexicon. Furthermore, whether a word is "regular" or an "exception" has no influence on the reading performance of these patients. This means they pronounce the word by retrieving the pronunciation as a whole without assembling it. Recently, we studied a developmental analog of this form of reading disability (Aaron et al., 1990). The subject was a 19-year-old female with a borderline IQ who could read words at about the fourth-grade level but could not read even a single item from a list of 36 nonwords. She also read "regular" and "exception" words equally well. Children described in the developmental reading literature as "word callers" are similar to this subject. Poor readers who tend to rely on sight vocabulary for reading may depend on only the word pronunciation lexicon.

The Semantic Lexicon

The semantic lexicon can be thought of as a store which contains all the meanings we associate with the words we know. There is evidence to show that a good portion of the information we have about the world is organized on a conceptual basis. The observation that the priming effect of conceptually related words on one another is larger than it is for conceptually unrelated words is taken as evidence for this conclusion. The verbal learning "free recall task" provides further support for the belief that the semantic lexicon is conceptually organized. In this task, the subject is presented with a random list of words and is asked to recall them in any order he or she wishes. The words may represent different categories such as clothing items, fruits, animals, etc. It is generally observed that even without specific instruction, subjects tend to recall items in categories rather than in a random fashion. For instance, subjects are likely to recall the names of animals and fruits in groups even though the list was not presented to the subjects on such a conceptual basis. This suggests that learners tend to organize and store what they learn in conceptual categories.

In addition to experimental evidence, clinical data obtained from deep dyslexic patients also support the notion of an independent semantic lexicon. As noted earlier, neurological patients described as deep dyslexics are poor in pronouncing nonwords but can demonstrate a better comprehension of real words, particularly nouns.

The Orthographic Lexicon

The status of the orthographic lexicon is not firmly established. It was noted in Chapter 2 that it is not clear whether orthographic memory is independent of phonological and semantic skills, or these features become "amalgamated" into one complex skill as a result of reading experience (Stanovich, & West 1989). As a matter of fact, orthography is defined as the visual pattern of the written language as it relates to the graphemic, phonological, and semantic features of the language (Henderson, 1984).

Do we have any evidence for the existence of an independent orthographic lexicon? It is said that some children lag behind in the development of word recognition skill even though they have adequate phonological skills. If phonological skill is all that is necessary for word recognition, these children should be good at this task. The poor word recognition of children with good phonological skill is, therefore, thought to indicate that word recognition requires some additional ability. It is speculated that this additional skill is visual memory for orthographic units. The status of the orthographic lexicon is an important issue because if it turns out that some children have specific weakness in orthographic memory despite adequate phonological skills, this would represent a second variety of SRD. Some learning disability (LD) specialists indeed claim that there are two forms of reading disabilities: auditory dyslexia and visual dyslexia (e.g., Johnson & Myklebust, 1967).

Other evidence cited in support of the orthographic lexicon is that children sometimes write correctly a few words they cannot pronounce. Another argument for it is that mature readers can spell exception words correctly, a task which cannot be accomplished by applying spelling–sound rules. The same statement can be made with reference to *homophones* (words with similar pronunciation but dissimilar meaning, e.g., *read, reed; meet, meat*). Obviously some form of visual memory for these words is necessary for spelling them correctly. Experimental studies also suggest there might be an independent orthographic lexicon. For instance, Seidenberg and Tanenhaus (1979), found that in an aurally presented rhyme detection task, words that were orthographically similar (e.g., pie–tie) were identified as rhymes faster than rhymes that were orthographically dissimilar (e.g., rye–tie). The difference in RT is thought to be due to the arousal of orthographic representations (dissimilar in the case of *rye–tie*) which creates a conflict.

Even though these observations provide support for the belief that an orthographic lexicon exists, its independence as a lexicon is not clearly established. Ehri and Wilce (1980) suggest that the orthographic representation may not be stored as rote-memorized visual images but as sequences bearing systematic relationships to acoustic and/or articulatory segments detected in the word's phonological identity. Stanovich and West (1989) studied college students and concluded that *some* of the variance seen in word processing skill could be attributed to differences in orthographic processing skill but that reading experience may contribute to the orthographic variance. A study by Olson et al. (1989a) also found that phonological processing skill associated with word recognition had a sizable heritability, whereas the variance associated with orthographic processing was largely nonheritable, suggesting that reading experience is an important variable associated with orthographic processing ability. By definition, failure to learn to read because of inadequate learning experience is not considered a specific reading disability.

The visual memory capacity for orthographic representation also appears to be limited to 2 or 3 items (Zhang & Simon, 1985). Orthographic representations that exceed this limit may have to be sustained by phonological support to be retained in working memory. Available evidence suggests that spelling skill is more closely associated with phonological skill than with visual memory skill. After reviewing related research, Levy and Carr (1990) conclude that orthographic and phonological factors are difficult to separate, and that orthographic deficits seen in some children may be secondary to phonological difficulties.

How Is Information Organized in The Lexicon?

A knowledge of the format in which lexicons are organized can be useful because such knowledge will place us in a position to choose between alternate explanations advanced to account for the slow retrieval of information by poor readers. Two explanations have been advanced to account for the slow retrieval of information by poor readers. One is that the neurological mechanism of the poor reader takes longer to process information. The second explanation is that the lexicon of poor readers is organized in a chaotic fashion or that the relevant information is not stored in the lexicon, neither of which would permit efficient retrieval of information. A knowledge of the organization of lexicons is not merely a matter of theoretical interest but has practical value: instruction will be most effective when the information presented to students is compatible with the organizational pattern of the lexicon.

Two basic organizational formats have been proposed for the semantic lexicon. These are the *network model* and the *set model*. Other proposed formats are either hybrids or modifications of these two basic models. While the contents of the semantic lexicon may be representations of concepts, it is quite possible that the contents of the phonological rules lexicon are phonological properties of the word and that of the orthographic lexicon are patterns of letter sequences. Models of the semantic lexicon are constructed almost solely on the basis of data obtained from RT studies.

The Network Model

The network model proposes that lexical entries are arranged on a conceptual basis in the form of a hierarchical network. As one moves up the hierarchy, the concepts become more and more generalized. For example, the superordinate of *canary* is *bird,* and the superordinate of *bird* is *animal.* Thus, *canary* is at the bottom of the network, *bird* above it, and *animal* further up. Concepts relevant to *canary* alone will be linked to that word, whereas concepts relevant to birds in general will be linked to the word *bird.* For example, "yellow" would be linked to *canary* whereas "wings" will be attached to *birds.* When information has to be retrieved, the subject enters the lowest level of the network and proceeds further up until information necessary to answer the question is obtained. For instance, in this example, it takes longer to answer the question, "Is a canary an animal?" than to answer the question, "Is a canary a bird?" It is, therefore, inferred that *canary* is closer to *bird* than to *animal.* Even though a temporal–conceptual relationship has been demonstrated for several concepts, too many exceptions have been reported so that the network model does not appear to provide the best fit for the mental lexicon (Bower & Hilgard, 1986). For example, it takes longer to verify the statement, "cantaloupe is a melon," than to verify the statement, "cantaloupe is a fruit," even though in the network model *cantaloupe* and *melon* should be closer to each other than *cantaloupe* and *fruit.* The fact that people use the word "fruit" more often than the word "melon" can explain this discrepancy. Thus, the semantic lexicon may be built on a combination of conceptual and experiential bases.

The Set Model

In this model, semantic information is thought to be arranged in discrete sets. Each set may be envisaged as a deck of playing cards which includes all instances of a particular semantic unit as well as all its attributes. For instance, the semantic unit *dog* may contain the names of all breeds of dogs as well as their defining characteristics such as "dogs are animals," "dogs bark," "dogs are pets," etc. Furthermore, the attributes within the set as well as the sets themselves may be stacked on top of each other, with the most frequently encountered units occupying the topmost level. It is also assumed that information search is serial and proceeds from top to bottom. This form of organization can explain the finding that in lexical decision tasks the RT for high-frequency words is shorter than for low-frequency words. A modified version of this model hypothesizes that highly familiar words may be represented twice, once in the main set and again in a subset. The subset contains highly familiar words and is somewhat like an abridged pocket dictionary, which contains common words and is used for quick reference. When the reader encounters a word, she/he may first search the quick reference subset, and if the search fails to turn up the word, the reader would then proceed to search the large set.

An implication of the set model, in its originally proposed format, is that all units of information in a set are checked against the input information, one at a time, until the correct match is obtained. The incredible speed with which we can recognize a word is not compatible with this model unless it is modified to adopt a search procedure in which all items stored in a set are matched with the input item simultaneously. This, of course, is parallel search. However, for parallel search a hierarchical organization of semantic units based on word frequency and familiarity is not necessary.

This brief review shows that both models of lexicon have their relative weaknesses. Perhaps lexical organization is far more complex than we have anticipated. Nevertheless, as we will see later, these two models have important implications for remedial instruction. A more important question, however, is how the written word is recognized, a question to which we now turn our attention.

How Is a Written Word Recognized?

Even though several models have been proposed to explain the word-recognition process, most of them can be placed in two broad categories: models which postulate that a word is recognized by matching it with the word representations stored in the lexicons, and those models which disregard a need for lexicons and propose instead that a word is recognized by constructing a pattern of neural representation to which the word corresponds. The former is referred to as a *Lexicon-based model* and the latter as a *Parallel Distributed Processing (PDP) model*. Because the PDP model is of recent origin and not much is known about it, we will present it first.

The Parallel Distributed Processing Model

The PDP model of word recognition has dispensed with the mental lexicon altogether. It proposes that patterns corresponding to written words are computed every time a word is presented. The pattern that corresponds to a particular word is the product of learning experience. Each written word (familiar to the reader) corresponds to a unique pattern of activated neuron-like units, and this pattern is "computed" every time the word is encountered. Such a computation is essentially a re-creation of a pattern of synaptic connections already established in neuronal configurations as a result of learning and experience. The corresponding output can be pronunciation, comprehension, or the spelling of the word. Because such a computed "pattern" is postulated to contain phonologic, orthographic, semantic, and other information about the word and can also generate all the corresponding outputs simultaneously, this method of word processing is referred to as "parallel distributed processing" (Seidenberg, 1990). It is considered as "parallel" and "distributed" because the model proposes that the activations that represent all the characteristics of a word are interconnected so much that inputting a single feature of a written word, say, its pronunciation, is sufficient to arouse the entire pattern, and consequently retrieve the word's meaning, spelling, and other associated features. Because of this property, the PDP model is also considered to be "connectionist" or "associative." Because of its recent origin, the PDP model has not accumulated much supportive experimental evidence even though successful computer simulations reportedly have been achieved.

The Lexical Activation and Lexical Search Models

Lexicon-based models propose two mechanisms for word recognition: lexical activiation and lexical search. The *activation model* assumes that the search is carried out simultaneously, in parallel, and that the word representation which is in tune with the sensory input stands out and is recognized. It is possible to describe the simultaneous comparison of many words with a target word by using an analogy borrowed from Just and Carpenter (1987). Suppose that from an array of tuning forks differing in pitch, one has to choose the one matching a standard fork. The task can be accomplished by hitting the standard tuning fork against an object so that it vibrates, and then holding it against the array of forks. The single fork corresponding in pitch to the standard will vibrate in harmony even though all the tuning forks are exposed to the standard fork simultaneously. In this analogy, the standard tuning fork is similar to the printed word, and the array of forks is similar to the set of word representations stored in the lexicon. The search is simultaneous and parallel.

The *lexical search model,* on the other hand, assumes that a systematic serial search of the lexicons is carried out until the word representation that matches the sensory input is identified. A modified version of the lexical search model, however, proposes that the search need not be carried out on an item-by-item basis, but subgroups of candidates in the lexicon can be searched on a set-by-set basis. This brings the lexical search model very close to the activation model. The reader will realize that after these modifications, the difference between the two basic models becomes rather blurred. In the present context, an explanation of the word-recognition process is presented from the perspective of the activation model.

According to one version of the activation model, when the visually coded information arrives at the lexicon, it activates the semantic, phonologic, and orthographic lexical representations of several words simultaneously. This activation is carried out in a parallel fashion and is presumed to activate several viable candidates which resemble the input. For example, the word "house" may activate in the semantic lexicon the representation *house* in addition to activating related representations such as *home, hut,* or *family.* In the phonologic lexicon, the target word may activate phonemes such as /h/, /ho/ (rhymes with *go*), /ho/ (rhymes with "ho" in *hop*), /hou/ (rhymes with *how*). In addition, it may also activate orthographic patterns such as "ho," "ou," or "se," and whole-word pronunciations such as *house,* and *hose,* and *horse.* When the *summed* contributions of these representations exceed a certain threshold, the code that represents the word stands out, and the word represented by that code is recognized. A model described by Morton and Patterson (1980) is representative of this family of activation models. The model also allows for the word frequency and recency effects by proposing that these factors lower the threshold needed for recognition. Consequently, familiar words and words that have been recently encountered are identified more readily than unfamiliar words.

The Concurrent Model of Word Recognition

One of the issues in word recognition that continues to be controversial is the role played by the phonological features of the written word. Not only the psychological mechanisms that underlie the pronunciation of a word and the point in time when they come into operation are debated, but doubts about the very need for pronunciation in reading are raised. Some researchers contend that conversion of the written word into its phonological counterpart is not necessary for word recognition. They believe that the meaning of the written word can be captured without resorting to pronunciation, whether overt or covert. Several other investigators, however believe that a phonological conversion of the written word is essential for reading, but they are not in agreement as to the stage when phonological representation of the word comes into play— before word recognition or after it. When phonological realization of the written word precedes word recognition, such a conversion is termed as *prelexical;* when the meaning of the word is first realized and phonological awareness follows, phonological conversion is *postlexical.* Apart from those who advocate the prelexical or postlexical conversion of print into phonology, there are also cognitive scientists who believe that the input races toward the phonological and semantic lexicons and the lexicon that is accessed first is used in word recognition. However, it is assumed that, generally speaking, visual representation reaches the semantic lexicon sooner than the phonological representation and, therefore, phonology plays a less important role, particularly in skilled reading. It should be noted here that children who fail to convert print into pronunciation quickly and accurately almost always remain poor readers. This points to the importance of decoding skill for beginning, if not for skilled, readers.

The present authors believe that even though prelexical and postlexical conversions of print into phonology are possible and that there may be differences in word-recognition processes adopted by beginning and skilled readers, all the representative lexical features of the written word are used *simultaneously* in the word-recognition process. That is, a word's semantic, phonological, and orthographic representations in the lexicons are used simultaneously for its recognition. Furthermore, weakness in utilizing any one of these representations can bias the recognition process and lead to errors. We call this view the *concurrent model* of word recognition. In some ways, this model is similar to the PDP model described earlier except that the PDP model postulates that a word is recognized by collectively *computing* its features whereas the concurrent model postulates that the word is recognized by simultaneously *accessing* the representations of all the features of the word from the lexicons. The concurrent model also differs from the activation model in that it does not postulate that word recognition results from *summation* of all the properties (as the activation model suggests) but is the result of a *matching* of all the available properties.

The concurrent model draws heavily from models that are proposed to explain speech recognition, particularly the *cohort model* proposed by Marslen-Wilson (1989). The cohort model is an attempt to explain the experimental finding that spoken words generally are recognized in context in less than 200 msec from word onset, a point at which the available sensory information alone is too incomplete to allow correct identification of the word. That is, a listener can recognize a word in a sentence even before the word is completely uttered. This means, during this early stage, additional information such as the semantic and syntactic properties, as well as contextual cues, converge and activate viable candidates in the lexicon. This initial group of representations constitute the word-initial cohort. As more of the word is heard, there is a successive pruning of the number of candidates that do not fit the accruing input stimulus. This process of winnowing continues until there remains only one candidate that still matches the sensory input. This is the recognized word. The concurrent model of written-word processing differs from the cohort model in two ways: first, unlike the spoken word, the written word requires a mechanism to convert the stimulus into its phonological equivalent; second, the concurrent model assumes that a word is recognized all at once without undergoing a successive reduction in the number of activated candidates. It proposes that a number of viable semantic, phonological, and orthographic candidates may be activated, but selection of the single representative is made all at once without a successive elimination process. The word-recognition problem is solved much like a problem of simultaneous equations. Consider the following example which contains two equations. Finding the correct solution to this problem requires the use of both equations simultaneously.

$$
\begin{aligned}
(1) \quad x + y &= 3 \\
(2) \quad \underline{2x + y} &= \underline{4} \\
x &= 1
\end{aligned}
$$

In this example, neither equation alone could provide the correct solution. Assuming we are dealing with positive integers, equation (1) alone would give four values for x (0, 1, 2, and 3), and four values for y (0, 1, 2, and 3). Similarly, equation (2) alone would give three values for x (0, 1, and 2), and three values for y (0, 2, and 4). When the two equations are solved simultaneously, however, only one value for x and only one value for y is possible, and the correct solution is obtained. It is proposed that during word recognition, representations from the semantic lexicon, phonological rules lexicon, word pronunciation lexicon, and possibly orthographic lexicon are treated like separate equations in an algebraic problem and are used simultaneously in a one-step operation. We will give another example because this concept is important for understanding different forms of reading disabilities.

Suppose you are provided information about the height and weight of a group of men. Further, you are assigned the task of identifying the person by name when data about the person's height and weight are given. This problem can be illustrated with the aid of a two-dimensional graph (Fig. 3.1). For example, given a height of 6'3" and weight of 200 pounds, we can identify the person as "D." Using only one piece of information, e.g. weight, may lead to incorrectly identifying "C" as the person. Word recognition, according to the concurrent model follows a similar process except that it may involve n dimensions. The concurrent model is illustrated with an example (Fig. 3.2). In this sentence, "The house has a pool," the word "house" activates semantic representations such as *house, home, hut, live,* and *place;* in the phonologic lexicon it activates rules for pronouncing the graphemes and syllables such as /h/, /ho/, /ou/, or /use/. At the same time, in the word-pronunciation lexicon, it activates pronunciations associated with the words *house, home,* or *horse,* and in the orthographic lexicon, it activates letter patterns such as "ho", "hou", and "ho..e." The matrix is entered simultaneously in all these lexical dimensions and the intersect is recognized as the word. The solid arrows result in correct recognition; the broken arrows represent the recognition process of a poor reader who has specific weakness in the phonological rules lexicon. Under this circumstance, the rules lexicon

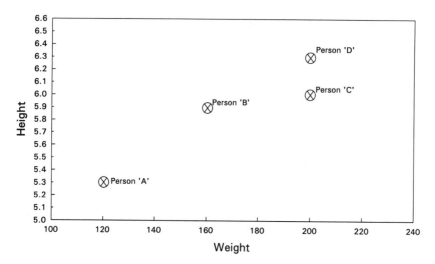

FIGURE 3.1. Person recognition as a two-dimensional problem.

has no significant input, and the semantic lexicon assumes an overriding power. The word is recognized as *home* because it agrees with the limited orthographic input *ho* and fits the sentence context.

The concurrent model is "form-based," not "time-based." That is, errors of word recognition are attributed not to an inability to retrieve information quickly but to the possibility that one or more of the lexicons is deficient in its content or organization. This conclusion is based on the observation that many children with SRD do not improve their word recognition performance even when allowed an unlimited amount of time. One implication of the concurrent model is that the conversion of the written word into its phonological representation is essential for the correct recognition of words. Weakness of this skill leads to approximations of the correct solution because under such a circumstance, word identification is accomplished by the semantic and orthographic lexicons alone. A large number of oral reading errors committed by children with SRD are semantically acceptable (e.g., *pond*—"pool"; *ponchos*—"pouches"). A smaller number of errors based on partial orthographic cues are not semantically acceptable (e.g., *house*—"horse"; *clean*—"clever"). Children with NSRD, on the other hand, tend to make many more semantically unacceptable errors than children with SRD. Therefore, analysis of oral reading errors can be useful in differential diagnosis. In this regard, the concurrent model of word recognition, in addition to being in consonance with the "interactive–compensatory model" of reading (Stanovich, 1980) and neuropsychological data, has practical utility.

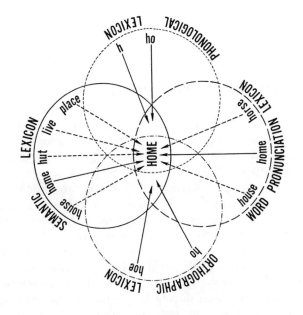

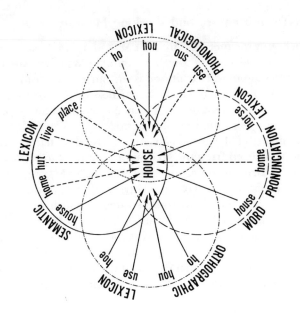

(A) Correct pronunciation of the word 'house'.

(B) Incorrect pronunciation of the word 'house' because of faulty phonological lexicon.

FIGURE 3.2. A schematic diagram of the concurrent model of word-recognition.

Correct recognition of the word ensures that the comprehension process is progressing along the right lines. Reading, however, is more than the ability to recognize individual words; it involves the comprehension of the entire sentence and the text.

SENTENCE COMPREHENSION

Once the word is recognized, it is thought to be kept in the short-term memory (STM) store for a brief period until a unit of meaning accrues due to the accumulation of words into a group. Subsequently, the meaning unit is processed further in the long-term memory (LTM). When all the units of meaning in a sentence reach LTM, the entire sentence is comprehended. The construction of meaning units is based on the accumulation of words and takes place in real time. For this reason, individual word representations have to be kept in a temporary store until a memory unit is completed. The STM is believed to play an important role in storing word representations temporarily and thus facilitate the building of meaning units. According to this view, acoustic STM plays an important role both during the word recognition stage and after the word is recognized. Any deficiency of the STM, therefore, can be a potential source of reading difficulty.

Short-Term Memory and Working Memory

A tendency to dichotomize memory into STM and LTM has a long history dating back to the end of the last century. Whether such a division represents psychological reality or is an outcome of our subjective experience has long been debated. Regardless of this argument, classifying memory into two components has been experimentally productive and is defensible on operational grounds.

Even though items in STM can be acoustic or visual in nature, the word representations realized from the lexicons are thought to be stored in some phonological form in the acoustic STM. The STM, much like the iconic store, is considered to have a relatively short duration. But unlike the iconic store, the STM has some strategies which help it to overcome its temporal and capacity constraints. The temporal limitation could be overcome through a process of covert rehearsal, and its capacity limitation by grouping or chunking input information. For instance, *deoxyribonucleic acid* contains letters that exceed the capacity of the STM, which is limited to 7–9 items. However, the word could be chunked into the following five units: *de oxy ribo nucleic acid,* which would reduce the cognitive load placed on STM considerably and facilitate rehearsal and retention of the information until its tranfer to LTM. Rehearsal and chunking could be accomplished more readily by converting the written word into its phonological representation than into its visual representation. The precise nature of the phonological representation, however, is not clear even though the ability to pronounce the written word overtly is closely related to the ability to form the phonological representation of the word. It is obvious, therefore, that individuals who have difficulty in converting the written word into its phonological equivalent (i.e., decoding) would encounter difficulty in retaining information in STM.

A number of studies can be cited to show that the written word is stored in the STM in phonological form. In a letter memorization task, more intrusion errors (and consequently, poor performance) were found for similar-sounding letters such as *b, v, p, c, t,* than for letters with dissimilar sounds such as *n, s, x, l, o* (Baddeley, 1966a). A similar finding for words is also reported by Baddeley (1966b). In the latter study, it was found that in immediate recall tasks, more confusion errors occurred for phonologically similar words (e.g., *mad, man, can*) than for dissimilar words (e.g., *cow, day, pen*). If, however, the words were recalled after a delay of 20 minutes, more intrusion errors occurred among words with similar meaning (e.g., *huge, wide, big*) than among words which differed in meaning (e.g., *late, thin, wet*). This indicates that STM is phonology-based but LTM is meaning-based. It follows that an inability to convert the written word into its phonological equivalent will severely restrict STM operation and secondarily affect comprehension. This, in fact, appears to be a proximal cause of SRD.

When STM is discussed from the perspective of its functions and strategies, it is referred to as *working memory,* an operational concept. One of the outcomes of this reformulation of the STM concept is that greater emphasis is placed on the function, rather than the structure, of the short-term store, and on performance over capacity. This conceptual shift is in line with the recent trend to explain differences in performance on memory tasks in terms of the speed with which STM carries out mental processes, rather than its capacity. Evidence for considering the speed of operation of the working memory being more important than capacity was presented in Chapter 2. The low digit span so often seen in individuals with SRD is, therefore, to be interpreted as an indication of slow processing of information rather than as a memory capacity limitation.

Propositions and Idea Units

In recent years, psychologists and linguists have studied comprehension processes extensively and developed a more or less coherent view about sentence comprehension. They believe that the basic unit in sentence comprehension is a group of words that forms a natural unit of meaning. These units are referred to as "propositions" (Kintsch, 1977) or "idea units" (Chafe, 1985). Propositions as well as idea units represent the smallest unit of knowledge that can stand as an independent assertion (Anderson, 1990). Whereas propositions are made up of explicit written text, idea units can be constructions such as inferences not directly expressed in printed words. In the following discussion, however, idea units and propositions are treated as synonyms and are used interchangeably. According to Chafe (1985), an idea unit is spoken with a single coherent prosodic contour ending in a clause-final intonation, and is preceded and followed by pauses. The idea unit is hypothesized to be a unit holding only the information a speaker can handle in a single focus of attention. In spoken language, an average idea unit contains about seven words, a number which corresponds to STM capacity. From a psychological point of view, a proposition or idea unit could, therefore, be defined as a unit of meaning made up of a sequence of words that can be held in STM at any given moment. It has to be added that the permanent nature of the written language permits idea units to be made up of a few more words. The additional words, however, are generally used for embellishing the written language and, therefore, may not add substantially to the memory load.

It is proposed (cf. Kleiman, 1975) that phonological representations of words recognized in the lexicon are held in the STM until they are reconstituted into idea units or propositions and then processed further in LTM. This momentary holding in STM provides an opportunity for the subject's knowledge of the world to be utilized in the comprehension process and thus facilitate the construction of propositions. If, for some reason, a word needed for the construction of a proposition is lost or not available, the reader uses his world knowledge to install an appropriate substitute for the missing word. Also, when such omissions are deliberately introduced by the writer, the reader infers the missing elements and makes appropriate restitutions.

At this point, when the semantic interpretation is added in the LTM, memory for the exact words in STM decays. This view is in agreement with the general observation that immediate recall of information, presumably from the STM, invariably is verbatim whereas in delayed recall, presumably from the LTM, content often is reformulated on the basis of meaning. For these reasons, sentence comprehension is considered to be an active, constructive process that requires information above and beyond that which is present on the printed page. Frequently, a writer creates sentences with the assumption that the reader already has related knowledge and therefore leaves some information out, expecting the reader to make appropriate inferences. In the previous chapter, we introduced the term "schema" to signify the world knowledge which is needed to make inferences. Now, we will take a closer look at the concept of schema which is considered to be an important component of comprehension.

Schemata

Many researchers believe that the reader's schematic knowledge has much influence on reading comprehension. Consider the following passage:

> Chicago hosts the LA Rams to determine the NFC's Super Bowl representative. There will be no sideshows in this one as it doesn't need any. Walter Payton running one way and Eric Dickerson the other is plenty, and add to that the Refrigerator and friends snacking on Rams quarterback Dieter Brock. (Hunt, 1986)

A correct understanding of the above statement requires a sound background knowledge of the current American football scene. In fact, some British psychologists who listened to this statement thought it was about a county fair or picnic. Inadequate information (schemata) often causes comprehension difficulties experienced by high school and college students.

The schema itself does not guarantee correct comprehension of a sentence. The appropriate knowledge must first be selected, and then activated. The importance of choosing a suitable schema for proper comprehension is demonstrated by a series of studies done by Pichert and Anderson (1977). As part of their research they required subjects to read about what two boys did at one boy's home while skipping school. The readers' schemata were manipulated by assigning different perspectives; one-third of the subjects were instructed to read the story from the viewpoint of a potential home buyer; one-third, from that of a burglar; and one-third were given no special orientation. It should come as no surprise that the assigned frame of reference had a powerful influence on learning and recall. The "home-buyer" group recalled more items regarding the quality of the home, whereas the "burglar group" remembered more information relevant to illegal entry and escape. Activation of the proper schema is, therefore, necessary for efficient learning and recall.

It should be remembered that schemata do not come in fully developed units but are complexes of interconnected ideas with fuzzy edges. According to David Memory (personal communication, 1991), when aroused, a single schema can overwhelm the reader. For example, background knowledge about American football can be made up of hundreds of ideas, and if such extensive schematic information were activated all at once, that might impede comprehension rather than facilitate it. Schemata must, therefore, be carefully focused and controlled in order for comprehension to proceed smoothly.

Our discussion so far indicates that even though STM can play an important role as a temporary store for information, activities such as selecting propositions and mobilizing appropriate schemata require the information stored in LTM. Operations of this kind which originate at higher levels and direct lower-level functions are described as "top-down" or "concept-driven" processes. Any process in the opposite direction, for example, from the iconic to the lexical level, is considered as "bottom-up" or "data-driven." Because of the simultaneous involvement of both top-down and bottom-up processes, reading is considered to be an *interactive* process. As we move from sentence to text comprehension, reading increasingly involves interactive processing.

TEXT COMPREHENSION

Just as a sentence is more than a collection of words, so is text more than a mere collection of sentences. The text usually contains a coherent theme and is, therefore, a more natural "unit" than a set of random words or sentences. Generally speaking, sentences within the text are arranged in such a way as to present information in a cohesive manner so as to avoid excessively taxing the reader's cognitive resources. Principles that govern the coherence and logical arrangement of sentences in narrative material (e.g., stories) constitute what is known as "story grammar." A closely related concept applicable to expository writing (e.g., textbooks) is "text structure."

Story Grammar and Text Structure

The concept of story grammar simply means that a text is not a haphazard collection of sentences and that both the writer and the reader have to be sensitive to principles of organization. Story grammar has recently received attention, but most of the investigations have been limited to children's stories. Such research shows that, in general, stories contain a theme, a plot, and a resolution. The theme is clearly indicated at the outset of the story or near its beginning. Even children in elementary school appear to be aware of this. For instance, in one study, Cirilo and Foss (1980) inserted the following sentence at two different levels in two different stories: "He could no longer talk at all." One story was about a king who was cursed by a witch so that he could not speak. The other story was about a soldier who was rewarded by the king for a good deed and was rendered speechless by the magnitude of the reward.

In the first story, the sentence contained thematic content essential for story comprehension, whereas the same sentence in the second story did not contribute significantly to the story's basic meaning. It was found that children spent more time reading the sentence in the first story as compared to the second story. It was reasoned that readers did so because they were aware of its thematic importance; so they spent more time processing it. An individual who is insensitive to story grammar may allocate equal time to all the sentences in the text, a practice which reduces the efficiency of the reader.

Texts and passages that students come across in high schools and colleges are primarily expository, that is, texts meant to inform rather than entertain. Nevertheless, story-grammar principles apply to them as well. For instance, the theme of the story is equivalent to the *main idea* in expository text. This is usually introduced in the beginning, and ideas that support the main idea are provided later on in the text. Awareness of this structure facilitates reading comprehension. Equally important is the fact that sensitivity to text grammar can help students write well-organized essays.

Identification of the main idea of the text also helps the reader to activate the appropriate schema early in reading and thereby build expectations and a contextual base. The following passage (Sanford & Garrod, 1981) illustrates that as we read each sentence we build up expectations based on the schema that is aroused. When the sentence does not fit the context, that particular schema is abandoned and a new one installed.

> John was on his way to school. He was terribly worried about the mathematics lesson. He thought he might not be able to control the class again today. He thought it was unfair of the instructor to make him supervise the class for a second time. After all, it was not a normal part of a janitor's duties. (p. 132)

The opening sentence in the passage activates the schema of a "school boy," which is replaced in the third sentence by the schema of the "teacher," which, in turn, is replaced by the schema of a "teaching assistant." This schema, too, is abandoned in the last sentence. Most expository texts do not lead the reader down the "garden path" in this way but make the main idea quite explicit early on. In the above case, the authors have deliberately misled the reader in order to make a point. Many poor readers, however, fail to anticipate necessary information sequences and unwittingly write confusing essays.

METACOGNITION

The term "metacognition" was introduced in Chapter 2. It can be described broadly as knowing what one knows and knowing what one does not know; it is a knowledge or awareness of one's own processing skills. Metacognition can also be defined as cognition about cognition. According to Garner (1987), because cognition includes perceiving, understanding, and remembering, metacognition involves thinking about one's own perceiving, understanding, and remembering processes. Reading teachers are familiar with children who plunge into text heedlessly and while reading aloud pay little or no attention to prosody and punctuation, rarely self-correcting their errors. These children are unaware of their poor text comprehension, an indication of deficient metacognitive skills.

Baker and Brown (1984) have classified reading-related metacognitive skills under two headings: reading for meaning (comprehension monitoring) and reading for remembering (studying). Reading for meaning has two components, *on-line monitoring* of comprehension and taking the necessary *corrective action* when difficulty is encountered. A number of studies show that as children grow older, their on-line monitoring skills also keep up with their development but that poor readers are less adept than skilled readers in using these strategies.

Metacognitive aspects of reading for remembering (study skills) involve three components: *self-knowledge, task knowledge,* and *text knowledge.*

Self-Knowledge

This aspect of metacognition includes an objective appraisal of one's own background knowledge (schemata), reading speed, and memory skills. For instance, if the student knows he is a slow reader, he can take appropriate steps to remedy the situation by allocating more study time. Similarly, corrective measures can be taken to improve memory performance and background knowledge about the topic being studied. An awareness of one's own cognitive style is another aspect of self-knowledge.

Task Knowledge

This includes assessment of one's own ability to identify what is required of the reading task: does it call for detailed study, or will skimming and scanning suffice? Does it require paraphrasing the major theme, or memorizing formulas? Poor readers up to sixth grade are known to equate reading with sounding out words correctly, not necessarily with comprehension. Reading specialists warn that task knowledge cannot be taken for granted and that poor readers may need explicit training in this aspect of metacognition.

Text Knowledge

In the context of understanding written material, metacognition enables the reader to evaluate his/her own knowledge about text organization, story grammar, main ideas, and supporting information. This aspect of metacognition also develops with age. Some older children, however, are found to be deficient in this respect. When metacognitive skill is lacking, the student may allocate equal time to all statements in the text, regardless of their importance. Also very useful are the abilities to recognize redundant content and to distinguish central ideas from trivia. This is particularly important for high school and college students who must read large quantities of material within a limited amount of time. A realistic appraisal of one's own ability to do this is another aspect of metacognitive skill.

Simple, informal means of assessing comprehension and metacognitive skills, and instructional methods to improve them, are presented in the following chapters.

4

The Nature and Diagnosis of Reading Disabilities

INTRODUCTION

In this chapter, the different kinds of reading disabilities are presented and the symptoms associated with each of these are described. Assessment procedures that can be used for diagnosing the different types of reading disabilities are also discussed. It should be noted that labels are attached to the various disabilities only for purposes of conceptual clarity and ease of communication between the authors and the reader (a potential consultant). Consultees (i.e., teachers or parents) are more interested in knowing why a child cannot learn to read well and what can be done about it than in knowing whether the child has reading disability and, if so, what kind of disability. It is, therefore, advisable, and even desirable, for the consultant to de-emphasize labels. It is also recommended that the consultant avoid terminology that has no relevance to treatment. For example, we neither know much about the nature of constructs such as "auditory memory," "visual perception," and "left-hemispheric functions," nor do we know how to improve or change them. It is better to state processes associated with these constructs in pragmatic terms such as "decoding skill," "the ability to learn sight vocabulary," and "word-recognition skill." The latter concepts are to be preferred because they can suggest remedial teaching techniques.

In the previous chapter we noted that reading skill is made up of two major components, decoding and comprehension, and either one or both these skills can fail to develop properly resulting in three different kinds of reading disabilities. Children with a decoding deficit but adequate listening comprehension are considered as having specific reading disability (SRD). This kind of reading disability is also referred to as Developmental Dyslexia. It needs to be reiterated that the term "developmental dyslexia," as used in this book, *does not* connote any neurological impairment or abnormality.

The second variety of reading disability is represented by children who have adequate word-recognition skills but are deficient in comprehension. Empirical studies show that word recognition skill is an independent predictor of reading skill (Stanovich, 1991); that is, an individual can have adequate word recognition skill but relatively undeveloped comprehension skill. According to one British study (Oakhill & Garnham, 1988), children who have adequate word-recognition skills but do not understand what they read make up about 10% of 7- and 8-year-olds. These readers have Nonspecific Reading Disability (NSRD). A Study by Carr, Brown, Vavrus, and Evans (1990) showed that nearly 25% of the poor readers of elementary school age who were referred to a reading clinic had impressive word-recognition skill but poor reading comprehension skill. Their listening comprehension was equally poor. Because reading and listening comprehension are mediated by the same underlying cognitive mechanisms, and because "reading seems to depend on a set of language processes that are common to both reading and listening" (Daneman, 1991, p. 526), individuals with NSRD are deficient in both areas.

In contrast to these two groups with deficits in either decoding or comprehension, the third group of poor readers have difficulties with both processes. These children are Low Ability Readers (LAR). They represent the largest proportion of students described by labels such as "learning-disabled" and "slow learners." The reading performance of

LAR generally is in line with their mental ability and, therefore, they are not considered as having reading disability per se. They simply are poor readers, not reading-disabled. Their reading difficulty is one manifestation of their overall poor cognitive ability. These three categories of poor readers are represented graphically in Fig. 4.1. Individuals with SRD and NSRD constitute only a small fraction of all poor readers—LAR make up the bulk of the group.

In the diagnosis of reading difficulties, sometimes a distinction is drawn between *process factors* and *content factors* (Pearson, 1984). Process factors refer to how well and how fast information is processed. Operations such as decoding, inference making, and metacognition are examples of process factors. In contrast, content factors refer to the kind of information that is processed. Vocabulary size and schemata of the reader are examples of content factors. Comprehensive assessment of the reading skill of an individual involves the evaluation of both process and content factors.

In recent years, reports have appeared that some forms of reading disabilities are caused by faulty physiological processes that mediate visual functions. Included in this are regressive eye movements and scotopic sensitivity. It was noted in the previous chapter that regressive eye movements indicate that the reader is monitoring his/her reading performance and that when difficulty occurs in decoding or comprehension, a "second look" is taken to remedy the situation. This results in

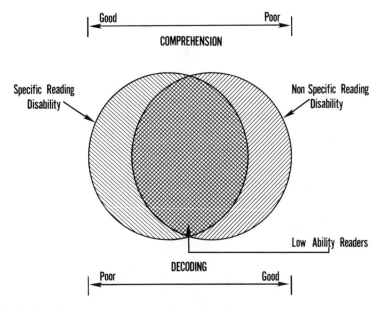

FIGURE 4.1. The three varieties of poor readers.

regressive eye movements. This explanation of regressive eye movements is further buttressed by several experimental studies which report that when nonverbal stimuli such as an array of lights is used, children with specific reading disability do not show regressive movements. According to Just and Carpenter (1987), some early training programs misguidedly thought that reading comprehension of poor readers could be improved by training these children to make short fixations and to reduce the number of regressive movements. Because these programs ignored the cognitive processes responsible for poor reading but focused on superficial phenomena associated with reading, they were unsuccessful.

Recently, it has been reported that the reading performance of some children with dyslexia improved significantly if they wore specially tinted prescription glasses. Even though it is claimed that such glasses could eliminate the dyslexia problem, in fact, what they appear to alleviate are symptoms of scotopic sensitivity. Scotopic sensitivity is a problem associated with photoreceptors in the visual system which increases the sensitivity of the eye to light and causes reddened or watery eyes, makes the print appear blurry and fuzzy, and results in erratic eye movements. If glasses could improve reading performance, it is obvious that some optical processes associated with the physiology of vision contribute to this form of reading difficulty. As Richardson (1989) puts it, dyslexia is a language disorder whereas scotopic sensitivity is a vision disorder. Because reading disabilities are psychological phenomena associated with cognitive processes, reading defects that arise from visual–optical processes are not considered reading disabilities.

The psychologist–consultant should, of course, be alert to the possibility that poor vision and hearing could cause learning problems in some children. If this is suspected, the child's vision and hearing should be evaluated by specialists.

The Nature of Reading Disabilities

INTRODUCTION

In this book, the term *reading disabilities* is reserved for reading problems that are attributable to some factor intrinsic to the reader. Examples of intrinsic factors include deficient phonological processing skill, comprehension deficit, and peculiar cognitive learning styles. Reading deficits that are caused by extrinsic factors such as poor motivation, limited reading experience, and an environment not conducive to learning are referred to as *reading difficulties*. Enabling the consultee to recognize the nature of the reading deficit, whether it is a form of reading disability or reading difficulty caused by environmental factors, is an important consultative skill because such a decision has implications for corrective instruction. In this section, the three kinds of reading disabilities—SRD, NSRD, and LAR—are presented and their symptoms described.

SPECIFIC READING DISABILITY

When the reading deficit is limited to the written form of language and does not extend to include the production and comprehension of spoken language, it is referred to as *specific reading disability* (SRD). Individuals with SRD also tend to have average or higher IQ scores and their listening comprehension is in line with their IQ rather than with their reading comprehension. The term *dyslexia* is also often used to refer to this condition. In this book, the use of the term "specific reading disability" is preferred because it is more descriptive of the reading disorder than "dyslexia," a term used by many as a catch-all label. As a matter of fact, even some teachers use the term "dyslexia" to refer to all kinds of academic problems. In addition, in the minds of many, dyslexia has come to be associated with neurological impairment. Because the term dyslexia is often misunderstood and misused, it may be prudent to avoid it. However, parents often ask the consultant directly whether their child has dyslexia. Under such circumstances, the label "dyslexia" should be used only when the diagnostic findings warrant it, and the term should not be applied indiscriminately to all forms of reading difficulties. Often, the use of descriptive labels such as "decoding difficulty with comprehension deficit" or "decoding difficulty without comprehension deficit" brings conceptual clarity to the consultation process. As noted earlier, using esoteric labels can be a source of communication problems between the consultant and consultee.

The incidence of SRD among children may not exceed 2% of the school population (Figure 4.1). The occurrence of SRD is even less frequent among college students. Studies claiming that nearly 10% of school-children have SRD or dyslexia usually fail to apply strict psychometric criteria in subject selection and, therefore, include a large number of borderline cases who are actually LAR. Inclusion of these borderline cases in the dyslexia category has caused a great deal of confusion regarding the nature of reading disabilities.

Symptoms of Specific Reading Disability

The most fundamental deficit of SRD is poor word-recognition skills. Skill at recognizing words is strongly correlated to the speed of initial reading acquisition (Stanovich, 1991). A major source of deficient word-recognition skills is weak phonological-processing skill. The phonological skills deficit theory of SRD (or dyslexia) can successfully account for the many symptoms individuals with this type of reading disability display, an accomplishment which neurological and perceptual explanations of dyslexia cannot match. The symptoms of SRD include: slow rate of reading, erratic oral reading, spelling errors, incorrect use of suffixes and function words in reading and writing, and below-average comprehension on timed reading tests. These symptoms are seen in the presence of normal listening comprehension. As will be seen later, all these symptoms could be accounted for by poor phonological skills. Research shows that a deficit in any particular process of reading results in greater reliance on other knowledge sources. This view, expressed as the *interactive–compensatory reading hypothesis,* has been supported by empirical studies (Stanovich, 1980). In agreement with this hypothesis, individuals with poor decoding skills, in addition to presenting a set of symptoms, tend to compensate for their poor phonological skills by relying on other strategies for reading. One such compensatory strategy is to rely excessively on context for *recognizing written words.* Thus, the SRD or dyslexia syndrome includes not only symptoms associated with deficient phonological processes but also indications of the use of alternative strategies. Because individuals with SRD differ in the extent of their decoding deficit, past reading experience, and amount of remedial instruction previously received, a certain degree of variability in symptoms can be expected among disabled readers. In the following section, the symptoms that characterize SRD are described.

Slow Reading Speed

A number of studies show that the speed with which words are recognized is a major factor contributing to individual differences in reading skill. Even though skilled readers may be able to recognize many written words without resorting to phonological recoding, poor readers are held back when they encounter unfamiliar words and function words. For this reason, individuals with SRD tend to remain slow readers relative to others their age in spite of many years of schooling (Aaron & Phillips, 1986). Many mature students with SRD, however, compensate for their decoding deficits by relying on strategies such as sight reading of words and context use with such success their reading comprehension appears to be within normal limits. When these students are assessed by untimed reading tests, their reading achievement tends to be normal or close to normal. Their performance, however, declines significantly when their reading comprehension is assessed with the aid of timed tests. In one study, Runyon (1991) found that college students identified as having LD performed much worse than college students identified as not having LD on the comprehension part of the timed Nelson–Denny reading test. When the test was administered without time restrictions, however, there was no difference between the two groups in reading comprehension. In fact, the difference in performance between timed and untimed tests can be used to differentiate SRD from NSRD and LAR. Students with NSRD and LAR perform poorly on tests of reading comprehension whether they are timed or not.

Individuals with SRD almost invariably have a below-average digit span as measured by the WISC-R subtest (Aaron, 1989). This observation is consistent with the fact that individuals with SRD are slow in processing verbal information. In Chapter 3 we presented evidence that suggests low digit span is indicative of slow processing of information by the STM rather than its limited capacity. The factor responsible for the slow processing of information by poor readers, however, does not appear to have a physiological or neurological basis because dyslexic children do not differ from normal readers in their speed of retrieving names of objects or pictures (Katz, Shankweiler, & Liberman, 1981; Liberman, Mann, Shankweiler, & Werfelman, 1982; Perfetti, Finger, & Hogaboam, 1978). Thus, the retrieval problem appears to be material-specific. Furthermore, it has to noted that the speed of retrieving word-name codes may be more related to reading speed than to reading comprehension (Daneman, 1991). For these reasons, it can be surmised that poor readers are slow in accessing verbal information because their phonological lexicon is either poorly organized or that the entries in the lexicon are incomplete and that slow readers need not necessarily be poor comprehenders.

Errors in Oral Reading

Poor decoding skill leads to an overdependency on sight-word reading strategy. Because poor decoders tend to identify words on the basis of minimal cues, usually the first few letters of the word, they tend to misread a large number of words and commit oral reading errors. SRD subjects misread content words and omit as well as substitute function words. Normal readers also tend to substitute function words, but the magnitude of errors committed by SRD subjects exceeds normal limits. When such errors are committed, the substituted function word invariably belongs to the same grammatical category as the target word. For example, the article *a* may be substituted for *the*, the verb *is* for *was*, and the preposition *on* for *above*. Because such errors do not alter the meaning of the sentence substantially, it may be concluded that despite the oral reading errors, subjects with SRD are able to monitor their own comprehension. Furthermore, because the target word and the substituted word do not visually resemble each other, visual confusion cannot be the reason for the misreading; nor can lack of familiarity with the word be used to account for the reading errors because function words occur more frequently in text than content words do. In addition to these errors, omission and substitution of suffixes are also frequently seen in the oral reading and writing of students with SRD. Even though these misreadings give the impression of grammatical errors, they may really be a manifestation of the underlying phonological problem. Teachers and parents are often surprised and frustrated by the difficulty encountered by disabled readers in learning to read correctly these apparently simple words. Misreading of grammar words, however, is common in beginning readers and poor readers. In fact, some teachers call these little words "demon words." The fact that function words and suffixes are semantically empty and, therefore, have to be kept in the working memory in a phonological form appears to be a good explanation of the misreading of such common words.

The misreading of content words by readers with SRD generally results in contextually appropriate substitutions. Furthermore, word-reading errors are as prevalent when these subjects read a list of isolated words as when they read sentences or passages (Aaron, 1987). The fact that subjects with SRD commit a significant number of errors when they read a list of unrelated words suggests that their problem can be tracked down to the word recognition level. Word-reading skill is, therefore, one index of an individual's reading ability, and for this reason most standardized tests of reading include a list of pronounceable nonwords.

Poor Spelling

Many studies of developmental dyslexia suggest that poor spelling is a concomitant of poor reading. This should come as no surprise because spelling-to-sound relational rules are used both in reading and spelling and because readers with SRD are deficient in grapheme–phoneme conversion skills. Two studies found that children who were poor spellers also performed poorly in phonological tasks (Rohl & Tunmer, 1988; Bruck & Waters, 1988). The correlation coefficients obtained between nonword reading scores and spelling scores of elementary schoolchildren usually range between .7 and .8, whereas the coefficients between tests of visual memory and spelling are usually negligible. This indicates that spelling as a skill may not be as much dependent on visual memory as it is on phonological skills. Genetic studies also report that phonology and spelling skills are highly heritable whereas orthographic memory is not (Olson, Wise, Conners, Rack, & Fulker, 1989; Szelezulski, & Manis, 1990). Without exception, all the college students with SRD studied by the authors of this book are poor spellers. Even though some adults with SRD manage to acquire adequate reading skill, probably by using a whole-word reading strategy and by building up a substantial sight vocabulary, they fail to make similar progress in spelling. The reason for this difference between spelling and reading may be due to the fact that reading is primarily a recognition task, whereas spelling is a recall task. Careful testing usually reveals that these so-called "good readers but poor spellers" have residual reading deficits (Joshi & Aaron, 1991). This phenomenon also brings up another point, that is, even though reading skill can be expected to improve in individuals with SRD, a corresponding degree of gain does not occur in spelling. Expectations regarding improvement of spelling skills, if any, should, therefore, be modest.

There have been attempts to classify spelling errors into subcategories such as "phonologically acceptable" and "phonologically unacceptable." For example, spelling *girl* as "gal" and *blue* as "bloo" is considered to be phonologically acceptable whereas spelling *girl* as "gril" and *stop* as "spot" is considered phonologically unacceptable. Boder (1973) describes children who commit "phonologically acceptable errors" as *dyseidetic,* and those who commit "phonologically unacceptable errors" as *dysphonetic.* It appears, however, that instead of representing two distinct subtypes of spelling and reading disabilities, these types of errors appear to represent two substages of spelling acquisition. Very young children and severely affected readers tend to commit numerous phonologically unacceptable spelling errors, whereas older individuals, who might have mastered many but not all the spelling rules, tend to make phonologically acceptable errors (Phillips, Taylor, & Aaron, 1985).

In summary, spelling errors indicate an accompanying weakness in phonological skill. Sometimes the presence of spelling errors in a student's writing may be the only residual symptom of a hidden reading disability. Therefore, an excessive number of spelling errors, seen particularly in the writings of mature students, should alert the teacher to the possibility of an associated reading deficit.

Errors of Syntax in Written Language

The written work of readers with SRD usually contains errors in the proper use of suffixes even though a considerable amount of intersubject difference exists in the quantity of such errors committed by college and high school students. Confusion of "homophonic words" (e.g., "were," "where"; "there," "their"; "won," "one") can also be seen in the written work of these students. It should be noted that some of these words are not homophones in a strict sense and that there are subtle differences in the pronunciation of these "homophonic" pairs. (Examples of true homophones are "meet," "meat" and "read," "reed.") Consequently, confusion of the spellings of "homophonic" pairs such as "won" and "one," and "were" and "where," often indicates the presence of subtle phonological deficits. A sample of one dyslexic college student's spontaneous writing, which contains errors of suffix and spelling, is shown in Fig. 4.2. Even though these errors appear to be grammatical, as

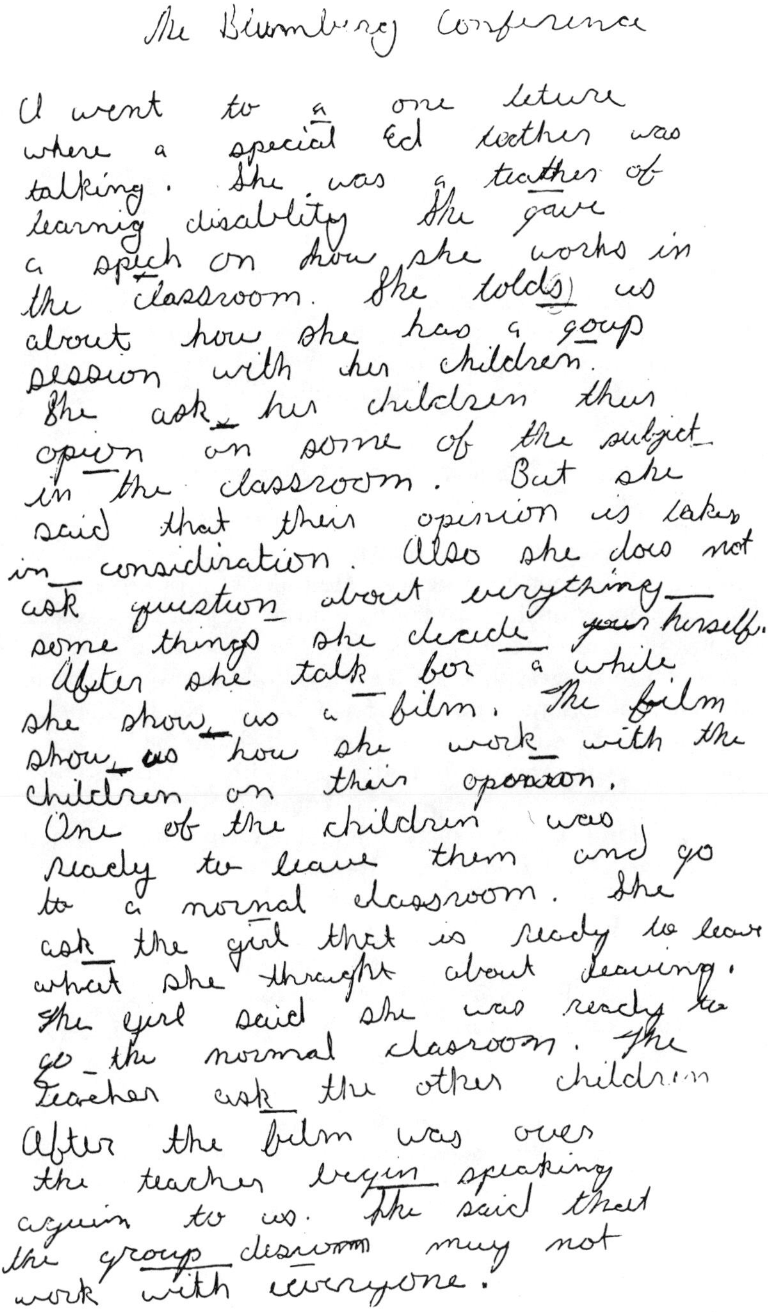

The Blumberg Conference

I went to a one leture where a special Ed teacher was talking. She was a teacher of learning disablity She gave a speech on how she works in the classroom. She tolds us about how she has a goup session with her children.

She ask her children thier opion on some of the subject in the classroom. But she said that thier opinion is taken in consideration. Also she does not ask question about everything some things she decide your hirself.

After she talk for a while she shows us a film. The film show us how she work with the children on thier opionon.

One of the children was ready to leave them and go to a normal classroom. She ask the girl that is ready to leave what she thought about leaving. The girl said she was ready to go the normal clasroom. The Teacher ask the other children After the film was over the teacher begin speaking aguin to us. She said that the group discusion may not work with everyone.

FIGURE 4.2. Spontaneous writing of a college student with reading disability.

noted earlier they could also be the result of an underlying phonological deficit. This conclusion is partly supported by a study in which the knowledge and use of grammar of five college students with dyslexia were assessed. Even though their written work contained spelling and suffix errors, their knowledge of grammar was found to be normal (Aaron, Olsen, & Baker, 1985). A recent study by Crain (1989) assessed the syntactical skills of normal and poor second grade readers. When the memory load created by the questions used in the study was reduced by utilizing pictures instead of written sentences, it was found that children with SRD performed as well as normal readers did. This led Crain to conclude that spoken language comprehension failures by poor readers arise from limitations in phonological processing involving working memory rather than defective syntactic skills.

Excessive Reliance on Context for Word Recognition

One of the college freshmen we had the opportunity to assess read the sentence "Baseball is a game played by many in America" as "Basketball is a game played by men in America." He then went on to "read" the remaining sentences in the passage by entirely fabricating basketball-related phrases as he went along. The errors he made when he read the opening sentence suggest that he did not decode the word "baseball" correctly but probably recognized correctly words such as "game" and "play" and guessed from context that the word should be "basketball." This case serves as an example of how subjects with SRD tend to rely on their stored knowledge and depend on contextual cues to recognize words. As noted in Chapter 3, reading is an interactive process wherein both *concept-driven* and *data-driven* processes operate simultaneously. Readers with SRD, being weak in decoding, depend excessively on context; those with NSRD, being deficient in higher level cognitive processes, depend much on print. This results in the former making contextually acceptable errors. Low Ability Readers commit a large number of contextually inappropriate errors.

There is some controversy about the extent to which good and poor readers make use of context. Some reading experts claim that good readers make an optimal use of context whereas poor readers fail to take advantage of context. A substantial number of research studies, however, indicate that this is not the case. One of the reasons for this controversy is a misunderstanding about the stage of reading in which context is thought to play a role. The two stages of reading in which context could be important are word recognition and sentence comprehension. Context, probably, is important for the proper understanding of sentences. For instance, consider the following pair of sentences:

(1) Jane's parents were very poor. They always fed her dog biscuits.
(2) Mary's parents were very rich. They always fed her dog biscuits.

In these sentences, whether the girl or the dog was fed dog biscuits depends on the context in which the phrase occurs. In contrast to the role played by context in sentence comprehension, its importance appears to be minimal in word recognition. Mitchell (1982), after reviewing the relevant literature, concluded that word recognition is not guided or helped by contextual information, the main reason being that word recognition is simply too fast an operation to rely on context. There is also evidence to show that even skilled readers can guess correctly only one word in four and that guessing from context invariably leads to errors (Gough, Alford, & Holley-Wilcox, 1981). We may, therefore, conclude that subjects with poor decoding skills are likely to rely on context for word recognition more than skilled readers do. One of the goals of many early reading instruction programs is to help students learn to recognize words correctly, not to play guessing games.

Normal Listening Comprehension.

Normality is not usually considered a "symptom" of a disorder. However, normal listening comprehension is important for differential diagnosis: *there is no discernable deficit in the listening comprehension of individuals with SRD, when comprehension is evaluated in terms of normal, oral communication or exchange of information.* When highly artificial tests made up of contrived sentences are used to assess comprehension, these sentences increase the listener's memory load. Under such a condition, the listening comprehension of subjects with SRD may appear to be deficient. The fact that the reading comprehension of college students with SRD tends to be close to normal when assessed by untimed tests indicates that the poor reading comprehension seen in these subjects under certain testing conditions is more apparent than real. It is highly probable that in these subjects, the phonological processing factor becomes a bottleneck during reading and operates as a limiting factor. In skilled readers, decoding has become a highly automatized task thus releasing attention to be directed at comprehension. In the case of subjects with SRD, decoding remains an attention-demanding operation, preventing them from directing attention entirely to comprehension. This may be why subjects with SRD tend to do much better in tests of listening comprehension (which do not require the grapheme—phoneme transformation) than in tests of reading comprehension. Thus, poor reading comprehension is not a primary deficit but is secondary to the phonological processing deficit. Studies of dyslexic children that have failed to find comprehension deficits in dyslexic children (Frith & Snowling, 1986; Mann, 1986) lend support to this view.

Before closing this section on SRD, we have to mention one "symptom" that is often mistakenly thought to be a marker for SRD or dyslexia. Many individuals who are concerned with children's education, including some elementary school teachers, associate dyslexia exclusively with letter and word reversals in writing. We noted earlier that Orton was one of the earliest investigators to draw attention to disabled readers' tendency to reverse letters and words. Orton, however, noted that reversal in writing was by no means a reliable and constant symptom of specific reading disability. Systematic investigations undertaken since that time have indicated that Orton was essentially correct in noting the variability of reversal errors in poor readers (e.g., Liberman et al., 1982). It must also be added that reversals are seldom seen in the writings of adult dyslexics, which suggests that a maturational factor is responsible for reversal errors. One possible explanation why younger children reverse letters more often than older children do may be that young children, having not mastered print-to-phonology conversion skills, tend to rely on visuo-spatial cues and treat letters and words as though they are pictures. It is known that memory for orientation of a picture decays very rapidly and that we tend to remember the picture's meaning, not the physical details (Anderson, 1990). This can be easily demonstrated. Without looking at any of the real coins, try to find out in Figure 4.3 how many are reversed drawings of the real coin. The chances are good that you failed this simple test because information about the right–left orientation is not retained in our LTM as part of our visual memory about coins. In other words, we can recognize any of these four coins regardless of its left–right orientation. Children who tend to process written words as visual information rather than as phonological information also may disregard the orientation of letters and words and, therefore, commit reversal errors. If this is true, these children may not reverse letters and words consistently, but may do so on a random basis. This, indeed, is borne out by observations. The point is that reversal of letters and words is an indication that the stimuli are processed as visual rather than as phonological information. Not having mastered the phonological strategy, young children tend to reverse letters and words.

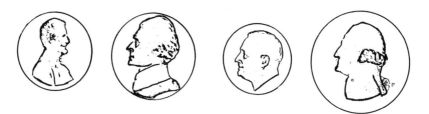

FIGURE 4.3. Which of these are reversed drawings of the real coin?

From such a visual strategy, beginning readers, however, make a transition to a phonological strategy as they mature (Frith, 1985). Consequently, reversals can be considered an indication of arrested phonological skills only in the case of older children, say beyond the age of 8 or 9 years.

One finding that has emerged unambiguously from the numerous studies undertaken during the past several years is that decoding skill, even though not a sufficient condition for successful reading performance, is a necessity (cf. Shankweiler, & Liberman, 1989). Studies that have probed the decoding skill further suggest that the decoding deficit seen in some young children could be traced to their poor *phoneme awareness* skill. Since phoneme awareness is perhaps the only diagnostic tool that can be effectively used with very young children, and also because training in phonological awareness is known to be a successful method of remediation, it will be discussed in some detail.

Phoneme awareness could be described as the knowledge that spoken words contain units of sounds and the ability to recognize them. Phoneme awareness helps the reader to eventually associate the letters of the written alphabet with their corresponding sounds. Ultimately, mastery of this skill enables the reader to articulate the written word (i.e., decode it) effortlessly and automatically. Many children fail to develop decoding skill because, to begin with, they are not aware of the fact that spoken words are composed of sound units. This is partly because phonemes in spoken words overlap each other in a shingle-like manner. In fact, some experts believe that phoneme awareness develops in children because of reading experience, even though there is evidence to show that it is also a product of maturation. Whatever the case may be, there is substantial evidence to show that children who are deficient in phoneme awareness tend to be poor decoders. This has been demonstrated not only in the case of the English language but in several other European languages as well (Alegria, Pignot, & Morais, 1982; Cossu et al., 1988; Fox, & Routh, 1980; Lundberg, Olofsson, & Wall, 1980; Stanovich, et al., 1984). It is also reported that preschool children who receive phoneme awareness training are less likely to fail at learning to read when they reach elementary grades than those who do not receive such training (Bradley, & Bryant, 1985; Lundberg, Frost, & Petersen, 1988). There is also evidence to conclude that dyslexic adults exhibit deficits in phonological awareness similar to the ones seen in dyslexic children (Byrne & Ledez, 1983; Liberman et al., 1985). More recently, Kitz and Tarver (1989) found that the performance of a group of dyslexic college students was inferior to that of their nondyslexic peers on two phoneme-awareness tasks. These investigators interpreted their results as suggesting that although the dyslexic subjects had improved their reading skills (probably by developing an adequate sight vocabulary), there remained a fundamental deficit in their ability to process phonological information quickly and accurately. These and many other studies show that phonological processing skill, as assessed by phonological awareness tests and nonword reading tasks, is an important correlate of reading skill. Phoneme awareness should be contrasted with two related skills: phoneme discrimination and phonetic skill. Phoneme awareness is an ability to analyze and isolate the different sound units in a word (e.g., *cat* = /k/ae/t/; *book* = /b/u/k/) whereas phoneme discrimination involves the ability to tell whether two phonemes such as /k/ and /r/ (in *cat* and *rat*) are the same or not. Phonetic skill refers to the ability to name the letters of the alphabet. Of these three skills, phoneme awareness seems to be the most difficult to acquire and, when not mastered, is known to adversely affect reading.

NONSPECIFIC READING DISABILITY

The most important feature of Nonspecific Reading Disability (NSRD) is poor comprehension in the presence of relatively intact decoding skills. As noted in Chapter 1, individuals with hyperlexia present an extreme form of this condition. It should, however, be noted that many hyperlexic children present additional symptoms such as autistic tendencies and social aloofness; they also have a unique childhood history of having started "reading" in a compulsive, ritualistic manner at a very early age.

The existence of children who can pronounce words and read aloud sentences rather well but fail to comprehend what they read has been well documented in reading research. Harris and Sipay (1980) noted that there are some children who can read rather fluently but do not pay attention to the meaning of the sentence and make no effort to remember what they are reading. They call such mechanical, thoughtless reading as "word calling." The number of children who can be considered to have NSRD is much smaller than those with SRD. This is more true of college students than children in elementary school. But, as noted earlier, a British study reports that as many as 10% of children in early primary grades have this form of reading problem (Oakhill & Garnham, 1988). Carr et al (1990) also report that nearly 25% of poor readers fall into this category. The existence of the NSRD condition is not totally unexpected because decoding is a modular skill and is independent of comprehension. Decoding skill, therefore, can be expected to have a developmental history that is different from comprehension.

Individuals with NSRD appear to be able to pronounce written words either by assembling the pronunciation or by addressing the whole-word pronunciation lexicon. A study of two subjects who could read aloud far better than they could understand what they read (Aaron et al., 1990) showed that one of the subjects, a 19-year-old female, read familiar words fluently but did very poorly in reading nonwords. This performance, in addition to her ability to read "regular" and "exception" words equally well, led to the conclusion that she was not able to use the spelling–sound rules to pronounce the word, but pronounced words by associating the whole word with its pronunciation. This process, however, imposed severe limitations because she could not read any unfamiliar word. The second subject, the 11-year-old hyperlexic girl, however, could read nonwords quite well but showed better performance in reading "regular" words than "exception" words. It appears that she could use spelling–sound rules for pronouncing words.

The most outstanding symptom seen in students with NSRD is their poor reading and listening comprehension which is in striking contrast to their oral reading skill. These subjects do not commit many errors while spelling familiar words. The "word class effect," namely, a pronounced difference in the accuracy and speed of reading function words and content words so often seen in subjects with SRD, is also not seen in these subjects.

LOW ABILITY READERS

By far the largest number of poor readers seen in schools have a combination of decoding and comprehension deficits and, therefore, are classified as low ability readers (LARs). This statement is also true of postsecondary institutions that are not very selective and have an open admission policy where many such students come to college underprepared. As noted earlier, LARs constitute the largest proportion of those labeled as learning-disabled in elementary schools. These children have deficits not only in reading but in all aspects of learning. In contrast to students with SRD and NSRD, LARs are deficient in both decoding *and* comprehension; their listening comprehension and reading comprehension are substantially below their age and grade level. They tend to be slow readers, and when comprehension is required, their reading rate declines even further. Even though they are poor in decoding skill, LARs do not rely excessively on context to recognize a word because of their limited vocabulary and background knowledge. As a result, while reading aloud they often produce words that are contextually inappropriate, and some of these could be nonsense words. The observation that they seldom correct their own reading errors indicates a weak metacognitive skill.

Many of these symptoms associated with LAR are also seen in students whose past academic history is marked by frequent absences, poor motivation, and limited reading experience. It was noted earlier that reading failure which is environmentally induced is not labelled as reading disability but is referred to as reading difficulty. Procedures helpful for differentiating reading difficulties from the various kinds of reading disabilities are presented in the next section of this chapter.

READING DISABILITIES AND METACOGNITION

Metacognition was described as knowing what one knows and knowing what one does not know. Included in metacognition are the ability to monitor one's own reading performance and the ability to take corrective actions when comprehension fails. In spite of its short history, this topic has received a good deal attention (Garner, 1987). These studies show that children with unspecified reading disabilities are deficient in metacognitive skills and that these skills could be improved with instruction.

While it is possible that many disabled readers also have poor meta-cognitive skills, it is uncertain whether deficient metacognitive skill alone, by itself, can produce reading disability. A number of studies have investigated the metacognitive skills of poor readers. In a study of fourth grade good and poor readers, Paris and Myers (1981) found that poor readers were deficient in their knowledge about the adverse effect of negative strategies on comprehension. In a similar study, Garner and Kraus (1982) compared good and poor readers from Grade 7 for their knowledge about reading. Important differences were found between these two groups. For instance, to the question, "If you are given something to read, how would you know if you were reading it well?" good readers gave answers such as "If I could understand it without reading it over and over again," whereas poor readers gave answers such as "If I read fluently loud" and "If I didn't pause much." It is the authors' experience that many college students who are average readers are also deficient in metacognitive skills and show improvement in test performance after receiving information about metacognition and related study skills. Even though there may not exist a subgroup of poor readers whose difficulty is attributable exclusively to poor metacognitive skills, its instructional utility makes a knowledge of metacognition important for the consultant.

READING DISABILITIES: COGNITIVE STYLES
AND LEARNING STYLE

Cognitive style has been defined as "consistent individual differences in the ways of organizing and processing information" (Messic, 1976, p. 5).

Nearly twenty cognitive styles have been identified, but three have been more thoroughly investigated than others. These are, *reflectivity–impulsivity, field independence–dependence,* and *successive–simultaneous processing.* Even though cognitive style is concerned with the manner in which behavior occurs rather than with the level of performance, studies which have investigated reading in the light of cognitive styles indicate that some cognitive styles are not conducive to reading. For instance, impulsive children are known to commit more oral reading errors than reflective children. A recent report indicates that many children diagnosed as having attention deficit disorder also are poor readers (Dykman & Ackerman, 1991). A weakness in successive processing style and an overdependence on simultaneous style has also been implicated in SRD (Kirby & Robinson, 1987).

Recently, a new cognitive style that has implications for reading consultation has been reported (Aaron & Whitefield, 1990). This cognitive style has been named *dysfluency* and is marked by extreme slowness in the processing of symbolic information. Subjects who are dysfluent show no symptoms associated with reading disabilities other than a slow rate of reading. Dysfluent readers tend to perform poorly on timed tests because they are very slow in reading. Consequently, their grades are not consistent with their level of intelligence and the time they invest in preparing for tests. Because of their slow processing tendency, they also do poorly on tests of STM such as the digit span subtest of WISC-R.

It is important to distinguish dysfluent readers from individuals who experience reading difficulties for want of sufficient reading experience. These underprepared poor readers also tend to have poor vocabulary and a mediocre academic history. Careful examination of the symptoms as well as the academic history of the students can separate dysfluent readers from students who have reading difficulties that are environmental in origin.

Learning style is a broad term which encompasses cognitive style as one of its elements. It is used for describing a learner's dispositions which interact with certain environmental factors and produce optimal learning. For example, according to the proponents of the concept of *learning style,* a child who tends to be a "simultaneous processor" is likely to learn to read better if taught through the whole word method than through the phonics method. According to Butler (1988), *learning style* refers to "Reasonably stable patterns of behavior that indicate learning preferences and abilities and have four component parts: cognitive, affective, physiological, and psychological" (p. 28). The cognitive component includes factors such as cognitive style, and modality preferences (auditory learner vs. visual learner); the affective component includes personality dimensions such as anxiety level, expectancy, and level of motivation; the physiological component includes gender differences, daily rhythms (morning vs. afternoon person), and level of arousal; the psychological component includes factors such as self-concept, locus of control, and sociability (loner vs. group person). Because the idea that matching the method of instruction with the learning style of the child should reduce learning difficulties is intuitively appealing, some educators attach much importance to the notion of *learning style* (e.g., Carbo, 1988; Dunn, 1988).

Research findings on the effectiveness of matching teaching with children's *learning style* are, however, equivocal. Some researchers (e.g., Cronbach & Snow, 1977; Stahl, 1988) found no evidence of useful interactions between student preferences and instructional treatments. Adams (1990) cites eight separate reviews of this literature, all of which have concluded that matching beginning reading methods to different aptitudes is not a solution to reading problems. There are other problems as well. The validity of some concepts such as "morning person," "afternoon person," "visual processor," and "auditory processor" is not established. The notion that teaching children through their preferred modality would bring better results than if teaching and modality are not matched is also thoroughly discredited (Kavale & Forness, 1987). As Johnston and Allington (1991) put it, "Individualized remedial instruction differentiated on the basis of learning style has received no more support than that based on modality preferences, though it continues to receive considerable popular press" (p. 994). Finally, as Harris and Sipay (1990) remark, it would be physically impossible to accommodate all the potential permutations of learning styles that might exist in a classroom.

Differential Diagnosis of Reading Disabilities

INTRODUCTION

The primary intent of the diagnostic procedure is not necessarily to classify the student into one of the three categories of poor readers described earlier in this chapter and label him/her, but to identify the weakness of the individual student and to provide appropriate instructional guidance. The severity of symptoms tend to vary in degree; therefore, it may not always be possible to unambiguously assign all children with reading disabilities to one of the three categories. In spite of this occasional uncertainty, the diagnostic procedure presented in this chapter can provide a broad orientation for the consultee to determine the general principles to be followed in corrective instruction and management procedures, as well as to help set up realistic academic goals for students on an individual basis. For example, students with

SRD may require special attention in developing phonic skills, whereas those with NSRD may need special coaching in improving comprehension. Whether a child is eligible for special education services or not is also not part of the evaluation procedure because such decisions are not psychological but are governed by administrative and fiscal policies.

Many students with reading disabilities tend to adopt compensatory techniques by excessively utilizing one or the other strategy. The diagnostic procedure, therefore, also attempts to identify such "strengths" of the reader with the disability. Sometimes, such compensatory strategies can be utilized to help the student circumvent weaknesses and, at other times, the student should be discouraged from using them. The diagnostic procedure is also simple enough to be carried out by the consultee in collaboration with the consultant. The procedures presented are not meant to be rigidly followed but have to be taken as broad guidelines which can be modified as circumstances demand.

Diagnostic conclusions reached are based on quantitative data and qualitative information obtained. Quantitative data are obtained by following two procedures: formal assessment and informal assessment. Formal assessment utilizes standardized tests, and the student's performance on these tests is usually compared against national norms. For this reason, such tests are referred to as *norm-referenced tests.* Informal assessment is based primarily on information collected regarding errors committed during oral reading, impromptu writing, and spelling. This is accomplished with the help of locally developed instruments which often, but not always, contain test items from curriculum material used in the classroom. When the tests contain curriculum-based materials, they are usually constructed by the consultee. Under such circumstances the student is tested to see if he/she has reached a criterion set up by the consultee in a certain skill. These tests are, therefore, referred to as *criterion-referenced tests.* When the testing procedure is aimed at measuring students' progress in the classroom and is based on items that are drawn exclusively from the material covered in the classroom, it is referred to as *curriculum-based assessment* (Idol, Nevin, & Paolucci-Whitcomb, 1986; Shinn, 1989). Both curriculum-based assessment and criterion-referenced tests generate numerical data, which are not compared with preset national norms but with informal criteria established by the consultee and the consultant. The distinction between norm-referenced tests and criterion-referenced tests in reading disability consultation is not, however, absolute. The assessment procedures described in this book are based on the "componential view" of reading and, therefore, differ in several important respects from the traditional procedures that are followed in the diagnosis of LD in children.

Qualitative information about the student is obtained primarily though interviews and observations in which details regarding the student's academic history, educational experience, level of motivation, and biological and genetic characteristics are obtained. Information obtained in this way is useful in determining whether environmental factors or some intrinsic factor is responsible for the reading problem. In other words, qualitative assessment is useful in separating reading disabilities from reading difficulty. A schematic outline of the overall format of the diagnostic testing procedure is shown in Table 4.1. The diagnostic procedure is described in detail here with the expectation that the consultant will demonstrate the evaluation procedure to the consultee (i.e., the classroom or special education teacher) who subsequently will carry out his/her own evaluation. Because the first step in the evaluation procedure starts with an interview, qualitative assessment procedures are described first.

QUALITATIVE ASSESSMENT

Information that is considered to be of a qualitative nature is obtained through interviews and informal observation of the student's behavior. Of course, if the classroom teacher is the consultee, he/she already has a good knowledge of the student and his/her behavior. If parents are consultees, an independent observation of the child, in the classroom, may be necessary. An interview with the parents, preferably along with the child, is the starting point in diagnostic evaluation. There exists no test which can separate students whose reading difficulty is environmentally induced from those who have reading disabilities. Information gathered about the student's previous academic history during the in-

TABLE 4.1. A Schematic Outline of the Assessment Procedure

	Quantitative assessment	
Qualitative assessment	Formal assessment	Informal assessment
Interviews and observation	Standardized tests of reading comprehension, listening comprehension, decoding, and vocabulary	Locally developed tests of decoding, spelling, reading speed, context dependency, errors of syntax in writing, metacognition, and cognitive style
Information about academic history, level of motivation, study habits, family background, health history, and biological/genetic factors		

terview perhaps will be the only basis for making a diagnostic decision in this regard. The questions asked during the interview should be such that they elicit information regarding the educational history and family environment of the client and his/her genetic, biological, and neuropsychological background.

Qualitative information, when obtained and carefully analyzed, can provide additional information for the differential diagnosis of reading disabilities. During an interview, it is important to obtain precise information rather than vague statements. For example, the question, "How much time does your child spend reading at home?" is expected to be answered in terms of hours spent with the books rather than with statements such as "not much," or "quite a bit." After explaining to the parents the reasons for obtaining this kind of information, the following set of questions can be asked.

Educational Environment of the Home

Is there a specific time allotted for studies? Does the child have a room of his/her own? How much time does the child spend watching TV? How much time with books? How many hours do parents and other siblings watch TV? Do parents keep close track of the child's performance at school? What are parents' educational level and what are their occupations? How many children do they have? How is the achievement of the other siblings at school? How many magazines and newspapers do they get? How much time do parents spend on reading? Is the child a behavior problem at school?—at home? Do the parents try to tutor the child or assist him/her with homework? How many times have they met the child's teachers this year? How would the parents describe the child—a hard worker, puts in minimum effort, or work avoider? Do the parents feel that the child is not succeeding in school despite his/her best efforts, or is he/she getting what he/she deserves? Is he/she strong in any one academic area such as math? Does the child have a special talent or interest in some area such as visual arts, music, or machinery repair?

Answers to these questions should give a fairly good idea about the academic environment at home. If the answers indicate that parents are reading-oriented, take time to help the child, and at least one sibling is doing well at school, it may be suspected that the poor reader in the family has reading disability, not reading difficulty.

Biological/Genetic Factors

SRD, or developmental dyslexia, is associated with certain biological characteristics, and information regarding these can be useful in separating SRD from NSRD and reading difficulties. There is evidence that there are more left-handers who are dyslexic than right-handers, and the incidence of immune-related health problems such as allergy is higher among dyslexic subjects than it is in the general population (Geschwind & Behan, 1982).

It has also been known for nearly a century that dyslexia has a genetic predisposition. However, the presence of relatives who are poor readers does not ensure that there is a genetic history of reading disability in the family. Parents themselves may not be good readers because of limited educational opportunities or because their occupation does not require any reading or writing. Extreme caution should be exercised before a genetic history of dyslexia can be assumed to exist in a family. A life style in which reading is not given much importance can mimic reading disability in the family. The following is a list of sample questions that can be asked in order to obtain information regarding biological and genetic factors.

Is the child left-handed, mixed-handed, or ambidextrous? (Mixed-handed individuals do certain things with one hand and other things with the other hand, whereas ambidextrous individuals can carry out activities equally well with either hand.)

Which hand does the child use for writing, brushing teeth, throwing the ball? Is any sibling, parent, or close relative left-handed, mixed-handed, or ambidextrous?

Is the child allergic to any substance, or does he/she have more allergic reactions during any particular seasons(s)?

Has either parent experienced difficulty in reading or spelling?

Is there any close relative who, in spite of his/her best efforts, remains a poor reader or speller?

Does any of the client's siblings have reading or spelling problems?

Neuropsychological Factors

Neurological impairment, when present, can cause reading difficulty. Such impairment can be caused by metabolic disorders such as infantile jaundism, and juvenile diabetes. The presence of any of these disorders by itself does not indicate neurological impairment. In contrast, epileptic seizures and cerebral palsy are symptoms of neurological impairment. Here, too, there is no one-to-one relationship between these disorders and the intellectual competency of the child. Some children with cerebral palsy can be very intelligent. When a neurological impairment is associated with reading problems, the child usually happens to be a LAR because the impairment can have adverse effects on all aspects of intellectual functioning. The following questions are asked to elicit the necessary information.

How was the child's birth history? Was the birth normal? What was the APGAR score? Did he/she at any time have convulsions, seizures, or was he/she involved in any accident? If so, was a head injury possible? Did he/she begin to walk and talk between 1 and 1½ years? How is his/her present health history?

QUANTITATIVE ASSESSMENT

Traditional Methods of Diagnosis versus Components-Based Assessment

Many children whose reading achievement is discrepant from their IQ are identified as having a learning disability (LD); a substantial number of children identified as having LD have reading disability. The individually administered intelligence test, particularly the WISC-R, is the most widely used instrument to estimate children's reading potential. The traditional method of diagnosing LD, which relies heavily on the child's IQ test performance, has been criticized, however, for several reasons. First, the validity of the assumptions that underlie the use of IQ in defining learning disabilities has been questioned (Siegel, 1989). In addition, the IQ score is not able to account for a large amount of variance seen in reading performance because the correlation coefficients obtained between IQ and reading achievement scores are rather low, ranging from .4 to .6. There is yet another problem. Administrative decisions regarding LD are based on the discrepancy between an individual's reading potential (estimated from IQ) and actual reading achievement. However, there is no consensus about the extent of this discrepancy which marks LD. A more serious, but pragmatic problem is that diagnosis based on IQ may satisfy administrative expediencies but does not lead to recommendations regarding remediation, instruction, and management. After reviewing the problems that arise in the use of IQ tests, Stanovich (1991) concludes that defining reading disabilities by reference to discrepancies from IQ is an untenable procedure.

In the place of IQ measures, performance on tests of listening comprehension are utilized in the diagnostic procedure recommended in this book. As a diagnostic tool, listening comprehension does not have the limitations of IQ tests. The advantages of using listening comprehension are that it is an integral component of the reading process; a test of listening comprehension is simple to administer; and more importantly, the diagnostic findings based on this procedure lead to recommendations regarding corrective instruction.

Diagnostic Procedure Based on the Componential View of Reading

Because the diagnostic procedure recommended in this book is somewhat new and departs rather radically from the traditional methods, the rationale that underlies this procedure is presented in some detail.

The diagnostic procedure to be described is based on the following propositions: (1) reading ability is, ultimately, the ability to comprehend written language; (2) reading comprehension (i.e., reading ability) is composed of two independent components—decoding and language comprehension; (3) the best measure of language comprehension is listening comprehension; and (4) apart from decoding and the differences attributable to the modalities of input, reading and listening comprehension are mediated by the same cognitive mechanisms. These propositions lead to two expectations. First, development of decoding and comprehension skill can be arrested independently of each other, resulting in the following three different kinds of poor readers—those with deficient decoding but adequate comprehension skills; those with poor comprehension but adequate decoding skills; and those with deficient decoding and poor comprehension skill. Second, listening comprehension can be utilized to estimate the reading comprehension potential.

It was noted in Chapter 3 that a substantial body of psychological evidence exists to support the two-component view of the reading process. There also is an impressive body of literature to support the second proposition that except for the modality differences, reading comprehension and listening comprehension represent a unitary cognitive process. For instance, Duker's (1965) review of 23 studies that compared reading comprehension and listening comprehension, and another review of an additional 12 studies (Kennedy, 1971) report correlation coefficients that range from .45 to .82. In a more recent review, Danks (1980) reported similar data. Stanovich, Cunningham, and Feeman (1984) compared the reading performance of children from Grades 1, 2, and 5 with measures of intelligence, listening comprehension, and decoding skill. Consistent with other studies, the correlation coefficient between reading and listening comprehension rose from .37 in Grade 1, to .59 in Grade 5. At all levels, listening comprehension was found to be a better predictor of reading achievement than were measures of intelligence. Wood, Buckhalt, and Tomlin (1988) obtained a higher mean correlation coefficient of .78 between reading and listening comprehension for a group of children classified as learning-disabled and mildly mentally retarded. In an unpublished study of 180 children from Grades 3 through 8, Aaron and Simurdak (1990) obtained correlation coefficients that ranged from .58 to .71. As Royer, Kulhavy, Lee, and Peterson (1986) noted, listening comprehension appears to place an upper bound on reading comprehension. In a review of this topic, Trabasso (1981) noted that studies suggest it matters little as far as comprehension is concerned whether the material is read or heard. Kintsch and Kozminsky (1977) administered reading and listening tasks to college students and found suprisingly small differences in the production of structural elements and propositions, which led them to conclude that reading and listening involve identical comprehension skills. In a study of college students, Palmer et al., (1985) obtained a correlation coefficient of .82 between reading comprehension and listening comprehension, which led them to state that reading comprehension can be predicted almost perfectly by a listening measure.

The high correlation coefficient obtained between listening comprehension and reading comprehension makes listening comprehension a viable means of estimating reading comprehension. The idea of using listening comprehension as a predictor of reading comprehension is not an entirely new one. Several years ago, Ladd (1970) noted that listening comprehension is one of the most important indicators of reading ability. Durrell and Hayes (1969) wrote that listening comprehension is more directly related to reading than are most tests of intelligence. Carroll (1977) was explicit in advocating the use of listening comprehension for assessing reading comprehension potential. In a recent study, Spring and French (1991) found that children with reading disabilities scored significantly lower on reading than on listening comprehension, while nondisabled readers scored slightly higher, but not significantly so, on reading than on listening comprehension. These authors suggested that identifying chidren with SRD on the basis of the discrepancy between their reading and listening comprehension scores is more appropriate than using IQ scores for this purpose. The validity of using listening comprehension measures for the diagnosis of different forms of reading disabilities has been recently documented by one of the authors of this book (Aaron, 1991).

The facts that comprehension and decoding are two major components of reading, and that listening comprehension is well correlated with reading comprehension, lead to certain expectations. One of them is the possibility that once the contribution of listening comprehension to reading is factored out, the remaining deficit could be attributed to decoding deficit. There is evidence to support such a proposition. In a study of 172 dyslexic children, Conners and Olson (1990) found that printed word recognition and oral language comprehension each contributed independent variance to reading comprehension and that reading comprehension of the dyslexic children was higher than their word recognition. When this finding is translated into pragmatic terms, it follows that the reading difficulty of a child who has good listening comprehension, but poor reading comprehension, can be attributed to poor decoding skill. Conversely, the intrinsic cause of reading disability of a child with poor listening comprehension but adequate decoding skill can be attributed to sub-optimal comprehension skill. In low ability readers, both listening comprehension and decoding skills are expected to be poor. Studies which investigated these type of poor readers, in fact, confirm such an expectation. For instance, Curtis (1980) found that among third and fifth grade poor readers, there was much common variance between word recognition and listening comprehension that accounted for poor reading comprehension; she also found that these children were poor in both listening and reading comprehension. A study of poor readers from fifth grade by Berger, (1978) and a study of adult poor readers by Sticht (1979) produced similar results.

The proposition that once the contribution of listening comprehension to reading is factored out, the remaining deficit could be attributed to poor decoding skills is advocated by investigators who subscribe to the componential view of reading. For instance, according to Gough and Tunmer (1986), reading (R) equals the product of decoding (D) and comprehension (C). That is, $R = D \times C$. It follows that if $D = 0$, then $R = 0$; and if $C = 0$, then also $R = 0$. They conclude that the linear combination of decoding and listening comprehension predicts reading so well that there is no room for improvement.

In spite of all the desirable characteristics of listening comprehension as a predictor of reading potential, the consultant needs to alert the consultee to a potential problem of the *Matthew Effect* which proposes that poor reading habits can depress the growth of vocabulary. If this happens, separating children with SRD from those with NSRD would become difficult. Stanovich (1991) recently cautioned that the use of listening comprehension scores as a means of estimating reading potential needs some refinement. While the confounding nature of the Matthew Effect should be given serious consideration, it may not seriously affect our ability to predict reading comprehension from listening comprehension since both forms of comprehension are equally subject to this problem. In our experience, we find that almost all the college students with SRD obtain listening comprehension scores at post-high-school levels.

Separation of the three different types of poor readers is based on this rationale. In addition to aiding in the identification of the three types of poor readers, this procedure also provides guidance for corrective instructional measures that are to be adopted.

Formal Assessment

Reading Comprehension. Reading comprehension can be assessed in more than one way. The simplest format requires the child to read a passage and then answer a set of questions. Performance on this test depends not only on the reader's comprehension skill but also on his/her memory ability. Consequently, the obtained result could be contaminated by memory factors. Tests that follow this format are usually timed tests. The *Stanford Diagnostic Reading Test* (SDRT) is an example of this form of test. Another way to assess reading comprehension is to adopt the *Cloze procedure*. In the Cloze test, the reader is required to furnish the words which had been deleted in a systematic way. The assumption is that the reader cannot supply the correct word unless he/she has understood the meaning of the sentence. Tests that follow this format do not usually impose time restrictions. Consequently, the reading comprehension measure obtained can be considered to be relatively free from memory demands. The *Woodcock Reading Mastery Tests* (WRMT) follow this format. One minor problem with this type of untimed test is that many individuals with SRD, particularly older subjects, given enough time, can "figure out" the missing word successfully. This can lead to "false negatives" in the sense that the score obtained under such conditions would not reveal any reading disability even though the testee may be a slow reader and a poor decoder. The *Peabody Individual Achievement Test* follows a different technique to assess reading comprehension. In this test, the child reads a sentence, after which he/she selects one picture, from a choice of four, that best illustrates the meaning of the sentence. Even though this form of testing reduces the memory load, the understanding of pictures can require a good deal of reasoning ability. This is particularly true at the higher level. The consultant can recommend the use of any test, depending on the circumstances. A more comprehensive list of standardized reading tests, along with brief descriptions, is provided in Appendix II.

We recommend the use of two tests: the Passage Comprehension Subtest of *Form G* of the *Woodcock Reading Mastery Tests, Revised* (WRMT-R; Woodcock, 1987) and the Reading Comprehension Subtest of the *Stanford Diagnostic Reading Test* (SDRT; Karlsen, Madden & Gardner, 1984). The WRMT battery has six subtests, passage comprehension being one of them. The SDRT is a timed test, whereas WRMT is an untimed test. This way of assessing reading comprehension by combining a timed and an untimed test not only increases the reliability of the test results, but also is helpful in differential diagnosis. For instance, children with SRD do better on WRMT than on SDRT because performance in the former test is not affected by reading rate. Children with NSRD and LARs do equally poorly on both tests.

The raw scores obtained on the WRMT are to be converted into grade equivalents and standard scores; the raw scores obtained on the SDRT are converted into grade equivalents and percentiles because there is no simple way to convert the raw scores into standard scores.

Listening Comprehension. This skill is assessed by administering the Passage Comprehension Subtest from WRMT-R, Form H, as a test of listening comprehension. The examiner reads each sentence aloud and the subject is required to furnish the missing word. If the subject requests it, the sentence is read one more time, but no more. A good test of listening comprehension should be valid in the sense that obtained results are free from contamination by variables such as memory and motivation. Furthermore, when listening comprehension is being compared with reading comprehension, the level of vocabulary difficulty, and both the complexity and cohesiveness of sentences should be equivalent under both listening and reading conditions. Good tests of listening comprehension that satisfy these requirements are simply not available. Taking these constraints into account, researchers have used equivalent forms of the same test for assessing reading and listening comprehension. Spring and French (1991) have adopted a different strategy by using odd and even sentences from the PIAT to assess reading and listening comprehension, respectively.

Because the two forms of the WRMT (Form G, which is used for measuring reading comprehension, and Form H, which is used for measuring listening comprehension) are similar in the number of inferential questions, length, and difficulty level, the two forms of the test provide comparable data. The raw scores obtained in the listening comprehension test are also converted into grade equivalents and standard scores. In their unpublished study, Aaron and Simurdak (1990) administered the two tests to 180 children from Grades 3 through 8 and obtained an overall correlation coefficient of .73 between reading comprehension and listening comprehension. The listening comprehension test has a test/retest reliability of .67.

Vocabulary. Reading vocabulary of the subject is measured with the aid of the word comprehension subtest of the WRMT-R. This subtest is comprehensive because it assesses the reader's knowledge of antonyms, synonyms, and analogies. The raw scores obtained by the subject are converted into standard scores and grade equivalents.

Decoding. The decoding skill of the subject is assessed with the help of the word-attack subtest from the WRMT-R. This test requires the subject to read either nonsense words or words with a very low frequency of occurrence in text. The raw scores obtained by the subject can be converted into standard scores and grade equivalents.

Initial Diagnosis. The objective of the formal assessment procedure is to identify the component(s) in which the student is weak and to make an initial judgment as to which one of the three categories of reading disabilities (SRD, NSRD, LAR) the subject fits. This initial diagnosis is made on the basis of the student's performance during the formal assessment procedure. As a first step, the student's WRMT reading comprehension results are examined. The manual provides grade equivalents (GE) up to the 16.9 level, which is roughly equivalent to the college-senior level. The grade equivalent is the most readily interpretable metric and indicates whether the student's reading comprehension is at or below the grade he is in. Freshmen entering college are expected to score equivalent to the 12th grade. For statistical purposes the standard score should be used, and its use for diagnostic purposes is also strongly recommended. The confidence interval for the grade equivalent score can then be calculated by using the standard error of measurement (SEM) provided in the test manual. The confidence range obtained by adding and subtracting 1 SEM to the obtained score indicates that the chances are 2 to 1 that the true score of the student falls within this range; the range obtained by adding and subtracting 1.96 times the SEM to the obtained score provides a range which reduces error of measurement and chance factors to a 5% level. For example, in the passge comprehension subtest, a college freshman obtained a score equivalent to 7.4 grade. There is a nearly 66% probability that his true score falls between 6.5 and 8.4 grades (i.e., ±1 SEM) or, there is a 95% probability that his true score falls between 5.3 and 10.7 (i.e., ± 1.96 SEM). Clearly, the student has comprehension deficit. In the WRMT, these statistics are somewhat cumbersome to calculate, but the microcomputer scoring program called ASSIST can make computation much easier.

What degree of discrepancy should indicate reading disability? There is no simple answer to this question and the decision is largely left to the consultant and the consultee. The test scores reveal whether the student's reading comprehension is at grade level or lower and what degree of confidence we can attach to this number. It is the personal philosophy of the authors that any degree of discrepancy found in a student who wants to improve his reading performance deserves attention.

The reading comprehension subtest of SDRT is a timed test and provides grade equivalents and stanine scores. A direct comparison of reading comprehension GEs obtained on the WRMT and SDRT can provide useful diagnostic information. In general, students with SRD do less well on SDRT than on WRMT because they have adequate comprehension but are slow in reading; students with NSRD and LAR do equally poorly on both tests.

The next step in the diagnostic procedure is to compare the reading comprehension score of the student with the listening comprehension score, both obtained from WRMT. The raw scores obtained in these tests are converted into standard scores for the purpose of comparison. The logic involved in this form of comparison is that if the student has a listening comprehension score that is average or better and a reading comprehension score which is lower, his/her reading difficulty is due to poor decoding skill. In contrast, if the student has below-average scores in both forms of comprehension, the deficit is not limited to the written language but includes spoken language as well. How large must the discrepancy between these two comprehension scores be for it to be considered as indicative of a genuine difference? At a very basic level, if there is no overlap between the confidence limits set up by ± 1.96 SEM, then it can be inferred that a true difference exists. For instance, a college sophomore obtains a raw score of 50 on reading comprehension and a score of 60 on listening comprehension on the WRMT. First, these are converted into W scores and the corresponding standard scores are obtained from the tables. The corresponding standard scores are 93 and 110 for reading and listening, respectively. When the 95% confidence range is computed by adding and subtracting 1.96 SEM to each of the standard scores, we obtain the following data:

Reading comprehension   : 87 ————101.
Listening comprehension :   104 ————112.

Given there is no overlap between these two estimates, we can conclude, with approximately 95% confidence, that a true difference exists between the listening comprehension and reading comprehension of this subject: the student is poor in reading comprehension but not in listening comprehension. The source of his reading disability is likely to be his poor decoding skill. The student's performances on the two remaining subtests of the WRMT—vocabulary and word attack—are also used in the initial diagnosis. In order to confirm the initial diagnosis of SRD, the student's vocabulary scores should be higher than the decoding scores. As we saw earlier, reading is a major means of vocabulary acquisition. Because of their poor reading habits and limited reading experience, poor readers of all kinds tend to have a limited vocabulary. This condition is much more evident in the case of students with NSRD and LAR. These students, therefore, may need intense instruction in vocabulary development.

It is necessary to interject a cautionary note here. Children in the early elementary grades tend to have a higher listening comprehension score than reading comprehension score. This difference gradually disappears after the fourth grade. A statistically acceptable way to adjust for these differences is to compute a regression equation that can predict reading comprehension scores from listening comprehension scores. Because it is a time-consuming project to set up regression formulas for local populations, this procedure is not presented here. The interested reader may get detailed information from an article written by one of the authors (Aaron, 1991).

Informal Assessment

Information obtained through the informal assessment procedure is used for validating the initial diagnosis that was made on the basis of formal assessment techniques. This informal procedure is useful for evaluating the student's decoding skill, reading speed, spelling, dependency on context, metacognition, cognitive style, and syntactical skill. Any or all these tests could be administered, depending upon the depth of analysis needed and the time available. With the exception of two, all these skills could be evaluated with the aid of tests developed by using the classroom curriculum. The two exceptions are decoding skill and reading speed. We recommend the use of tests shown in Appendix IV to assess these two variables. The best way to assess decoding skill is to require the student to read a list of words with which he/she in unfamiliar. Familiar words would not serve the purpose because they can be read wholistically as sight words without utilizing decoding skills. For this reason, words taken from the student's textbooks cannot be used. Furthermore, pronounceable nonwords, rather than real words, are recommended because students vary a great deal in their vocabulary. Spelling-to-sound rules become progressively more complex, and children master them as they mature; a good test should sample all these rules. The list of nonwords provided in Appendix IV is developed with these rules in mind. Some caution needs to be exercised while determining the decoding skills of mature students by using of nonwords. Some students can, by using the analogy strategy, successfully pronounce even nonwords. For instance, the subject can pronounce correctly the nonword "greak" if he/she knows the word "break" by sight. For this reason, it is prudent to take into account the performance of the student on the non-word reading test, and the word attack subtest of WRMT. The amount of time it takes to read the list of nonwords also provides an index of the subject's decoding skill.

Two lists of function words provided in Appendix IV can be utilized for assessing reading speed. There is a good reason for not using passages taken from textbooks to assess reading speed. This is because during oral reading, even normal readers have a tendency to ponder over unfamiliar words. Thus, a handful of unfamiliar words in a passage can bias the measure of speed and make even a skilled reader appear slow. The use of lists of very common function words words shown in Appendix IV can eliminate much of the problem encountered in using text passages. Two lists of content words that are matched with the two lists of function words for word length and frequency are also shown in Appendix IV. A comparison of the speed with which function and content words are read can be useful in differential diagnosis. Children with SRD are *much* slower in reading function words than content words;

LARs also show a similar discrepancy, but the difference in the speed is much smaller than the one seen in SRD readers.

The remaining tests could be developed from curricular materials used in the classroom. However, certain precautions are to be observed in developing these tests. These precautions are noted as each test is discussed.

Decoding. A list of 36 pronounceable nonwords shown in Appendix IV is utilized for evaluating the student's decoding skill. The list of pronounceable nonwords used in this test was developed after examining the literature and identifying spelling-to-pronunciation rules that are progressively mastered by children (Calfee, Venezky, & Chapman, 1969; Venezky, 1976; Wijk, 1966). By the time they reach sixth grade, a majority of children have mastered the skill of decoding written words and should be able to pronounce almost all the words in this list. This test was standardized on a group of children from Grades 3 through 8.

Spelling. It was noted that one manifestation of decoding deficit is poor spelling. In individuals who have compensated for some of their reading deficits, poor spelling remains as the only identifiable residue of the reading problem. A list of 38 common words that can be used for evaluating the student's spelling skill is presented in Appendix IV. These words were selected on the basis of the same rules as was the list of nonwords. The consultee can, however, develop a list of spelling words from textbooks used in the classroom. In selecting these words, care should be exercised to see that mastery of all the spelling-to-pronunciation rules shown in the Appendix are tested. We noted earlier that phonologically acceptable spelling errors indicate a mastery of lower-level rules of pronunciation but a failure to master the more complex rules. The temptation to interpret phonologically acceptable spelling errors (e.g., *girl* as "gal"; *certain* as "sertain") as an indication that the child is "phonologically" strong should be resisted.

First, the subject is asked to read the list aloud. After some time, the subject is asked to write down these words. Only those words the subject was able to read but misspelled are counted as errors.

Reading Speed. The speed with which words are recognized and passages read is an important correlate of reading skill. Poor decoders are slow readers because they take more time to identify words than good decoders do. Thus, students with poor decoding skills tend to be slow readers regardless of their comprehension skills. Reading speed is traditionally assessed by asking children to read a passage and then noting the time. The use of passages, however, introduces factors that confound the results. To avoid this problem, lists of 20 function words and content words are used for estimating reading speed. The words in

Level 1 lists occur very frequently in written text—more than 500 times per 5,088,721 words of running text (Carroll, Davies, & Richman, 1971). Words in List 2 occur with less frequency but, nevertheless, are common words. List 1 can be used for children below Grade 5.

Context Dependency. It was noted earlier that when a reader has problems with "bottoms up" processing, decoding becomes difficult. Under these circumstances, the reader tends to rely heavily on his/her previous knowledge as well as the contextual cues found in the text. Conversely, the disabled reader who has poor comprehension ability and insufficient background knowledge is likely to depend more on print than on context. Removal of the context from the material to be read will, therefore, have greater negative impact on the performance of the poor decoder than on NSRD or LAR subjects. Thus, the effect of context removal can provide a measure of context dependency. Context dependency is measured in the following manner: the student is asked first to read aloud two passages that match his/her grade level, and the oral reading errors/he makes are noted. After a day or so, the student is asked to read aloud the same words that made up the passages but which are arranged randomly in the form of a list. Taking the words out of the sentences eliminates contextual cues. The number of errors committed while reading the word list is noted first. Then, the child's reading of the text is analyzed to see how many of these incorrectly read words from the list had been correctly read. This number provides a measure of context dependency. The passages shown in Appendix IV come from a list of 24 graded passages that have been calibrated for syntactic density and readability (Aquino, 1969; Miller, & Coleman, 1967). If material for this test is taken from the child's own textbook, the passages used should be the ones not yet introduced in the classroom. Otherwise, some children may be able to guess many words correctly from having listened to them during classroom instruction.

The passage-reading task also provides an opportunity to examine the nature of errors made while reading aloud. Students with SRD tend to make context-appropriate errors, whereas students with LAR make errors that are meaningless; also, these students occasionally produce neologisms.

Metacognition. Knowledge of one's own cognitive processing and the ability to undertake deliberate corrective actions when comprehension fails are aspects of metacognition. The two corresponding features of metacognitive skills that can be assessed during the testing process are accurate self-evaluation and comprehension monitoring. The metacognitive aspect of self-evaluation is assessed in terms of the accuracy of the student's perception of his/her own ability or weakness. This can be accomplished by asking the child to predict how many questions s/he thought s/he could answer correctly when the word comprehension subtest of the WRMT is administered, and then comparing this figure with the scores obtained. Striking discrepancy between these two figures is an indication of poor self-evaluative skills. Similarly, as mentioned earlier, an absence of a tendency to correct oral reading mistakes also indicates that the student is not actively monitoring his/her own comprehension.

Cognitive Style. In a way, SRD or dyslexia can be viewed as the result of using a unique cognitive style wherein, to recognize the written word, the individual relies more on meaning and visual cues than on the phonological features of the word. Even though nearly 20 cognitive styles have been identified in psychological literature, the impact of only a few of these on reading has been studied. It seems that children who are described as impulsive make many more errors while reading aloud than do those described as reflective. It is important for the consultee to decide if what appears to be a reading disability could be an artifact of attention deficit. Another cognitive style, *dysfluency*, described earlier, is an extreme slowness in the processing of symbolic information. A subject is considered dysfluent if s/he reads the list of 20 function words very slowly but does well on tests of comprehension, decoding, and spelling. A significant difference between the subject's performances on WRMT and SDRT is also an indication of slow reading. Even though both dysfluent and SRD readers do poorly on timed reading tests, dysfluent readers perform fairly well on tests of decoding and spelling. The dysfluent reader's digit span is also low. In contrast to students with a mediocre academic history, the dysfluent reader usually has a reasonably good academic record and presents evidence of high motivation and sustained effort.

Syntax in the Written Language. It was noted earlier that the errors of suffix omission and substitution seen in the writings of SRD poor readers may be indicative of phonological weakness. These errors can be detected if an informal sample of the student's writing is obtained. For example, the student could be asked to write a paragraph on a prescribed topic, and the written material then analyzed for errors of syntax. The written sample, however, cannot be relied upon as an index of the student's language skill. This is because, in order to avoid spelling errors, some students use in their writing only words whose spelling they are sure of. This leads to the selection of very ordinary words and creates an impression of immature language skills. Table 4.2 presents the appropriate measures for differential diagnosis, together with the distinctive patterns of test results which identify the underlying problem.

TABLE 4.2. Diagnostic Profiles of Different Types of Reading Disabilities

	Specific reading disability	Nonspecific reading disability	Low ability reader
Reading comprehension:			
Untimed test	Close to normal	Poor	Poor
Timed test	Poor	Poor	Poor
Listening comprehension	Normal	Poor	Poor
Decoding skill	Poor	Normal	Poor
Spelling	Poor	Normal	Poor
Reading speed	Slow	Normal	Slow
Context dependency for recognizing words	Yes	Rarely	Some
Oral reading errors:	Many, errors fit context	Few, mechanical pronunciation; many do not fit context	Many, some are nonwords; do not fit context
Self-correction of errors in oral reading	Often	Rarely	Rarely
Suffix dropping and substitution in writing	Often	Rarely	Rarely

DIAGNOSTIC PROCEDURES WITH VERY YOUNG CHILDREN

Many parents with children in the first grade become aware, for the first time, that their child may have a reading problem. This often happens during the first parent–teacher meeting, which usually takes place before the end of the first semester. Teachers at that time may recommend a psychological evaluation of the child. These instances are becoming increasingly common. A diagnostic assessment of the child's reading is extremely difficult at this stage when he/she is just beginning to learn to read. The child has not had time to master sufficient reading skills to be tested. Results of standardized reading tests cannot, therefore, be meaningfully interpreted. A similar situation arises when the consultant's advice is sought by parents who are told that their kindergarten child is not quite ready to move to the first grade but would be better off being placed in a "transition class." Many parents view such a recommendation as a humiliation and would like to see their child promoted to the first grade. Under these circumstances, parents often consult with the school psychology clinic.

In such cases, assessment must focus on prereading abilities because many of these children have not acquired more than rudimentary reading skills. It was noted that "phonological awareness" is an important prereading skill and a good predictor of reading achievement in later grades. Consequently, a combined measure of the child's phonological awareness and cognitive ability or IQ can be used for decision-making purposes. A phonological awareness test is presented in Appendix III. The consultee also may wish to develop local norms for this test, or reach diagnostic conclusions by comparing a child's phonological awareness scores with those of good and average readers from the same classroom. It should be cautioned that while poor phonological awareness presages poor reading performance, the converse need not be true. That is, some children may demonstrate good phonological awareness but still encounter reading difficulties later on. These children usually have depressed IQs and turn out to have Nonspecific Reading Disability.

5

Intervention Strategies:
Word Recognition and Spelling

INTRODUCTION

This chapter is concerned with the improvement of reading-related skills such as decoding and spelling in those children who have not mastered them. The consultant and the consultee, in collaboration, make decisions regarding the intervention strategies they think will be most suitable for achieving improvement of these skills. The consultant and the consultee make decisions also about the setting in which the remedial strategies will be implemented. The remedial work can be carried out in the regular classroom or special classroom, on an individual basis or in a group setting. Even though the consultant may have personal biases and preferences regarding the strategies and the settings, it is desirable that decisions are mutually agreed upon by both the consultant and the consultee.

Reading disabilities differ in their nature, and so does the severity of the reading problems children have. Consequently, children differ in the amount of progress they make as well as the time they take to reach the desired academic goals. The consultant and consultee should, therefore, be flexible enough to abandon methods of instruction that are unproductive and try alternative approaches. This policy is sometimes referred to as *trial teaching*. During trial teaching, the student's progress in learning to read is monitored and a decision is made as to which beginning reading approach is likely to yield satisfactory results. Harris and Sipay (1990, p. 252) give detailed information about the steps to follow in implementing trial teaching. Among the different methods to be tried for improving decoding skills, they recommend *whole word method, synthetic phonic method, linguistic method, visual–motor method,* and *kinesthetic method.* Step-by-step procedures that utilize these methods have been developed by reading specialists, and these are briefly presented later in this chapter. Methods designed to improve comprehension focus on vocabulary development, comprehension of sentences and text passages, and improvement of inferential and metacognitive skills. These are presented in the next chapter.

Remedial procedures can be carried out in more than one setting. Clark (1988) identifies three different settings and labels their respective models accordingly: tutoring model, the small group model, and the whole class model. It is generally acknowledged that the tutoring model, in which direct instruction is provided on a one-to-one basis, is the most effective for remediating reading problems. This arrangement, however, places great demands on the consultee's time and resources. In this connection, it has to be noted that taking the child out of the classroom for special instruction would deprive him/her of exposure to the regular classroom curriculum. This practice, in the long run, can produce the *Matthew effect.* Therefore, a decision to "pull out" the child from the regular classroom for special tutoring, which will make him/her miss the regular instruction, is not recommended as a routine policy.

Regardless of the method and setting chosen, it should be remembered that reading is a skill and, like any other skill, improves only with practice. In other words, to become a skilled reader, children have to read and read. Children persist in reading activity only when they are interested in what they read. The implication for consultation is that any method of intervention, no matter how good it is, will assuredly fail if it cannot arouse the interest of the reader and hold his/her attention. For this reason, the materials used for remediation should be, as much as possible, meaningful, purposeful, and interesting. Great care should be exercised to see that instruction does not become a chore and a drudgery, particularly when phonics is the method of choice.

In this book, a distinction is made between the teaching of word recognition skills and the teaching of reading for comprehension. Earlier in this book these orientations were referred to as "learning to read" and "reading to learn," respectively. Some authorities describe these as *skills instruction* and *meaning instruction.* Even though some reading specialists dismiss the value of separating beginning reading from skilled reading and do not view "skills instruction" as an independent component of reading instruction (e.g., Goodman, 1986), both experimental data and clinical observations suggest that such a distinction has practical value. This two-stage view of reading instruction recognizes that the goals of teaching beginning readers are distinct from those of teaching older pupils. Mastery of word recognition skills which appears to be a necessary condition for learning to read is the goal of beginning reading. Stanovich (1991) cites more than 20 research studies to show that skill at recognizing words is strongly related to the speed of initial reading acquisition, and that development of word recognition skill leads to increases in reading comprehension ability. Because words have to be recognized before their meaning can be comprehended and appreciated, a certain amount of skills training is necessary. In this respect, learning to read is no different from the acquisition of skills such as piano-playing or typing. Once this basic skill is acquired, the focus of teaching reading turns to the ultimate objective of reading: getting meaning from print. This does not mean that beginning instruction has to be meaningless, purposeless, and uninteresting. What it means is that unless the written word can be recognized first, the ultimate goal of reading, that is, extracting meaning from a sentence or a passage, will be difficult to accomplish. The most efficient way to develop word-recognition skill is by acquiring an ability to break the code. These statements are based on substantial research. After discussing the issue of beginning reading instruction, Perfetti (1991) concludes:

> Failure to help the child acquire this coding system puts the child at risk of treating printed English as if it were a list of thousands of arbitrary associations between print symbols and words. "Phonics" programs try to make sure such a failure does not occur. How could anyone disagree with this? (p. 75)

Several reading specialists have developed procedures and materials for teaching beginning reading. In most instances, these materials and methods grew out of the practical experience of those who have taught reading to children for many years. In the revised edition of *Approaches to Beginning Reading,* Aukerman (1984) lists 165 approaches to the teaching of beginning reading. These range from straightforward methods such as *Professor Phonics Gives Sound Advice,* to methods such as *Colorsound,* which use specialized procedures. A few of these methods are presented in this chapter. The criteria for their inclusion here are the following: ready availability of the materials, ease of implementation of the recommended procedure, and empirical evidence that documents the effectiveness of these methods. Of necessity, descriptions of methods and strategies are brief, the intent being to present an overall picture and omit details. The consultant and consultee should feel free to modify any of these methods to suit local needs or combine two or more methods as necessary. Certain principles, however, are to be observed when such modifications are introduced, and these are presented at appropriate places. In this chapter, methods for improving decoding skill and strategies for improving spelling are discussed under separate headings.

STRATEGIES FOR IMPROVING WORD RECOGNITION

A survey of the history of reading instruction in the United States makes it clear that the teaching of beginning reading was influenced by two diverse philosophies, one emphasizing skill acquisition and the other emphasizing text understanding. Educational practices that emerged from these two orientations are broadly referred to as those which emphasize "code" and those which emphasize "meaning," respectively. Methods that were developed with code emphasis in mind focus on the teaching of decoding skill and, therefore, utilize the "phonics approach." Methods that emphasize meaning are less structured than the "phonics approach" and may use words, sentences, or whole texts as the starting point. The different approaches that emphasize code and meaning are shown in Table 5.1.

TABLE 5.1. Different Approaches to Teaching Beginning Reading

Code emphasis	Meaning emphasis
Phoneme awareness training	Whole word method
Synthetic phonics	Language experience method
Analytic phonics	Whole language method
Methods that recommend the use of syllables and subsyllabic units	

CODE EMPHASIS

Phoneme Awareness Training

Phoneme awareness is an ability to recognize sound units in the spoken word. It was noted in Chapter 2 that such an awareness is a prerequisite for the development of a knowledge of grapheme–phoneme correspondences. It also was mentioned earlier that training in phoneme awareness improves reading skills of young children. Phoneme awareness can be particularly useful in helping children who are kept back in kindergarten classes and children who fail to demonstrate progress in learning to read in first and second grades. It is not surprising, therefore, that a number of reading specialists have developed phoneme awareness training programs.

Phoneme awareness training programs attempt to develop in children a knowledge of the link between the sounds of speech and the units in written language. In other words, these programs attempt to develop in children a knowledge of the phoneme–grapheme relationship. A phoneme is the smallest speech sound that distinguishes one word from another (e.g., "*c*at vs. "*r*at"), and a grapheme is the written symbol that represents a phoneme. A grapheme can be a single letter (e.g., *c* as in "cat"), can be a digraph (e.g., *ck* as in "truck") or a trigraph (e.g., *que* as in "unique").

Before describing phonological awareness training methods, we want to enter two caveats.

First, it is commonly observed that very young children, 5 and 6 years of age, show a great deal of variability in their awareness of phonemes. It is known that even before children become aware of phonemes, they are aware of "onset and rimes." It is also documented that children who are taught about rhymes are more successful at reading than those who are not given such training (Goswami & Bryant, 1990). If, after a few attempts, it becomes apparent that the child is not ready for phoneme awareness training, he/she may be introduced to rhymes and sound patterns of words. This can be done in informal, game-like settings. Once an awareness of these sound patterns is established, phoneme awareness training can follow.

Second, we recommend that phonological awareness training be carried out hand in hand with spontaneous "writing" by children. This draws children's attention to spelling. (The kind of spelling produced by children without deliberate tutoring is known as "invented spelling.") The goal of encouraging invented spelling in very young children is not to turn them into accurate spellers, but to draw their attention to the relationship between written language and its sounds. Studies show that phoneme awareness progresses rapidly as children begin to read and write and that being taught to read and spell is also an effective way to advance phoneme awareness (Goswami & Bryant, 1990). The implication for the reading consultant is that he/she should not lose sight of the observations that, "Learning the code must be central in reading instruction. The additional emphasis on linguistic awareness, invented spellings, and other early reading activities promotes the . . . integrated reading activity" (Perfetti, 1991, p. 72).

Phonological awareness programs, in general, follow these steps: (1) creation of an awareness of phonemes in spoken words, (2) development of auditory–visual associations by relating phonemes to graphemes, (3) development of phoneme analysis skills by decomposing the written word into its constituent phonemes, and (4) development of synthesis skills by blending the phonemes in the written word.

Generally speaking, the child is first given training in recognizing the first and last sounds of several *spoken* words. After this skill is mastered, the child is taught to count (by tapping on the desk) the number of phonemes in *spoken* words. After this, the teacher may pronounce the phonemes in these words, and the child is taught to put the phonemes together (i.e., to blend) and pronounce the words. Up to this point, the training is entirely auditory; no printed word is introduced. This stage is followed by the auditory–visual association training. During this stage, the child is presented with line drawings of familiar objects or animals. Below each drawing is a rectangle divided into sections equivalent to the number of phonemes in the word that represents the picture. Thus, under the picture of the sea, there would be a rectangle with two sections, and under the pictue of a man, there would be a rectangle with three sections. The child is taught to say the word slowly so that the three units of sound in the word "man" become recognizable, and then to put three check marks in the appropriate sections of the rectangle. After this exercise has been completed with many different pictures, the pictures are removed and the child is taught to put the correct number of check marks in the boxes after hearing the teacher say the words.

After this step is mastered, the printed word is introduced in the place of the line drawing and the child repeats phoneme analysis of the written word instead of the picture. Subsequently, the idea of vowels and consonants is introduced and two different color pencils may be used to mark the boxes, one for vowels and the other for consonants. These exercises can be presented as games, and teams of children can compete with each other. In the place of line drawings, photographs of children in the classroom can be used and children can learn to read the names of their classmates. One program, developed by Blachman (1988) is based on procedures recommended by Elkonin (1973) and follows the general procedure described here. Liberman, Liberman, Mattingly, and Shankweiler (1980) have also developed a similar program. A slightly different method in which plastic letters are used to develop phoneme awareness is described by Bryant and Bradley (1987).

Once the principles of phoneme awareness training are understood, the consultee can develop his/her own methods and materials. When developing indigenous materials, the consultant should keep in mind the following principles selected from recommendations made by Leukowicz (1980), Liberman et al. (1980), and Williams (1980):

1. Phoneme analysis requires a very slow, "stretched" pronunciation of the word to be segmented.
2. All the tasks are first auditorily presented; only after these tasks are mastered, is visual presentation made of drawings, letters, and words.
3. In auditory tasks, children learn first to analyze short words into phonemes; blending phonemes into syllables and words is introduced later.
4. Stop consonants (*b, d, g, k, p,* and *t*) are introduced first; other consonants (*v, f, h, s, v,* and *z*) are introduced later.
5. Analysis of words with two phoneme segments is mastered before segmental analysis of three phonemes is presented.
6. Vowel consonant syllables such as *in* and *am* are introduced before consonant-vowel syllables such as *no* and *go* are presented.
7. Decoding of simple words is introduced after these skills are mastered.
8. Care should be taken to see that children do not get bored. (These exercises, preferably presented in a game format, need not be practiced for more than thirty minues per day.)

Synthetic Phonics

This approach is also referred to as "explicit phonics" because it teaches the grapheme–phoneme relationship first and then teaches the blending of sounds into syllables or words. In contrast, *analytic phonics* introduces a few words first, and the student is then taught to take the constitutent sounds apart. Therefore, the analytic approach is referred to also as "*incidental phonics*". Phonics approaches generally consider the teaching of letter–sound relationships to be of primary importance. Consequently, words which are used for instruction are selected with the teaching of grapheme–phoneme relationships in mind, not for meaning or story value. This can make the nature of reading materials somewhat artificial, which has frequently drawn criticism. In this chapter, three methods that are specifically developed to teach children with reading disabilities to read through the synthetic phonics approach are described. These are the *Orton-Gillingham Approach, The Spalding Method,* and the *DISTAR* program.

The Orton-Gillingham Approach

This approach was first presented in 1960 by Anna Gillingham, a close associate of Samuel Orton, and by Bessie Stillman. The original publication was revised several times, the seventh edition appearing in 1979. Even though the procedure is intended for children from Grades 3 through 6 who have reading disability, the same principles apply in teaching junior-high and high-school students with reading disabilities. The three important features of the Orton-Gillingham approach are that (1) it teaches phonics directly by introducing letter names and sounds first, and blending skills soon after; (2) it uses a multisensory approach by teaching letter–sound associations through auditory, visual, and kinesthetic modalities; (3) it follows a systematic, step-by-step approach proceeding from simple to complex in an orderly progression. The authors of this approach presume that dyslexic children have formed the bad habit of processing words as ideograms of "wholes" and that this old habit should be broken. For this reason, children under treatment are discouraged from reading outside materials.

In the Orton-Gillingham approach, an association of the written letter and its *name,* as well as an association between the written letter and its *sound,* are taught. Individual letters written on cards are exposed one at a time, and the *name* of the letter is spoken by the teacher and repeated by the pupil. After this, the *sound* of the letter is produced by the teacher and repeated by the pupil. Following this, the teacher makes the *sound* represented by a letter and the child is encouraged to tell the *name* of the letter. After this, the pupil traces the letter with his/her finger and copies it on a sheet of paper. The three kinds of associations thus taught are visual–auditory, visual–kinesthetic, and auditory–kinesthetic. Initially, two vowels and eight consonants are introduced with the aid of key words (for example, *a* in "apple"). Once these associations are well formed, words made of three letters are introduced, and the same three kinds of associations are practiced. These words are preselected, written on cards, and stored in a file box referred to as the *Jewel Case.* Each set of words in the Jewel Case is intended to teach one-letter/one-sound association. For example, the Jewel Case contains the following words which are meant to teach the letter-sound association of *d:* "don," "dad," "dug," "dam," "dim," "dash," "bid," "hid," and "kid." Once the words in the Jewel Case are learned, the child is encouraged to speed up his responses.

Each lesson lasts from 40 to 60 minutes a day, and usually no more than two new letters are introduced in a day. Only one sound of the letter is introduced at a time because it is believed that introducing more than one sound (e.g., *c*at and *c*ity) will confuse the child. Some digraphs such as *th* and *ch* are introduced before some of the single letters because, having a fixed sound, these digraphs are easier to learn than letters with multiple sounds. Spelling is also taught soon after word reading is introduced and children's attention is drawn to certain spelling rules. Once the words in the Jewel Case are mastered, sentences and stories made up of these words are presented. These stories are in the teacher's manual and, at this stage, are made up entirely of phonetically regular words. The authors admit that some of these stories may appear to be infantile, but this is justifiable because they are intended for developing reading skill and not for entertainment or literary appreciation. The same stories are also used for dictation. Gradually, phonetically irregular words and multisyllabic words are introduced following the same procedures that were used for introducing single syllable regular words.

According to Clark (1988), even though this method has been practiced extensively with dyslexic children and adolescents, little research has been conducted to validate the effectiveness of the Orton-Gillingham approach. According to her, the primary reason for the paucity of research is that this method is used primarily in clinics on a one-to-one basis, which does not generate extensive data that can be statistically analyzed. In addition, many practitioners may not follow the recommended sequence rigidly, but modify the method and introduce their own set of words or words from *basal readers,* thus rendering an evaluation of the unadulterated Gillingham method impossible. One study (Kline & Kline, 1978), however, reports that of the 92 dyslexic children taught through the Orton-Gillingham approach, only 4.4% failed to show improvement; older children gained in reading as much as younger children did. This study also noted that at least two years of remedial instruction was necessary to effect substantial gains. In addition to the absence of empirical studies, the Orton-Gillingham method has two features which are a source of concern to us. One is the fact that letter *names* are taught as the first step in instruction; the second feature that is worrisome is that the child is drilled in a one-letter/one-sound association before the letter's second sound is introduced. When the letter *name* is taught first, dyslexic children may not be able to suppress the tendency to call out the letter name rather than use the *sound* or *sounds* the same letter stands for. It is the authors' clinical impression that one of the impediments to the progress of dyslexic children is the tendency for them to be stuck inextricably with a one-letter/one-sound notion so much so that when needed, they are unable to apply another sound to the grapheme. This is also a source of their spelling problems. For example, they invariably spell "necessary" as "nesessary" because they associate /s/ sound with the letter *s* only and cannot consider the possibility that the letter *c* also has the /s/ sound.

Methods and materials that are used in the Orton-Gillingham approach can be found in *Remedial Training for Children with Specific Disability in Reading, Spelling, and Penmanship,* by Gillingham and Stillman (1979). Another set of materials prepared by Henry and Redding (1990) known as *Structured, Sequential, Multi-sensory Lessons Based on the Orton-Gillingham Approach* can also be utilized in implementing the Orton-Gillingham approach. The Orton Dyslexia Society conducts several workshops around the country every year to provide training in the Orton-Gillingham approach.

A closely related guide for teaching children with specific language disability (dyslexia) through the multisensory approach has been developed by Slingerland (1977). In many respects, the Slingerland procedures are very much similar to the Orton-Gillingham approach. In fact, Beth Slingerland spent some time with Anna Gillingham and Bessie Stillman, authors of the Orton-Gillingham method. The Slingerland procedure, according to its author, is most effective when used as a preventive measure. Slingerland has developed also a screening test for the early diagnosis of potential reading problems (Slingerland, 1974). The Slingerland procedure starts with the introduction of single letters of the alphabet. During the initial stages, a special time block is arranged for learning the *names* of the letters of the alphabet. Children are shown specially prepared cards which contain the letter to be taught, a word that starts with the letter, and a picture of the object the word represents. Every child in the group is called upon to pronounce the letter. This is the auditory approach. This is followed by kinesthetic exercise; the teacher writes the letter on the chalkboard, and the child is asked to trace it with his/her finger as he/she pronounces it. After children have mastered several letters, they are asked to reproduce them from memory by writing the letters on a piece of paper. Then the child's attention is drawn to the *sound* the letter makes. The visual approach is carried out by teaching children to pronounce letters written on the chalkboard. After the children have learned several consonants and vowels, three letters that make up a word are placed on a board, and blending is introduced. First, the teacher pronounces the word, and children repeat it. Tracing and spelling exercises are also carried out simultaneously. Eventually, simple sentences are introduced.

The effectiveness of the Slingerland approach has been better studied than the Orton-Gillingham method. Clark (1988) describes three studies which found the Slingerland method to be more effective for young children with and without reading disability than conventional methods. Being very similar to the Orton-Gillingham method, the Slingerland procedure is subject to the same criticisms.

Spalding's Writing Road to Reading, or the Unified Phonics Method

The *Writing Road to Reading* program was developed by Romalda Spalding and has been extensively tested, with good results (Spalding & Spalding, 1962, 1969, 1986). It is a structured method of teaching phonics and is available in the form of a single book which makes the implementation of the procedures relatively easy. Even though this method is intended for use in the regular classroom, "it is equally valuable to remedial or group teachers at any point" (Spalding & Spalding, 1962, p. 9). It is also called the Unified Phonics Method because it incorporates hearing, speaking, and writing as well as reading comprehension.

Spalding acknowledges her indebtedness to Samuel Orton, under whom she practiced her remedial methods for a period of 3 years. Even though much of the material is borrowed from the Orton-Gillingham approach, the Spalding method differs from it in two important respects: emphasis on letter *sounds* rather than letter *names,* and the emphasis on spelling through writing. According to Spalding and Spalding (1962), the core of the method is a technique in which the child is taught how to write down the sounds of the spoken language in isolation and then in combination. Once this skill is mastered, the child can pronounce any printed word. In practice, however, children are taught the sound of each grapheme, or *phonogram* (to use the authors' terminology). A phonogram is a single letter or a combination of letters that represents a single sound. Examples of phonograms are: *b, p, qu, th,* and *ough.* According to the authors, there are 70 phonograms in the English language, representing 45 basic sounds. Each phonogram is printed on a card and the teacher shows one phonogram at a time to the children and pronounces it. Children repeat the sound in unison. After pronouncing the phonogram, the children write the grapheme on a sheet of paper. The correct pronunciation of the phonogram and the word that represents it are printed on the back of the card and are for the teacher's use only. Children are not shown the words until the phonograms are mastered. The method prohibits the use of letter *names.* Mastery of the phonograms is frequently tested by seeing if the children can correctly write down when the sound of phonograms are given by the teacher.

As soon as the phonograms are fairly well learned, words from a prescribed list are dictated, and children write and say them at the same time. After writing the word, they pronounce the word. Writing and pronunciation of the written word are stressed because the authors recognize, quite correctly, that spelling is more reliant on the ability to pronounce the word than to visualize it. After the word has been learned, its meaning is discussed and illustrated with the help of pictures. A system of spelling rules and notations is also introduced to enable the reading and spelling of difficult words. It has to be noted, however, that modern research has cast much doubt upon the usefulness of learning rules for reading and spelling. After these 70 phonograms are mastered and the child has learned to write and read a few hundred words, he/she can be encouraged to write and read sentences. At this point, the child may be introduced to conventional textbooks or literary material. Reading from a book is not begun until the child has learned enough common words to comprehend the meaning of simple sentences.

As noted earlier, the Spalding method has a good track record. According to Aukerman (1984), it has been tried and is now used in a number of schools from coast to coast and in Hawaii. He further states that "a significant and up-to-date body of data has been assembled showing the *indisputable* success that many schools are enjoying with the Spalding Method" (p. 541). In support of this conclusion, Aukerman provides statistics collected in Grades 1 through 6 from 20 different schools widely separated geographically, such as Hawaii and Illinois. It is worth quoting Aukerman once again because he makes these comments in the context of 164 other instructional approaches:

> Scores that are consistently far beyond the national norms and testimonials of gains made by illiterate adults, new arrivals from the rim of the Pacific, learning disabled children, and others who had not previously learned to read in regular classrooms using standard means should be proof enough of the effectiveness of *Writing Road to Reading* when it is taught according to the precepts delineated by Romalda Spalding. (1984, pp. 545, 546)

The DISTAR Method

DISTAR is an acronym for Direct Instructional System for Teaching Arithmetic and Reading. It was originally developed by Carl Bereiter and Siegfried Engelmann in 1964 and was intended primarily for socioeconomically disadvantaged children. DISTAR, however, has also been used for teaching learning-disabled children. At present, it is available from Science Research Associates as *DISTAR Reading Mastery*, I and II (Englemann & Bruner, 1983) and from Charles E. Merrill as *Direct Instruction Reading* (Carnine & Silbert, 1978). It is essentially a teacher-centered direct method of teaching reading; it follows a predetermined rigid sequence of procedures; and it uses highly structured materials. The program is intended for preprimary level to Grade 6 and provides instruction in reading, language, spelling, and arithmetic. According to Becker (1977), another reading specialist associated with DISTAR, all children, regardless of their background can be taught; basic skills acquisition underlies all successful learning; and teachers must, therefore, be held accountable for student failure.

The essential features of the DISTAR program are that it follows a carefully structured daily curriculum and is based on teacher-directed small-group instruction. The amount of teacher–student interaction is high, with emphasis on positive reinforcement. Continuous monitoring of performance is maintained with the aid of criterion-referenced tests administered biweekly. It is also a fast-paced program. According to Aukerman (1971), "creative teachers are admonished not to resort to a language-arts approach. Direct instruction does not provide for pleasantries or side trips that might embellish the lesson; for, by so doing, the sequential steps in instruction would be broken" (p. 452). As will be seen later, this type of program is in direct conflict with the philosophy of the *whole language* approach.

The reading–language program has six levels. Levels I and II are intended for children from preschool through the second grade. During initial stages, instruction focuses on developing oral language skills, vocabulary, and attention skills. Prereading skills are developed in the preschool stage, and letter sounds are also introduced at this time. At the beginning, a limited number of consonant and vowel *sounds* are introduced. Each sound is slowly pronounced by the teacher, and children are asked to repeat it. Then two sounds are introduced and blended. Children first sound out words slowly, and then they are urged to say the words fast. Written letters that correspond to these sounds are introduced later in Level I. Rhyming activities are carried out by introducing "sound families" (e.g., in, fin, sin, bin). This phase of instruction, therefore, can be considered a form of phoneme awareness training. After six sounds have been learned, reading instruction begins by introducing simple, phonetically regular words. Subsequently, these words are incorporated into simple sentences and stories.

DISTAR uses a modified alphabet in which silent letters are shown in half size, with a bar over vowels. Consonant blends are printed as joined letters, and upper case letters are not used except for *I*. These modifications are phased out when the child has mastered the basics of reading, sometime in Level II. Comprehension is attended to from the very beginning, starting with interpretation of pictures, leading to interpretation of written sentences, and finally stories. Intensive interaction between the teacher and children is a feature of the program, with the teacher asking many "wh" questions. Spelling instruction is also part of the program even though the entire class may be taught spelling at any given time, unlike reading instruction which is carried out in small groups. Acitivities are allocated the following amounts of time: group instruction, 25 to 30 minutes; independent work, 15 to 20 minutes; group spelling, 10 minutes. Children are given take-home assignments every day. Reinforcing the responses of children is an integral part of the program. Rewards are in the form of praise as well as tangibles such as candy and small take-home books.

The DISTAR method of teaching has received more research attention than most other methods because several Head Start programs have used it. Positive gains in reading have been reported by programs using DISTAR since 1968 (e.g., Biloine, 1968; Meyer, Gersten, & Gutkin, 1983). What is more interesting is the fact that these gains appear not to be lost as children move up the grades. For instance, Meyer (1984) found that from a group of children who have been exposed to DIS-TAR, 34% were accepted by colleges, as compared to 17% of non-DISTAR students. This study also reported a significantly lower drop-out rate for DISTAR students, as compared to students taught through conventional methods. Aukerman (1984) has briefly described four large-scale follow-up studies and notes that all these studies have pro-duced very positive results in favor of DISTAR.

Understandably, the DISTAR program is criticized for its highly structured format, fast-paced teaching, and the pressure it exerts on very young children. It also requires a high degree of commitment from teachers who have to give undivided attention to several groups of 4- and five-year-olds all working at the same time. According to Aukerman (1971),

> it is a high-presssure, hurry-up program, structured in method and materials, the objective of which is the training of the child so that he will not be a failure when he joins his more privileged classmates in Kindergarten or First Grade. The program appeals to teachers who feel the need for structured statements and a rigid step-by-step approach to teaching facts and skills. (p. 455)

The implication for consultation is that highly structured programs are likely to be more effective with children who have reading disabilities than with children without reading problems. Many teachers have, in fact, found DISTAR to be effective with slow learners (Wallace, 1981).

Analytic Phonics

Analytic methods teach reading skills by introducing words first and then by analyzing these words into their phonological elements. Even though a sentence or a passage can be the starting point, usually instruc-tion begins with teaching the child to read a set of preselected words by sight. In this respect, analytic phonics is similar to the "whole word method." It was noted in Chapter 2 that during the middle of the 19th century, Horace Mann very strongly advocated the use of the word method. Strictly speaking, however, a teaching method can be called the word method only if it never resorts to phonic analysis during the entire course of instruction. In contrast to the pure word method, analytic phonics uses words only as a means to an end, the end being phonics instruction, which may be taught directly or incidentally. Nevertheless, in actual practice a distinction between word method and analytic pho-nics is hard to maintain because teachers differ from one another in the number of sight words they teach before starting phonics analysis. According to Aukerman (1984), many, but not all, basal readers in-troduce phonics as a "strand" after teaching children to recognize a list of selected words by sight. The phonics strand is introduced by encouraging children to analyze words already learned by sight and by drawing their attention to the phonics elements in these words. Some basals that are described as "linguistics–phonics" also use a similar procedure and can be considered as following the analytic phonics approach. As noted in Chapter 2, a few basal readers provide for direct instruction in phonics. Changes have been introduced in the most recent versions of the basal readers, and these are described in Appendix I.

Analytic phonics attempts to teach phoneme–grapheme relationships by drawing the learner's attention to letter patterns that have similar pronunciation. The teacher introduces a new word and encourages the child to recognize the letter or letter pattern he/she has seen in words that were already learned by sight. The child is then taught to pronounce the new word by analogy. Thus, if the child knows how to pronounce the words "car" and "ball," he/she can pronounce the word "call" even though he/she has not seen it before. This reasoning has some empirical support because some experimental psychologists claim that skilled readers read unfamiliar words almost exclusively by "analogy" (Glushko, 1979).

A teacher who uses an unadulterated form of analytic phonics (even though such a purist may not exist) would proceed along the following lines. First she/he would select a number of letter sounds or sound patterns to be taught. Then she would select words which contain these letters or letter patterns. If the students are not already familiar with these words, she will teach the students to read them by sight as whole words. For example, the teacher would write the words "can," "cap," and "cat" on the chalkboard and teach them as sight words. The teacher would then ask the students how these words are alike. (Answer: all these words have /ca/ sound at the beginning.) Now the teacher would write a new word ("cab") on the chalkboard and ask the children to pronounce it. When a sufficient number of such patterns are introduced, simple sentences and stories are constructed by using words based on these spelling–sound patterns and children are encouraged to read them aloud.

Unlike synthetic phonics, very few patented methods based on analytic phonics have been developed. One procedure that comes close to satisfying the analytic phonics designation is the *Glass Analysis for Decoding Only* (Glass & Glass, 1976). The Glass analysis method teaches decoding skills by helping learners identify orthographic patterns within words. For example, the student may be given the word "stronger" and asked the following questions. What letters make the /ong/ sound? What letters make the /str/ sound? What letters make the /er/ sound? In the word "stronger" what sound do the letters "ong" make? What sound do the letters "str" make? The following steps are recommended by the Glass approach: (1) identify the whole word and ask the child to repeat the word; (2) give sounds and ask for the letters; (3) give letters and ask for the sound; and, (4) take away letters and ask for the remaining sound (i.e., phoneme deletion).

According to Clark (1988), research on Glass analysis training has produced somewhat conflicting results. For dyslexic children, the Glass method may not be indicated until they have learned the letter–sound associations. Clark believes that after letter–sound associations are learned, the Glass method may facilitate word recognition process because it trains the student to recognize orthographic patterns.

Another program which can be considered as following the analytic phonics strategy has been developed by Stern and Gould (1965) *(The Stern Structural Reading Series)*. As the name implies, much emphasis is placed on the structure of the words taught, as well as the method of instruction. In the readiness part of the program, children are taught to recognize the initial sounds in spoken words and to associate the sounds with their corresponding graphemes. This part of the structural method, therefore, resembles synthetic phonics rather than analytic phonics. After the readiness program is completed, CVC words, along with pictures that represent the words, are presented. Words shown on one page of the workbook usually have the same vowels or consonants and, therefore, can be considered to belong to a single word family (e.g., "cat," "pat," "bat," "mat"). The child's attention is drawn to the sound patterns within these words, in this case, /at/. Reading, writing, and comprehension skills are encouraged. Even though very little published evaluative research is available, according to Aukerman (1971), the Structural Reading Series has several features in its favor. This includes color-cued vowels, root words, interesting pictures and stories, and the presentation of words that are phonemically and structurally related as a group. In addition, the first-grade program introduces more than 800 phonemically related words, a number far higher than what is encountered in most programs.

Linguistics–Phonics

Methods that call themselves "linguistics–phonics" follow an analytic phonics approach to teach decoding skills. The linguistic approach introduces words with similar pronunciation as a family. For example, words such as "cab," "bad," "ban," "has," and "tan" which use the short vowel /a/ are taught before the long vowel sound /a/ (e.g., call, fall) is introduced. Nonwords which conform to this sound pattern may also be introduced. Even though words are introduced in an effort to make reading meaningful, the selection of words based on restricted phonological rules usually results in stilted and odd sentences (e.g., "Dan is a bad cat. Dan has a tan van. Sal is Dan's fat gal."). An underlying premise of the linguistics–phonics system is that language is systematic and words made up of contrasting patterns represent different meanings. These patterns of similarity and contrast should be made use of in the teaching of reading. Consequently, the child's attention is drawn to a pattern by presenting words that share a common graphemic unit; at the same time, the child is taught to notice the differences among words belonging to the same phonemic family. For example, the words "rag," "sag," and "bag" have the digraph "ag" in common but differ from each other in the initial letter. Consequently, they also have different meanings. Books such as *Let's Read, A Linguistic Approach* (Bloomfield & Barnhart, 1961) and *Linguistics and Reading* (Fries, 1963) are better known than other publications that advocate the linguistic–phonics method of teaching reading.

The Bloomfield–Barnhart program introduces 86 monosyllabic words with the /a/ sound in the first book. Short vowels /i/ and /u/ are introduced after this. Consonants are added to the words introduced earlier. Subsequently, long vowels and double vowels are introduced. Inflected words and words with irregular spelling patterns are also introduced about this time. Once these are mastered, reading instruction focuses on comprehension.

Fast and slow readers from schools in Arlington, Virginia, and from nine schools in Pennsylvania were taught using the Bloomfield–Barnhart method and were monitored for progress. According to Aukerman (1984), all these children performed above expectation.

The *Merrill Linguistic Readers* (Wilson & Rudolph, 1980) is an outgrowth of Fries's *Linguistics and Reading*. Similar to the Bloomfield–Barnhart approach, the Merrill Linguistic Series is also based on the philosophy that recurrent writing patterns in the English language can serve as guidelines for teaching children how to read. These recurring patterns are called "pattern words." The pattern words to be encountered in a sentence or a story are first written on the chalkboard and presented to the children. The teacher pronounces it, spells it, points to each letter or digraphs in the word, and sounds them out. Then the pupils say the word, spell it, and may use the word in a sentence. After this exercise, children start with their first reader in which the same words are found. Because the words selected are based strictly on linguistic rules, normal stories or materials from children's literature are not seen in primary readers. The 1989 version of the Merrill Linguistic Reading Program, however, has a language enrichment component which contains appealing stories and poems. According to Aukerman (1984), one of the studies of the United States Office of Education showed that children taught through the linguistic method scored higher on a reading test based on word patterns than a group of children taught by using another basal reader. However, there were no differences between these two groups on ordinary reading materials.

Comparison of Synthetic and Analytic Approaches

A good deal of family dispute has been going on about the merits and drawbacks of these two phonics approaches. The complaint against the synthetic approach is that it is mechanical and uninteresting and, therefore, makes learning difficult. Proponents of the synthetic method, however, argue that the number of letter–sound associations that have to be learned is within reasonable limits, whereas the number of words to be learned by sight in the analytic method is very large. This requirement taxes memory. Research, in general, favors the use of the direct synthetic approach when first-grade children are taught to read (Bond & Dykstra, 1967). As noted earlier, the review of studies by Chall (1967, 1983) came to a conclusion in favor of synthetic phonics. Chall noted that a knowledge of letter–sound relationships appears to be more essential for success in the early stages of reading than other factors such as intelligence. Systematic phonics instruction has been found to be quite effective in also teaching children with reading disability (Williams, 1980). The implication for consultation is that it is possible different children may respond differently to the different teaching approaches. The consultee should, therefore, be flexible enough to try more than one method or any combination thereof.

Recently, a widely advertised commercial program, *Hooked on Phonics,* has attracted the attention of many parents and has become a matter of concern to professional organizations such as the International Reading Association. Since it is very likely the consultant's opinion may be sought in this matter by consultees, particularly parents, some comments about this program are in order. *Hooked on Phonics* contains eight 20-minute cassette tapes; nine decks of flash cards depicting letters, letter sequences, and words; four books of word lists; and one book of sentences constructed from these words. The International Reading Association has recently published opinions expressed by experts who were asked to review the program (*Reading Today;* Vol. 8, No. 6, June 1991). The opinions include statements such as "*Hooked on Phonics* concentrates only on decoding; the materials fail completely in engaging the learner; the learner gets insufficient feedback when using the program; the program appears to require support and instruction from others; it teaches phonics in a way that is not engaging, motivating, enriching, or fun" (p. 22). Finally, one of the reviewers raised the question: How can the program move through 10 years of reading instruction, practice, and experience in a mere 2 hours? The implied answer is that the program makes unreasonable promises that no single reading instruction program can keep.

Principles to be Observed in Using the Phonics Approach

Whether one uses the analytic approach or the synthetic approach, and regardless of which phonics method is used, certain principles uncovered by studies of language development are to be followed when implementing the remedial program. It is known that phoneme acquisition starts somewhere between 10 and 14 months of age, with most children becoming proficient in the use of their native language sounds by the time they are 7 or 8 years old. There is some variation in this timetable, some children taking longer to reach this goal. Even though there is considerable variation concerning the order in which these sounds are acquired, psycholinguists have noted general tendencies in the acquisition of sounds. For instance, nasals (/m/, /n/), glides (w, j) and stops (/p/, k, t, b, d, g) are produced earlier than liquids (l, r) and fricatives (f, v, s, z). It also appears that phonemes which occur in the initial position of words are learned earlier than those in the final and medial positions. Similarly, it is argued that voiced consonants (e.g., /b/, /d/, /g/ whose articulation produces vibration of vocal folds) are acquired before voiceless consonants (e.g., /p/, /t/, /k/). A discussion of how children acquire the sound system of their native language and the sequence of phonological development is presented by Edwards and Shriberg (1983).

The following principles, adopted from Tanner (1988) will be of interest to the consultee who wishes to develop her/his own phonics program.

1. Consonants are attended to before vowels because consonants are more consistent than vowels and most words begin with consonant sounds.

2. Stop consonants, nasals, and glides are introduced before liquids and fricatives. Simple consonants can be introduced at the kindergarten level.

3. Consonants are first taught in the initial position, then in final position, and then in medial position.

4. Short vowels are introduced earlier than long vowels. [Generally speaking, the short vowel sound of a letter is different from its name, whereas the long vowel sound of a letter is similar to its name (e.g., "mat" vs. "mate"; "cut" vs. "cute"; "hostel" vs. "hotel").] Short sounds can be introduced at the preprimer level and completed before the end of first grade. Once these are mastered, long sounds are introduced.

5. Consonant blends and digraphs can be introduced early in first

grade. Blends are letter groups in which the constituent letter sound can be identified; digraphs are letter groups in which the constituent letter sounds are not maintained. Examples of blends are: /bl/, /fl/, /br/, /tr/; examples of digraphs are /ch/, /th/, /ng/, /nk/.

6. Vowel digraphs and dipthongs are introduced in the first grade after children have mastered simple vowel consonant usage. Dipthongs refer to sounds represented by two adjacent vowels in the same syllable (e.g., /oi/ as in "oil", /ou/ as in "house" and /oy/ in "joy").

7. Phonologically consistent words (e.g., "cave," "gave") are introduced before inconsistent words (e.g., "have") are taught. (Note: Inconsistent words occur frequently in the written language and, consequently, may not pose a major problem if introduced along with consistent words).

8. Common rhymes (phonograms such as /ight/, /ing/, and /tion/) can be introduced soon after consonants are learned. Auditory training in onset and rimes, if introduced in kindergarten level, could facilitate the learning of phonograms. It is recommended that syllables be introduced in the second grade and syllabication skills also be taught at the same time. However, some researchers think that the syllable constitutes a natural unit and can be introduced quite early in reading instruction.

Methods that Recommend Syllables and Subsyllabic Units

Even though we have a general notion what a syllable is, it is difficult to define it with precision. A syllable can consist of only one vowel (e.g., a, i) or it can be VC, CV, CVC, and CVCC. Structurally, a syllable is a pronounceable unit and, therefore, must have one or more vowels. Because syllables are more easily identifiable in the spoken language than phonemes, some researchers have argued that the syllable can be a natural unit of reading instruction (e.g., Rozin & Gleitman, 1977). Whereas the syllable boundary can be readily recognized in spoken language, it cannot be always easily identified in written language. For example, how should the syllable be marked in the following words: "button" = but/ton or butt/on; "reading" = rea/ding or read/ing? Some researchers (e.g., Taft, 1979) believe that these written words are parsed as butt/on and read/ing respectively because *on* and *ing* are more frequently encountered orthographic units than *ton* and *ding*. However, the decomposition of a large majority of multisyllabic words into their constituent syllables follows an orderly pattern.

It is thought that the ability to divide an unknown word into syllables can be helpful in decoding unfamiliar words. For this reason, children are made aware of certain rules of syllabication. Examples of such rules or syllabication are "divide between two consonants that are not a digraph or a blend"; "final *le* and the preceding consonant usually form a syllable (e.g., ta–ble; can–dle)" etc. There are several such rules. These rules are applicable to about 70–80% of the VCCV words. While a methodical application of such rules can be useful in deomposing a word, can it really improve the decoding skill of the beginning reader? Many authors are critical of "teaching" such rules to children because they think it is wasted time and that such rules also create confusion. An awareness of the syllabic nature of words, however, may be helpful in increasing reading speed. According to Harris and Sipay (1990), many children who have difficulty in blending single phonemes find it easier to blend syllables and make spoken words. These authors also conclude that although teaching syllabication generalization has been criticized, the fact remains that if properly taught, it can be helpful for dividing "big words" into decodable units. A few major rules of syllabication are provided by Tanner (1988).

It is, however, important to know how to pronounce written monosyllabic words because monosyllabic words occur in elementary school textbooks more often than multisyllabic words. It is suggested that many monosyllabic written words are processed as units that are intermediate between the phoneme and the syllable. As has been mentioned previously one such intrasyllabic unit is referred to as "onset and rime." (Again, the onset of a syllable is the initial consonant or consonant cluster in a word; its rime is the vowel and any following consonants.) According to Treiman and Chafetz (1987), in the English language an onset can contain up to three phonemes. For example, "sip" has the onset /s/ and the rime /ip/; "slip" has the onset /sl/ and the rime /ip/; and "strip" has the onset /str/ and the rime /ip/. Note that the rimes of these three words are identical and, therefore, can be learned as a single unit common to these words. Examples of other common rimes are /ing/, /ion/ and /ough/. Similar to rimes, many words can share the same onset. For example, the onset /str/ is shared by words such as "strip," "strap," "string," and "strike." Remember that these are orthographic units and their main contribution to reading is that they provide "orthographic redundancy" and thus reduce memory load. This can make word recognition fast and effortless. The linguistics–phonics approach discussed above actively promotes the use of these units in the teaching of reading and calls them "phonograms." Teaching methods based on Linguistics–phonics have developed families of words based on phonograms to be used in beginning reading instruction. It is well documented that children find rhyming tasks much easier than phoneme-analysis tasks, probably because of the fact that words which rhyme share rimes with each other.

Apart from the inherent appeal of onset and rime, is there any evidence to show that these units are effective in teaching reading? Very few studies have investigated this question directly, but these studies lend support to the notion that training children in the recognition of onset and rime has a positive effect on reading achievement. In one study, Cunningham (described in Goswami & Bryant, 1990) investigated three groups of 6- and 7-year-old children. There were two experimental groups which received training in segmenting words into onset and rimes as well as phonological-awareness training. At the end of the 10-week training period, greater improvement in reading was seen in the experimental groups than the control group. Because in this study children were given both segmentation and phoneme awareness training, it is not possible to attribute improved reading performance to onset–rime segmentation training alone. More convincing evidence comes from two studies by Bradley and Bryant (1983, 1985) which found that 6-year-old children who received training in rhyming and alliteration in addition to recognition of letter sounds in words did better than children who received rhyming training only. Both groups did better than children in a control group who were given training in categorizing words. Thus, there is evidence that exposure to rimes facilitates reading acquisition, but a combination of rhyming and phoneme awareness training produces the best results. In a series of short- and long-term studies, Olson, Wise and Rack (1989) used personal computers equipped with speech synthesizers to present words to dyslexic children from Grades 1 through 6. The computer was equipped to provide speech feedback for words targeted by the reader. The overall finding that emerged from these studies was that segmented feedback of syllables and onset–rimes improved dyslexic children's phonological coding skills. The studies by Olson and his associates also suggest that segmental presentation may not be effective with words that have more than two syllables, and exception words.

In summary, the studies described above indicate that teaching children to read by drawing their attention to the syllabic and subsyllabic features of words improves their decoding skill. Teaching children to read by segmenting words into syllables and subsyllabic units can be undertaken *after* phonological awareness has been established. A "most complete" list of phonograms can be found in *The New Reading Teacher's Book of Lists* by Fry, Fountoukidis, and Polk (1985, p. 124). These authors, however, describe the phonogram as a vowel sound plus a consonant sound. Memory (1986) has provided guidelines for fostering independent decoding skills in subject matter area classes by utilizing context clues and knowledge of word families and root words.

The implication for consultation that can be derived from these studies is that the teaching of phonograms of orthographic patterns as one of the strategies of beginning reading instruction should be seriously considered as part of the development of word recognition skills.

MEANING EMPHASIS

Whole Word Programs

Several educators have developed devices and techniques to present lists of preselected words as part of the reading program. These devices include words printed on cards, filmstrips, audiotapes that accompany visual presentation, tachistoscopes, and computers. Invariably, the vocabulary taught is tightly controlled and the words are preselected on criteria such as frequency and phonic complexity. Many of the programs introduce word analysis after a certain number of words are learned as sight vocabulary. As a result, many of these programs are indistinguishable from analytic-phonics programs.

A procedure that straddles "word" and "sentence" approaches is a technique referred to as *cut-up stories* (Clay, 1982). Developed as part of the Reading Recovery Project in New Zealand, the cut-up stories system provides the child with practice in assembling sentences and helps in building knowledge about one-to-one correspondence of printed and spoken words. The procedure is as follows. First, the child tells a story or dictates a narrative which is written down by the teacher on a sheet of paper. The child is then asked to read the story and copy it. The story is then cut up into language units such as words, phrases, or even sentences which the teacher thinks the child is capable of assembling. Larger segments are used for weaker students; smaller segments such as syllables, digraphs, and trigraphs are used as units if the teacher feels the child needs to improve his/her phonic structural analysis skills. The cut-up units are put in a shoe box, shuffled, and then given to the child who has to put them back together and construct the story.

Language Experience Approach

Language experience refers to a philosophy of education rather than to any specific method of teaching reading. Nessel and Jones (1981) define the language experience approach (LEA) as

> a means of teaching students to read by capitalizing on their interests, experiences, and oral language facility. Students dictate stories and accounts based on their experiences; these materials are then used as the basis of the reading program. (p. 1)

LEA is based on the belief that the language and experience of children can be a much better vehicle to impart reading skills than a set of preselected words and sentences which may not match the language pattern of the child and is likely not to be very meaningful to the learner. According to Allen and Allen (1982), what the child can think, he can also talk about; what he can say, he can also write; what he can write; he can also read. To be able to talk, the child should have the experience about the topic he wants to discuss. Of course, very young children do not have numerous experiences to converse about; the teacher, therefore, creates situtations in order to provide such experiences for the child. Such experiences can be a trip to the zoo, baking cookies in the school kitchen, a visit to the library, etc. Following this, children talk about what they saw, they write about it, and read what they have written. This is the essence of LEA.

The idea of using children's dictated stories and experiences as the springboard for teaching reading is historically an old one. As noted in Chapter 2, materials developed from children's comments were used even during the last century for teaching reading; this practice was known by names such as "teaching with experience charts" and "experience methods." One problem in relying on LEA as the sole means of reading instruction is that the vocabulary of young children varies a great deal from one topic to another, as well as from one child to another. A solution to this problem is to write textbooks or guidebooks which use a wide selection of vocabulary that children actually use. Even though such a modification minimizes the problem, it squelches the true spirit of LEA and deprives it of its unique advantage—that is, reading material that is pertinent to ethnic, cultural, and geographic backgrounds of individual children. According to Aukerman (1984), to produce a universally acceptable language-experience set of readers would be almost impossible. Teachers who attempt to develop their own reading materials, therefore, will have to adopt a middle-of-the-road approach and utilize experiences, language, and vocabulary that are the norm for children. Packaged commercial programs are published, and if available locally, the consultee may use these as a source of guidance and adopt vocabulary and sentences generated by children in her/his own classroom.

Typically, a Language Experience class may follow these steps. An opportunity is created for children or groups of children to experience some event—watching a movie, taking a walk outside the classroom, visiting a hospital, etc. After this, children sit in small groups and talk about the experience. Children also may describe their families, holidays, animals they have seen and games they play. Following this, they report to the teacher, who writes these sentences on the chalkboard. Older children are encouraged to write these down on their own notebooks, in which case the teacher provides individual help. The written material is then read by the children and copied on individual sheets of paper. These sheets of paper are eventually bound together to create the child's own book. The teacher provides individual help when children copy down what is written on the chalkboard. Phonics and spelling are taught "incidentally" when children read and copy the sentences written on the chalkboard. Once the basics of reading are acquired, instruction may utilize traditional materials such as basal readers.

Detailed guidelines for teaching reading and writing through LEA can be found in the following books: *Language Experiences in Reading* (Allen & Allen, 1982), *The Language-Experience Approach to Reading* (Nessel & Jones 1981), and in *Language Experience Approach to the Teaching of Reading* (Stauffer, 1980). Materials used in LEA vary from classroom to classroom; therefore, it is impossible to compare it with other methods for its effectiveness. One study carried out in the San Diego schools (Aukerman, 1984), in which approximately 750 first-graders were studied, showed significant differences in comprehension favoring the traditional method which used basal readers; no differences were found in word meaning and vocabulary. However, boys from low socioeconomic groups who were taught through LEA showed higher interest in reading. Hall (1978), after reviewing a number of studies, found the overall reading achievement of students who received language experience instruction to be satisfactory and, in some instances, superior to the achievement of children instructed by other approaches. According to Hall, the persistent criticism that students taught through LEA do not develop a satisfactory reading vocabulary is refuted by research. This can be true if children in a classroom share their stories and writings with each other. It is highly desirable to implement such cooperative ventures when LEA is used for reading instruction. The following suggestions for implementing LEA are adapted from Newman (1980).

1. Establish a good relationship with the learner.
2. As you proceed, ask questions as needed to help enrich the story or the narrative.
3. Make the written material easy to see and read.
4. Write or print slowly so the children can follow the process.
5. Write the learner's words just as he/she says them, but use standard spelling.
6. When the story is written, read each sentence aloud, pointing to each word.
7. Have the child read the sentence aloud, pointing to each word.
8. Repeat the process until the child develops some fluency in reading each story.
9. Keep the written material in files and ask each child to read his story periodically.

Whole Language Approach

In spite of its current popularity, there is no satisfactory definition of the whole language approach (WL, or WLA). According to Bergeron (1990), any approach or program that supports *literature-based instruction* which integrates reading, writing, and literature is described under the umbrella of *whole language*. It has been described as an "approach," a "belief," a "method," a "philosophy," a "theory," an "orientation," a "movement," a "program," and an "educational perspective." As a matter of fact, this absence of clarity has caused concern in some circles that WL may suffer the same fate many other educational fads have experienced and may ultimately become extinct (e.g., Watson, 1989). In spite of not having a clearly definable set of characteristics, the roots of WLA can be traced to certain philosophical foundations from which it appears to have evolved. These are humanistic education, emphasis on meaning so that reading is purposeful and interesting, and the integration of reading and writing into a unified learning task. These educational principles, however, are not unique to WLA but are shared by many methods of reading instruction, including those which emphasize the code approach. The distinction between WLA and other approaches of teaching reading is so blurred that WLA can claim to have the advantages of all successful methods of teaching and the disadvantages of none. For instance, Newman and Church (1990), in an attempt to clarify misunderstandings of what WL is really about, include the following in their list of *myths* about WLA: in WL, you do not teach phonics; WL is limited to a literature-based curriculum; WL is a way of teaching language arts only, but not other subject areas; there is no evaluation in WL; in WL classrooms there are no standards, anything goes; WL teachers deal just with process and not outcome; there is one set of prescribed principles for teaching WL.

Because WLA is "more an implementation of a philosophy than a methodology" (Harris & Sipay, 1990, p. 74), it is impossible to present a specific method of teaching through this approach or to compare its effectiveness with other methods. Moreover, from our experience we can say that no teacher is a WL purist; wittingly or unwittingly, all teachers provide at least some direct instruction in phonics.

Whole language, however, differs from methods that emphasize the code approach in certain important ways: WL is based on the premise that learning to read is as natural as learning to speak. It assumes that because the goal of teaching reading is to help the beginning reader comprehend the meaning of the written language, explicit teaching of phonics is unnecessary and even counterproductive. The distinction between learning to read and reading to learn is viewed by its proponents as artificial. The learning environment must allow "risk-taking," and when the child is uncertain, he/she should be encouraged to guess the written word. Underlying all these assumptions is the basic premise that one learns to read by reading, not by acquiring component skills. Consequently, word-recognition skill development is not among the goals of this approach. According to Klesius, Griffith, and Zielonks (1991), WL differs from the phonics approach in that unlike phonics instruction, WL keeps language whole, deemphasizes decoding, and recommends the use of literature instead of basal readers. WL also denounces the use of practice exercises and worksheets. These principles are, however, based on premises of questionable validity: "In contrast to code-based instruction, whole language rests on dubious scientific foundations" (Perfetti, 1991 p. 75). Some of the differences between WL in general and instructional methods with a code emphasis are shown in Table 5.2.

According to some WL supporters (e.g., Altwerger, Edelsky, & Flores, 1987; Goodman, 1986), virtually all human babies learn to speak their home language remarkably well in a very short time, without any formal training. Learning to read should also be just as natural. Children have difficulty in learning to read because educators have taken apart the language and turned it into words, syllables, and isolated sounds. Many

TABLE 5.2. Major Differences Between the Whole Language Approach and Methods with a Code Emphasis

Whole Language Approach	Methods with a Code Emphasis
1. Learning to read is as natural as learning to speak	Learning to read is not a natural act; explicit instruction is often needed
2. Comprehension of meaning is the goal of instruction even in beginning reading	Word recognition is necessary for comprehension; therefore, skills training is necessary
3. No distinction is maintained between learning to read and reading to learn	Learning to read precedes reading to learn
4. Risk-taking and guessing from context are encouraged	Reading is a precise act; guessing the word from the context is discouraged
5. Literature is recommended as the main material for instruction	Basal readers (which contain literary selections) are the materials for instruction
6. Practice exercises, drills, and the use of worksheets are discouraged	Exercises, drills, and worksheets are part but not the core of the instructional program

researchers, however, point out that learning to read is not as natural an act as learning to speak (e.g., Liberman, 1989; Gough, 1981). The argument is that while spoken language has a history as old as the human race, written language was invented, perhaps only 5,000 years ago. Every human society has a fully developed spoken language but not all societies have written languages. Even in societies that have a written language, not all individuals learn to read.

Another argument frequently seen in the WL literature is that children in China learn to read their language, which is written in the form of logographs. Being nonalphabetic, it is argued, logographs do not depend on phonological analysis for reading. Decoding skill, therefore, is not essential for learning to read English, either. This may not be an entirely correct argument for the following reasons. The nature of Chinese orthography requires that in order to become a proficient reader, a large number of logographs must be remembered by rote. The size of Chinese speakers' sight vocabulary is limited to less than 4,000 logographs, and even a scholar may be unable to recognize by sight more than twice that number (Goody, 1968). In fact, the nature of orthography is considered one of the reasons for a low level of literacy in China. In contrast, an English-speaking high school student can read more than 20,000 words with ease. More importantly, a child with proficient decoding skill is *empowered* to sound out even words he/she has not encountered before. Furthermore, Chinese characters are not entirely morphemic but have phonemic elements which are made use of by readers of that script (Leong, 1987). According to WL, learning goes from the whole to the part; teaching, therefore, should also start with the whole and go to the part. This means children learn to read texts because texts and not words constitute the meaningful unit. Research, however, shows that vocabulary and word-recognition skills are two strong correlates of reading skill and that a major cause of reading disability is poor word-recognition skills (Perfetti, 1985; Liberman & Liberman, 1990). A number of studies also show that context may facilitate comprehension of the meaning of sentences but it is not of much help in word recognition (Mitchell, 1982; Stanovich, 1980). Furthermore, it is documented that poor readers depend on context for word recognition more than skilled readers do and that even skilled readers can guess correctly only one word in four and that guessing from context invariably leads to errors (Gough, Alford, & Holley–Wilcox, 1981). In spite of the disavowal that the belief in the dichotomy between learning to read and reading to learn is unfortunate and not acceptable in a whole-language program (Goodman, 1986), many studies show that children learn word-recognition skills in the first three grades and if this skill is not well developed, this deficiency impedes further acquisition of reading skills. For instance, the correlation coefficient between reading achievement and decoding skills is higher in Grades 1 through 3 than it is from Grades 3 up; an opposite pattern of lower correlation between reading achievement and listening comprehension in lower grades and a higher correlation between these variables is seen in higher grades (Sticht & James, 1984). We also noted in Chapter 3 that comprehension and word recognition are independent skills.

Many review studies that have compared the code emphasis with meaning emphasis (not WL in particular) indicate that teaching methods with a code emphasis have some advantage over others (Chall, 1983; Anderson et al., 1985; Adams, 1990). A study by Stahl and Miller (1989) is noteworthy because it carried out a meta-analysis of studies that compared the effectiveness of basal readers, which emphasize the code approach, with that of the WL and language experience methods. After analyzing the results of 15 studies, these investigators concluded, "The studies that met more of our rigorous criteria for inclusion tended to favor basal reading programs over whole language/language experience programs" (p. 107). These researchers also suggest that WL programs may be more effective when used prior to starting a formal reading program. They also note that in the reading mastery phase, a more systematic approach to decoding than WLA may be needed, at least for some children. Reading experts such as Harris and Sipay (1990) also remark that children need to acquire decoding and word-recognition skills to a level that allows comprehension to proceed smoothly.

The implication for consultation is that empirical evidence as well as expert opinion suggests that WL, when it excludes phonics instruction, is not desirable for children with Specific Reading Disability and for children who have word-recognition difficulties.

STRATEGIES FOR IMPROVING SPELLING

The correlation coefficient obtained between scores on a test of decoding words and a test of spelling is in the neighborhood of .7 (Aaron & Simurdak, 1989), which indicates that phonological skills play an important role in spelling. Visual memory, in constrast, appears to play a less important role. It was noted in Chapter 3 that memory for orthographic units (spelling patterns) may, however, be necessary for correctly spelling exception words and homophones. It was also noted that such a memory is limited to units of about two or three letters in length, and that the acquisition of memory for such orthographic units is a product of reading experience. Longer units may have to be sustained by phonological knowledge. Spelling errors, therefore, often indicate a weakness in phonological skill and should not be interpreted, without strong evidence, as an indication of poor visual memory.

On the basis of her research, Frith (1980) concluded that production of the correct spelling of a word involves three stages: correct analysis of speech sounds and identifying the constituent phonemes in the word; conversion of phonemes into graphemes; and selection of the conventionally correct graphemes from all the phonologically plausible graphemes. This shows that there is a close relationship between decoding and spelling because pronunciation of the written word also involves phoneme identification and phonological analysis. Phonological processing of the written language is rule-governed and it is thought that as these rules are progressively acquired, children become increasingly proficient in reading and spelling. Research (e.g., Beers, 1980; Henderson, 1980) shows that at early stages of learning to spell, children use a letter–name strategy for spelling (e.g., *lef* for "leaf"). Next emerges a "vowel transition" stage in which long vowels are marked by doubling the vowel (e.g., *leef* for "leaf"). Some children fail to make satisfactory progress beyond this stage, and their spelling, even though incorrect, may be "phonetically acceptable." By a pure phonological strategy, nearly 70% of the words in the English language can be spelled correctly. The remaining 30% of the words are phonologically more complex or irregular. Spelling these words correctly requires the mastery of the more complex and idiosyncratic grapheme–phoneme relationships. Spelling errors that are phonologically unacceptable (e.g., "girl"—*gril*) and errors that are phonologically acceptable (e.g., "girl"—*gal*), therefore, reflect different degrees of spelling mastery and not different types of spelling disability. Sometimes, the only symptom that can be seen in mature students with reading disabilities is their poor spelling. It was noted in Chapter 4 that these students have acquired adequate word recognition skills by developing a substantial sight vocabulary but that careful testing would reveal subtle reading difficulties and slow reading speed (Joshi & Aaron, 1991). If this were not so, the so-called "good reader but poor speller" should be able to read his own writing and correct spelling mistakes. It should be noted that skilled readers also tend to spell phonetically words with which they are unfamiliar, or words whose meaning they do not know. Thus, spelling a word correctly involves phonological skills, familiarity with the word, and its meaning. In other words, spelling depends on phonological, orthographic, and semantic skills. Spelling instruction should, therefore, include all these aspects of language.

Individuals with reading disability generally do not show a degree of progress in spelling comparable to that in reading, probably because spelling is a recall task which requires the reproduction of all the graphemes in a word in correct sequence, whereas reading is primarily a recognition task which can be accomplished on the basis of partial cues.

For this reason, spelling is a more difficult task to master than reading. Consultees should be urged to keep this in mind and be modest in their expectation of children's progress in spelling. In spite of this pessimistic expectation, providing instruction in spelling has one advantage: it draws the attention of children to phonological features of words and thereby improves their decoding skills. The success of synthetic phonics such as the Spalding method may be due to its incorporating spelling instruction in the early stages of reading.

The most frequently encountered spelling errors seen in older students arise because of confusion among similar-sounding words or between a word and a similar-looking nonword (e.g., "there"–*their*, "piece"–*peace*, "elicit"–*illicit*, "disease"–*decease*, "separate"–*seperate*, "necessary"–*nesessary*). Under such circumstances, correct spelling depends on making the right choice, thus making spelling almost a forced choice test. A knowledge of the word's meaning, its origin, and its structure can increase the probability of selecting the correct spelling. This will probably produce some positive results, but even here the expectation should be modest. Students' attention can be drawn to these word features when they learn to spell.

Word Meaning

It was noted in Chapter 3 that the orthographic pattern of the English language is often more conducive to the extraction of meaning than to pronunciation. As stated by Venezky (1980), English spelling is a phonemically based system that preserves morphemic identity wherever possible. This psychological advantage, in addition to the fact that—unlike spoken language—printed language is formal and resistant to change, has helped to preserve the spelling pattern over a period of time. Even if by some miracle a reform which makes English spelling into a "one-letter/one-sound" system could be brought about, it would not bestow any additional advantage to the reader; in fact, the quick extraction of meaning, an advantage of the present orthographic system, would be lost. This idea can be illustrated with a few examples. The word "separate" comes from *apart*, therefore, it is not spelled sep*e*rate; "negative" comes from *negation*, therefore, it is not spelled as "neg*i*tive"; "there" comes from *ere* (which means *before*), therefore, it is different from "their." Or compare the sentence written in "reformed" spelling with the sentence written in conventional spelling: *They rode along the rode until they reached the river and rode across it* versus *They rode along the road until they reached the river and rowed across it.* The usefulness of conventional spelling in facilitating the extraction of meaning is obvious.

Word Origin

Many words in the English language have been borrowed from other languages. A knowledge of the origin of words can be sometimes helpful in avoiding common spelling errors. For example, "bacteria" (not bakteria) comes from the Latin word *bacillus;* "necessary" (not nessary or nesessary) comes from the Latin words *ne cesse;* "aerobatics" (not arobatics) comes from the Greek morpheme *aer;* "clear" (not cleer) comes from the latin word *clarus;* "calendar" (not calender) comes from the Latin word *calendra;* "quiet" (not quite) comes from the Latin word *quiescens.* Information regarding word origin can be found in any standard dictionary.

Word Structure

When a word is stripped of its suffix or prefix and the root morpheme identified or segmented into its constituent syllables, spelling ambiguity can sometimes be resolved. It has to be noted that the root morpheme represents a unit of meaning. Some examples are: "decease" = *de/cease,* versus "disease" = *dis/ease;* "definite" = *de/finite* (not defanite); "bargain" = *bar/gain* (not bargen); "noticeable" = *notice/able* (not noticable). There are, of course, several exceptions to the above principles, and English orthography abounds with these exceptions. Sometimes application of these principles leads to misspellings.

In spite of all these efforts, students with reading disabilities may not register noticeable improvement in spelling. Many students also have a limited vocabulary and tend to spell phonetically words with which they are not familiar. For this reason, efforts to improve spelling should go hand in hand with vocabulary building. The severity of the spelling problems in written essays could also be considerably minimized by using spell-check programs that come with word processors. Indeed, the computer can be a useful aid in teaching spelling even to very young children. Some available computer software programs are presented in Chapter 7. Lists of words classified according to their etymological origins and word structure can be seen in *Words: Integrated Decoding and Spelling Instruction Based on Word Origin and Word Structure,* by Henry (1990).

What are the implications for reading consultation? The discussion so far presented suggests that rote memorization of spelling patterns and the learning of grapheme–phoneme correspondence rules do not bring about appreciable results. This is understandable because it is easier to remember meaningful material than meaningless material. To make words and their spellings meaningful, spelling should be taught in the total context of reading, writing, and understanding. A certain amount of class time can be allocated for creative writing. When children write and read, their attention can be drawn to word patterns, root morphemes, suffixes, prefixes, the distinction between long and short vowels, and to special features such as consonant doubling. In summary, spelling is not taught in isolation but as part of the language arts program. Consultees should also remember that spelling is a skill and not a good index of an individual's total reading ability. As such, scores obtained by a child on spelling tests should not become a major determinant of the letter grade he/she receives in reading.

6

Intervention Strategies: Vocabulary and Comprehension

INTRODUCTION

Children who have symptoms of nonspecific reading disability and those who are considered low ability readers have comprehension deficits. According to Oakhill and Garnham (1988), nearly 10% of schoolchildren who have adequate decoding skills are poor in comprehending what they read. We noted in Chapter 4 that comprehension is a generic term which refers to both reading and listening comprehension. Consequently, strategies which are designed to improve comprehension are applicable to listening as well as to reading. Comprehension is not simply translating what is heard or read but involves an active construction of a cohesive body of information. Comprehension, therefore, is not a passive process but an active one wherein the reader makes inferences and builds up a cogent body of information above and beyond the information present on the printed page. The reader's schemata and the ability to properly interpret the author's intentions play important roles in the comprehension process. Many students, particularly, in high school and college, are able to comprehend the literal meaning of text but fail in inferential comprehension.

Ideally speaking, reading instruction in the first two grades of the elementary school should focus on word-recognition skills. Empirical and experimental data in support of this position were presented in the previous chapters. This is not to say that reading material should be uninteresting and meaningless. What this means is that in the selection of materials and methods for teaching reading in early primary grades, special attention is to be given to skills development. In grades beyond this level, and certainly in junior and senior high school, the focus of reading is comprehension of text and appreciation of literature. The strategies recommended in this chapter are intended primarily for students who have achieved an acceptable degree of mastery in word recognition skills. There is ample experimental evidence to show that unless word recognition has become automatic, it continues to be an attention-demanding process and, therefore, interferes with comprehension. In other words, decoding skill can be a limiting factor as far as reading comprehension is concerned. Once the student has developed adequate word recognition skills, instructional methods that promote comprehension can be quite effective.

In recent years, cognitive psychologists and psycholinguists have turned their attention to comprehension processes and have identified several factors that facilitate comprehension. Included in the list of such factors are vocabulary, the reader's schemata, and metacognitive processes. Possible means of improving the reader's vocabulary, schemata, and metacognitive ability are described in the following section.

STRATEGIES FOR IMPROVING VOCABULARY

Vocabulary is a very important correlate of reading ability. Studies which have examined the relationship between vocabulary size and reading comprehension report correlation coefficients that range from .66 to .75 (e.g., Just & Carpenter, 1987; Thorndike, 1973). A meta-analysis of vocabulary studies by Stahl and Fairbanks (1986) suggests that vocabulary knowledge plays a causal role in comprehension. This conclusion, however, is not endorsed by some researchers, who accept it only after adding certain qualifications to it. According to Beck & McKeown (1991), prior to the present decade, evidence of comprehension improvement through vocabulary instruction had not been impressive, many studies reporting no effects. More recent studies, however, suggest that in order to influence comprehension, vocabulary instruction needs to go beyond simply providing dictionary meanings of words, and provide opportunities for the "deep processing" of words. This can be accomplished by helping the learner to establish a variety of connections between words and their many semantic features through discussion, elaboration, presentation of synonyms, antonyms, and by providing multiple examples of sentences.

Vocabulary and comprehension have also a reciprocal relationship in the sense that the skilled reader has a larger vocabulary than the poor reader; the student with a larger vocabulary comprehends more than the student with a limited vocabulary; the more the student comprehends, the more she/he reads; and the more she/he reads, the larger his/her vocabulary knowledge becomes. Some authorities, therefore, believe that the best way to acquire new words is to meet them in context. They believe that rote memorization of individual words and their meanings is not usually a very effective means of building up vocabulary because it is difficult to remember isolated bits of information. Words become meaningful when they are encountered in sentences and are, therefore, easier to remember. This makes the teaching of vocabulary by pairing a word or list of words with their respective dictionary meanings less effective than presenting these words embedded in sentences. Meeting words in books also provides an opportunity for repeated encounters with the same word and thereby facilitates retention. This means extensive reading is an effective way to improve vocabulary.

Many experts, however, believe repeated encounters with a novel word in text is fortuitous and, therefore, cannot be relied upon as a means of vocabulary development. They recommend that a certain amount of explicit vocabulary teaching be undertaken to increase the size of students' vocabularies. In addition, learning words in a meaningful way is not limited to encountering them in sentences and passages. Words can become meaningful also when their linguistic origins and etymology are appreciated, and when presented in association with their antonyms, synonyms, and a group of words belonging to the same semantic family. Direct teaching of vocabulary, therefore, includes efforts to teach words with reference to their etymology, synonyms, antonyms, and the families to which they belong. After discussing the pros and cons of direct and incidental instruction in vocabulary development, Beck and McKeown (1991) arrived at the following conclusions: (1) all instructional methods produce better word learning than no instruction; (2) no one method has been shown to be superior to others; (3) there is advantage to methods that use a variety of techniques to facilitate deep processing of words; and (4) vocabulary acquisition is facilitated by repeated exposures and wide reading. These conclusions are supported by research studies. In a meta-analysis of studies of vocabulary instruction, Shepherd and Marmalejo (1991) found that compared to the incidental approach, direct vocabulary instruction produced better results. Furthermore, semantic-based direct technique, which utilized word-knowledge and networks of related concepts and ideas produced the best results. The studies that were subjected to the meta-analysis involved poor readers.

A lack of consensus about the effect of vocabulary improvement on comprehension shows that even though vocabulary knowledge is necessary for comprehension, such knowledge is not a sufficient condition. However, not knowing the meaning of a word can certainly impede comprehension. Bringing the word knowledge of reading-disabled students up to a level that is necessary for comprehending subject matter areas is, therefore, a basic goal of vocabulary instruction.

But what is word knowledge? Commenting that knowing a word is not an all-or-none proposition but falls on a continuum, Beck and McKeown (1991) proceed to identify four levels of "knowing": (1) the word has not been seen before; (2) the student has heard it, but does not know what it means; (3) the word is recognized in context; (4) the student knows the word well. In order to be an aid in comprehension, vocabulary knowledge should be at Level 4. That means, the reader should know the word, should know about the word, and be in a position to use the word meaningfully in a sentence.

As noted earlier, wide reading can be a source of vocabulary knowledge. Students with reading disabilities, however, are known not to be avid readers. This necessitates the need for direct instruction in vocabulary development. Three different approaches are recommended for the direct teaching of vocabulary. They are: *semantic mapping, cluster analysis,* and *morphological analysis.*

Semantic Mapping

This is a process whereby the relationship between a word and related words and concepts are portrayed in the form of a visual display. Such a semantic map is assumed to match the organizational format of the semantic lexicon. Johnson and Pearson (1984) have provided guidelines for teaching vocabulary through the semantic mapping procedure. The steps recommended for the construction of semantic maps presented here is a slightly modified version of their procedure. Methods that can be useful in constructing semantic maps along with illustrations are provided also by Heimlich and Pittelman (1986). Once demonstrated, students can follow this procedure and construct their own semantic maps for words and concepts found in their textbooks. This procedure can be more effective when students work in groups or as a class than when they carry out the project on an individual basis. The following steps are followed in constructing semantic maps.

1. Choose a word or topic from the textbook.
2. Write the word or concept on a large sheet of paper.
3. Think of as many words or concepts as possible that are related to the target word, put them on the paper, and connect them to the target word in some systematic way. For example, synonyms of the target word can be placed on one side of the paper, and antonyms on the other side. After this, refer to a dictionary or a thesarus and add additional words and concepts to the diagram.

Semantic mapping can also be used as a study-skill device while reading the textbook. Under such circumstances, the main idea becomes a pivotal point to which the major and minor supporting details are connected with lines. Such a graphic representation of information can be helpful for many students with reading disabilities who have poor verbal memory. Semantic maps correspond to the network organization of the mental lexicon.

Cluster Analysis

This is very similar to semantic mapping but is limited to the development of a family of related words or concepts. The process includes identifying words that are related to a single concept or idea and then teaching these words by noting the similarities and differences among them. The following is an example taken from Marzano and Marzano (1988). The basic concept is *mental activities.* Words that are related to this concept include common words such as "think," "forget," "remember," "guess," "wonder," or "solve," and unusual words such as "ponder," "perceive," and "cognize." Related concepts such as *intelligence, artificial intelligence,* and *subconscious* can also be introduced in this context. These groups of words and concepts are referred to as category lists. The similarity between category lists and the "set model" of the mental lexicon is obvious. If vocabulary improvement is one of the goals established in a learning skills course, students can be asked to construct sentences using words from these lists. Such an exercise not only focuses the attention of the student on the words to be learned, but also provides a context for the meaningful use of these words.

Morphological Analysis

A large number of words encountered in the text are combinations of root morphemes and affixes. Sometimes two words are combined to make a compound word. In Chapter 3 it was noted that root morphemes and suffixes are thought to be stored in separate lexicons, and that errors in the proper use of suffixes are quite common in the oral reading and writing of disabled readers. Analyzing words into root morphemes and their affixes is, therefore, likely to increase the awareness of disabled readers about the morphological structure of words.

It is thought that morphological analysis of words enables the student to capture the meaning of some of the unfamiliar words. Morphological analysis appears to have an added advantage of being able to improve decoding and spelling skills of poor readers. Henry (1990) reports that dyslexic students who were taught the structural nature of words and trained to use structural analysis showed significant gains in both reading and spelling. In her training program, Henry required elementary schoolchildren to identify structural and morphemic patterns (consonants, digraphs, trigraphs, prefixes, and suffixes) of words with three different etymological origins, namely, Anglo–Saxon, Romance, and Greek. As she describes, Anglo–Saxon words are common, everyday words, and most of them have a consistent pattern of pronunciation (e.g., "cap," "stand," "sister," "forbidden"). There are, however, several words which do not conform to the common spelling–sound pattern, and these have to be rote-memorized. Many of the Romance words are technical words and primarily of Latin or French origin. Many of these words also follow simple letter–sound correspondences even though the stress pattern can be complex (e.g., "excellent," "direction"). Suffixes such as *tion, tious, tial, sion, cial, cious* are also Romance in origin. Knowing that many affixes are of Latin origin can be helpful for realizing many word meanings (e.g., *aud* = "hear" as in audience, audible; *dict* = "speak" as in predict, verdict; *fac* = "make" as in factory, facsimile). Greek words are generally compound words (e.g., "microscope," "hemisphere," "physiology"). A knowledge of Greek root words can facilitate an understanding of the meaning of some uncommon words (e.g., *ast* = "star" as in aster, astronaut; *phon* = "sound" as in phonics, phoneme; *andr* = "male" as in androgynous, polyandry; *gyn* = "female" as in misogynist, monogyny; *morph* = "shape" as in amorphous, morphology). Lists of words along with descriptions of the nature and origins of these words can be found in these books: *Words, Tutor I; Tutor II,* by M. Henry (1990) and *The New Reading Teacher's Book of Lists* by Fry, Fountoukidis, and Polk (1985). Alexander (1988) has provided a small list of "root words" which can account for nearly 10,000 words in a typical desk dictionary. This list contains less than fifty such roots and, therefore, can be memorized even by children in primary grades.

In spite of the fact that a large number of words have come into English from other languages, words tend to change their meanings over a period of time. Some of these changes are: *generalization,* wherein the word acquires additional meanings (e.g., chair, grass); *pejoration,* wherein a word takes on a negative connotation (e.g., maverick; machiavellian); *amelioration,* wherein a word takes on a positive connotation (e.g., cowboy; black); and *euphemism,* wherein a somewhat negative meaning is expressed by neutral words (e.g., "revenue enhancement" instead of "tax," "patient outcome negative" instead of "the patient died").

Very often students will encounter unfamiliar words which do not lend themselves to easy analysis, and whose meanings, therefore, remain obscure. The meaning of some of these words can be inferred by examining the context in which the word occurs. Textbooks use several types of context cues to elucidate the meaning of words, and children's attention can be drawn to these cues. Context cues include the following: *restatement* (e.g., "The point he was making was banal and commonplace"); *definition* (e.g., "Altrusitic behavior, or sacrificing one's own interest for the welfare of others, can be seen even in animals"); *contrast* (e.g., "John was brusque in his behavior, but his wife was more agreeable"); and *comparison* (e.g., "John can be described as an ingenuous person, but his wife is shrewd and clever").

Some textbooks on study skills contain exercises that are aimed at building vocabulary (e.g., *Vocabulary Drills,* by Fry, 1986). These books can be used in junior-high and high school classes. In addition to these exercises, reading specialists also recommend allocating a designated time for silent reading, during which time students read individually materials of their own choice. In elementary grades, children may be placed in small groups and, when a request is made, the teacher may assist them in getting through their reading. Known as *Sustained Silent Reading* (McCracken, 1971), it is designed to promote vocabulary development by creating interest in reading. Because creating interest is the objective of sustained silent reading, external demands such as a report or summary are not required of the students.

The computer provides an excellent opportunity to build students' vocabulary. Some computer programs for vocabulary improvements are described in Chapter 7.

Strategies for Improving Reading Comprehension

The instructional strategies described in this chapter are intended to be used with children in the upper primary grades, high schools, and colleges. Reading comprehension is facilitated when the reader (1) can identify the main ideas in the text and separate them from major and minor details, (2) is aware of the organizational pattern of the chapter or essay, and (3) is able to summarize and paraphrase the information in the text. Reading comprehension also involves critical reading of the text whereby the reader is able to evaluate the information presented, accept what is valid, and reject what is questionable. These three subskills that facilitate reading comprehension, namely, the ability to identify main ideas and major details, the ability to recognize the organizational pattern of an essay, and the ability to summarize and paraphrase—are described in the following section.

Identifying Main Ideas and Major Details

Comprehending a written passage involves relating the content of the passage to the schemata the reader has and then retaining the relevant information so that it can be recalled on a subsequent occasion. This means that, first, the gist of the passage has to be identified and then related to the relevant schema. Second, the many details present in the passage must be reduced to a manageable number so that they can be retained in memory. This is accomplished by relating these details to the schema of the reader so that relevant details can be organized into a "gestalt" and irrelevant information discarded. These two goals can be accomplished by identifying the *main idea, major details,* and *minor details* contained in the passage. If the main idea is not quickly identified, the reader may be forced to retain the main details and supporting details in the form of far too many unrelated bits of information. This can put excessive stress on memory. The main idea functions as an integrative device to bring cohesiveness to the seemingly unrelated bits of information. This is why identifying the main idea in a passage is considered the most important single act necessary for proper reading comprehension. It should be noted that what is true of reading comprehension is true of listening comprehension as well. As will be seen later, the same principles apply when the student writes an essay; that is, the student's written work also should contain a clearly identifiable main idea to which the main details and supporting details are tied.

The most important requirement for reading comprehension is that the reader be aware of the concept of main idea and actively try to identify it in the passage she/he reads. Many expository texts are written in such a way that each paragraph in a chapter contains one main idea which is usually stated in one sentence (Cortina, Elder, & Gunnet, 1989). Often, the opening sentence of the chapter and the first sentence of the paragraph contain the main idea. Exceptions to these statements are far too numerous to consider them as rules. Sometimes a paragraph may be a continuation of the previous paragraph; sometimes the main idea may not be explicit, the writer deliberately avoiding a direct statement. Such writing is frequently encountered in literary prose. It is a good practice, however, for the student, when he/she writes, to keep in mind the idea that a paragraph should not contain more than one main idea and that it should be clearly stated.

The following tips can be helpful in identifying the main idea. As a first step, the chapter title and the subtitle tell the student the general area from which the main idea comes. It is expected that the student has some background knowledge about the subject matter under discussion. If not, the teacher has to ensure that the child acquires this background knowledge through direct instruction or practical experience.

Children's attention should be drawn to the fact that a general notion about the main idea can be gained by reading the titles and subheadings. Scanning the pages for words printed in boldface also can provide an inkling about the main idea contained in the lesson. Pictures and diagrams, when present, also give clues to the main idea. In advanced textbooks, a summary of the chapter is often provided at the beginning or end of the chapter, and the student can profitably read the summary before starting to read the chapter. It is also a good idea to read the questions that accompany the chapter before starting to read the text. The main idea of a paragraph usually answers the "what" question. Teachers also can prime the students by asking questions that relate to the matter at hand. Memory (1983) found that open-ended questions which required below-average readers to answer cause–effect questions improved their comprehension of such relationships.

Sentences that elaborate on the main idea are referred to by several descriptors such as "major detail" and "minor idea." We will use the phrase "major detail" to refer to these descriptive statements. Children's attention should be drawn to the following factors regarding these major details. Writers make a number of statements to support the main idea presented in the paragraph. These statements are generally descriptive and answer "who," "how," "how many," and "when" questions. According to Sotiriou (1989), sentences that present major details come in four different forms: They are sentences that present examples, a sequence of steps, description of characteristics, and cause-effect relationships. Often sentences that contain major details are prefaced with phrases such as "for example," "after that," "subsequently," "furthermore," or "because." Identifying major details helps the reader understand the main idea more fully and remember it better.

In addition to major detail, some reading experts identify another class of sentences, the "minor detail." Sentences that are considered to be representative of this kind often are used to qualify, embellish, or elaborate major details. Sentences that contain minor details often start with words or phrases such as "incidentally," "in other words," "as an aside," or "a corollary to this statement." The following passage illustrates the relationship between main idea, major details, and minor details.

I [designed,] after my first voyage, to spend the rest of my days at Baghdad, but it was not long ere I grew weary of an indolent life, and I put to sea a second time, with merchants of known probity. We embarked on board of a good ship, and after recommending ourselves to God, set sail. One day we landed on an island covered with several sorts of fruit-trees, but we could see neither man nor animal. We walked in the meadows along the streams that watered them. Whilst some diverted themselves with gathering flowers, and others fruits, I took my wine and provisions, and sat down near a stream betwixt two high trees, which afforded a delightful shade. I made a good meal, and afterwards fell asleep. I cannot tell how long I slept, but when I awoke, the ship was no longer in view. In this sad condition, I was ready to die with grief. I cried out in agony, beat my head and breast, and threw myself upon the ground, where I lay some time, overwhelmed by a rushing current of thoughts, each more distressing than the last.

Main idea; answers the questions "what" and "why." (The writer sets sail and reaches an island.)

Major detail; elaborates on the main idea. Major detail; elaborates on the main idea. (Describes the island.)

Major detail. (The writer is marooned.)

Minor detail; rephrases the writer's state of panic.

Williams (1986) has described an instructional program which can be used for developing comprehension skills in poor readers. In this instructional program, the main idea is called "the general topic," and major ideas, "specific topics." The 10 lessons of instructional sequence are divided into two parts. The first part focuses on identifying the general and specific topics of the lesson and the writing of summary sentences. During the initial stages of instruction, children are given training in producing superordinate labels (e.g., first they are presented with the names of individual items such as "ball," "wagon," and "balloon"). After this, they are asked to identify the general concept these objects represent. In this case, children have to come up with the response "play things" or "toys." Subsequently, the children are given training in identifying specific topics through a question–answer sequence. For example, if the child reads a paragraph about bicycle safety, he/she may be asked questions such as "Does this paragraph tell us everything about bicycles?" (Answer: no); "Does this paragraph tell us about how bicycles are made?" (Answer: No); "Does this paragraph tell us about traffic rules to be followed while riding the bicycle?" (Answer: Yes). In the second part of the program, paragraphs that contain anomalous sentences are introduced, and the reader is asked to determine whether an anomalous sentence is present in the passage and, if so, to cross it out. After this, the children are required to write a summary of the paragraph in one sentence. When a group of learning-disabled children were trained using this method, they showed substantial improvement in their abilities to identify the main idea in paragraphs and to summarize them. Williams suggests training should start with simple and short paragraphs, and notes that a great deal of practice is necessary for developing these skills.

In many passages, particularly the ones which deal with literary material, the intended message is not explicitly stated, but the author assumes that the reader possesses the world knowledge necessary for making the appropriate inferences. For example, the sentence "Jack and Jill went to McDonald's and had a great time" expects the reader to have knowledge about McDonald's and make the inference that Jack and Jill had a meal there. Generally speaking, inferential comprehension of text-book material requires a sophisticated background knowledge or schema of the subject matter. When the intended information is not explicitly stated, identifying the main idea could become difficult. Under these circumstances, the reader is expected to make inferences regarding the main idea based on his or her background knowledge. Sometimes inferential comprehension is encouraged by authors who want to encourage the reader to arrive at his/her own conclusions. The same device could be used by the student to enliven the essays she/he writes.

Recognizing the Organizational Pattern of the Essay

In addition to enabling the identification of the main idea, main details, and minor details, an awareness of the organizational pattern of the text also promotes reading comprehension. Children may need explicit instruction regarding the organizational pattern of the lesson they are about to read. Writers usually present the information they want to communicate in a systematic and coherent manner, which facilitates comprehension and retention of what is read. Written material that does not follow an organizational pattern obscures the main idea and imposes additional cognitive load which makes retention difficult. Conversely, the reader who is insensitive to the organizational pattern of the text also finds comprehension difficult (Baker, 1984). A study by Marshall and Glock (1978) shows that good readers are sensitive to text organization and are able to recall more information than children who lack this awareness. Reading specialists have identified the following patterns of organization:

1. Taxonomic
2. Sequential, chronological or process-based
3. Compare–contrast
4. Cause–effect
5. Expository–explanatory

Taxonomical organization usually contains information about different items that are classified according to some criterion. Sometimes the listing can be narrow, and at other times it can be quite broad. The three means of improving comprehension described in the section on reading comprehension are an example of a narrow list, whereas the chapter as a whole is an example of a broad list. Text that follows a taxonomic organizational pattern can be recognized by phrases such as "there are many reasons" or "the three species of birds described are."

Sequential patterns of organization present chronological progression of events or successive stages of some process in the form of narratives. Most of the information presented in history books is organized in a chronological sequence, whereas information found in science books about physical and biological phenomena is usually organized on a sequential basis.

The compare–contrast pattern is followed when two objects, ideas, or events are compared. Comparison focuses on the similarity between items, whereas contrast deals with the differences between them. Phrases such as "similarly," "likewise," "contrary to," and "unlike" are indicative of the compare–contrast pattern.

The cause–effect pattern is utilized when an attempt is made to relate two phenomena to each other and one of them is thought to be the consequence of the other. Children must be advised to be careful in interpreting two events happening at the same time as having a cause–effect relationship. For example, the number of churches in a city and the number of crimes committed in that city are usually positively correlated, but this correlation does not have a direct cause–effect relationship but may be related to a third factor: the size of the city. The reader, therefore, has to exercise caution when she/he reads statements that contain phrases such as "due to," "because of," or "it follows then." A similar critical attitude is necessary when the student writes his/her own essays.

The expository–explanatory format of organization is used in presenting a large portion of the material found in textbooks, particularly those used in higher grades. In expository writing, ideas may simply be listed and not be linked to each other with the aid of any of the devices presented above. This makes remembering such information somewhat difficult. Linking the separate ideas with the aid of a "semantic map" described earlier in this chapter can be a useful device to facilitate retention of such information.

Summarizing and Paraphrasing

Summarizing and paraphrasing are activities that involve both reading and writing. They are an important means of promoting comprehension and could be practiced even in elementary grades. Summarizing is an exercise in compression and requires the student to express the main idea and major details in as few words as possible. Summarizing is not simply retelling what is in the text but requires the structuring of main ideas and major details in a coherent, meaningful manner. Anyone who reads the summary may be able to grasp the main points and the general tone of the passage summarized. Summarizing improves comprehension because it requires the reader to focus on the essentials contained in the passage. Summarizing usually requires that the contents of a text lesson be expressed in a single paragraph. A summary is always shorter than the original.

One procedure that will make summarizing a relatively easy task is to underline the main idea in each paragraph and then rewrite each of them in the student's own words making certain that a meaningful gist emerges. According to Cortina et al. (1989), observing the following principles can be helpful in preparing summaries:

1. All of the author's main ideas should be included in the summary.
2. Only those major details that clarify the main idea are to be included.
3. The student must not include any of his/her own views or opinions in the summary.
4. Unless they affect the meaning of the summary, main ideas should be presented in the same sequence as they are in the textbook.
5. Sentences that express similar ideas should be grouped together and redundant statements should be deleted from the summary.
6. General terms and higher-order concepts should be substituted for lists of words and items.

The following additional points are to be stressed when teaching students to summarize passages:

1. The summary should be in the student's own words. It should not be a patchwork with phrases and quotes taken from the original.
2. The summary must be a connected whole. It may be in the form of more than one paragraph, but must be cohesive.
3. The summary must be complete and self-contained.

Reading specialists have often remarked that summarizing is a difficult skill to master and requires much practice before proficiency is acquired.

Paraphrasing, which in Greek means "equivalent sentence," involves an accurate restatement of a sentence or sentences in the reader's own words. In one sense, paraphrasing is a form of translation; it is the translation of the author's writing in the reader's language. In contrast to summarizing, condensing the information present in the original passage is not an essential feature of paraphrasing; in fact, a paraphrase can be longer than the original statement. A paraphrase must reproduce all the essential details contained in the original passage. In this sense, it is a full reproduction of the original. Usually, paraphrasing involves a sentence or a few sentences rather than an entire chapter. Two important points to remember while paraphrasing are that the original statement is to be recast in the student's own langauge and that a long sentence can be broken down and expressed in the form of many short sentences.

It is worth stressing the following points when children are given training in paraphrasing:

1. A paraphrase must faithfully reproduce the contents of the original passage.
2. A passage written in a terse or compressed style must be expanded and paraphrased to read more smoothly.
3. A verbose passage must be condensed without losing details.
4. While paraphrasing, the student must treat the passage as a whole such that the paraphrase can be read as an independent and complete composition. The habit of taking one sentence at a time, translating it into another sentence, and then putting them all together, should be discouraged. Paraphrasing also requires the ability to identify the main idea in a passage.

Critical reading is part of comprehension skill, and the development of critical thinking is one of the goals of education. Children in junior high and above can be expected to be critical about what they read. By becoming a critical reader, the student learns to reach his/her own conclusions, is able to separate fact from opinion, and is not unduly influenced by authors and the printed page. Critical thinking, as far as reading is concerned, involves at least four abilities: distinguishing facts from opinions, distinguishing an author's interpretation of facts from the facts themselves, recognizing the author's attempts to persuade the reader, and realizing when the author arrives at conclusions based on insufficient data.

Improving Comprehension through Writing

Because writing draws the attention of the student to phonological, syntactic and semantic features of words and sentences as well as to the main and major ideas in the passage, it is not surprising that exercises in writing often improve comprehension. Even though reading and writing can differ from each other in some important ways, both activities involve generative processes in which meaning is constructed. A large number of studies that have investigated the relationship between reading achievement and writing skill report a positive correlation. For example, Stotsky (1983), after reviewing the literature, observed that a number of studies suggest that writing activities improve comprehension and help retain information. Of the many studies she included in her review, 15 investigated the influence of writing on reading. The writing exercises used in these studies required children to combine sentences, paraphrase text, write one-sentence summaries of a paragraph, and do creative writing. The dependent variables in these studies were measures of reading comprehension, retention of vocabulary, and comprehension of the subject matter. Stotsky reports that 13 of the 15 studies found a positive effect of writing on reading, which led her to conclude that almost all studies using writing activities for improving reading comprehension or retention of information found significant gains.

Teachers of English have noted that good writing accomplishes three goals: it communicates the ideas of the writer to the reader clearly; it convinces the reader of the writer's viewpoint; and it clarifies the writer's own thoughts on the subject matter he/she is writing about. (These objectives constitute the three C's of writing.) This means that writing in higher grades should strive not only to communicate effectively, but through logical presentation of ideas, should also convince the reader. It also means that in order to produce writing of good quality, the writer must have a clear idea of the subject matter he/she is about to address.

Many of the subskills that have been presented with reference to reading are equally applicable to the writing process. A knowledge of key concepts such as the organizational pattern, identification of main idea and major details, and format of the passage (such as cause–effect, compare–contrast, expository), are also useful in improving writing skill. There is, however, one important difference between writing and reading: in writing information is produced, whereas in reading it is recognized. Therefore, writing is more demanding than reading. Writing is not just spoken language put down on paper. Spoken communication is informal and is carried out on the fly, whereas writing is formal and adheres strictly to rules of grammar. While the speaker and listener interact in person, the writer and reader are separated by space and time. The writer, therefore, has the obligation to anticipate the reader's questions and write without ambiguity. This is an important feature of good writing and can be accomplished to some extent by the writer switching to the role of reader to "monitor" the work in progress. This does not mean that written language is rigid, sedate and lifeless. In fact, many noted authors have used conversational and even a colloquial style and have achieved great success.

Spoken language contains prosodic features such as pause, stress, and elongation which are useful in highlighting certain aspects of the information conveyed. These features are absent in written language, even though punctuation is a limited means of attaining a similar effect. For this reason punctuation plays an important role in written language.

Another difference between written and spoken language is that idea units in spoken language contain, on an average, seven words, whereas idea units in written language contain an additional two or three words. These words are used primarily to embellish and adorn the language. Consequently, written language provides an opportunity to use a wider vocabulary.

Students' attention should be drawn to the three essential steps of good writing, namely, planning, writing, and revising–reviewing.

Planning

Good planning starts with the writing down of a summary even before starting to write the essay. While planning an essay and writing it, the student should keep in mind the three C's of good writing mentioned earlier. In addition, at this time it is also important to determine the format on which the article is to be based. As discussed earlier, the format can be expository, taxonomic, or based either on a cause–effect or compare–contrast model. Planning also can include creating a rough sketch of the main ideas and major details. Both the summary and the sketch should take into account the principle of story grammar, namely, that every essay has a beginning, a body, and a conclusion. Before putting down an idea on the paper, it will be helpful to visualize the subject matter that is to be written down. Scenes, settings, and events become lively when they are visualized first and then described with words.

Writing

While engaged in writing, it will often be necessary to refer to the summary and the diagram developed during the planning stage. It is important to keep in mind that each paragraph should contain a main idea and that it should be stated clearly in a straightforward manner.

Care should be exercised to see that all major details in the paragraph relate to the stated main idea. The writer has to remind himself whether he is communicating facts or his own opinion to the reader. Statements that reflect opinion can be qualified by phrases such as "perhaps," "probably," "according to some authors," or "in my opinion." Facts should be authenticated by quoting their sources. It is also important not to plagiarize by quoting clauses and sentences verbatim from books in such a way as to create an impression that they are the writer's own. Preparing a set of prompts beforehand and incorporating these into the writing at suitable intervals introduces variety to the writing. Examples of such prompts are the following: "A new idea is," "No one would have thought of," "Another way to put it would be," "The reason I think so," or "Even though it is generally believed that" (Bereiter & Scarmadalia, 1987).

At this point, the writer should not be too much concerned with the mechanical aspects of the product such as grammar and spelling. Paying excessive attention to these aspects will divert the attention of the writer away from the creative aspects of the process. Errors of grammar and spelling can be corrected when the essay is reviewed. An excessive concern about the correctness of the essay undermines its creativity and originality; this is a special problem experienced by students with SRD. If concern about spelling and grammar impedes the free flow of ideas, the student may dictate his essay into a tape recorder and correct these errors when it is transcribed.

Revising and Reviewing

Revising the essay that has already been written can also be seen as part of planning because revising involves improving or changing some of the ideas or even the overall plan and format of the essay. Revising is different from reviewing in the sense the latter involves checking the essay for errors of grammar, spelling, and punctuation. Reviewing, therefore, is the last step in the production of an essay. While reviewing, the student should focus on one type of error at any given time. For instance, during the first review, the student may check for spelling errors, and during the subsequent review, he can check for errors of grammar.

The following suggestions are adopted from an article by Lehr (1981), which contains specific instructions for the mechanics of integrating reading and writing, particularly with children. The teacher first presents model sentences and breaks them into various parts; children are then asked to assemble the sentences. Next, children are encouraged to write their own sentences based on concepts such as "same–different," "cause–effect," "past–present," and "problem-solving." These sentences are then combined into paragraphs. Finally, children are shown how to combine paragraphs into a story. This type of exercise has been found to increase the understanding of children about the nature of stories.

In a review article, Scott (1989) has presented some of the weaknesses commonly found in the written compositions of high-school and college students. The following is a paraphrased version of the problems and her suggestions for avoiding them.

1. Lack of coherence in text organization.
2. Conclusions do not flow from the body of the essay.
3. Opening sentence and main idea are vague.
4. Main idea too narrow and specific.
5. Main idea too broad to be recognizable.
6. Sentences too simple as indicated by short clause length.
7. Fragmented and run-on sentences.
8. Syntax errors relating to conjunctions and errors of agreement among words that represent the same object in successive phrases and clauses.
9. Overuse of terms such as *and* and *but*.
10. Inappropriate use of personal pronoun by using *you* and *I* interchangeably.

Problem: Lack of coherence in text organization. This problem arises because the student does not have a clear overall view of the yet-to-be-written essay. Nor has he/she given serious consideration to the format of its organization (e.g., cause–effect, expository, temporal–sequential).

Solution: Develop a summary and outline of the yet-to-be-written article; depict the organizational plan of the essay in the outline.

Problem: Conclusions do not flow from the body of the essay. Conclusion has no logical relationship to information presented in the essay.

Solution: Paying close attention to the outline sketch can eliminte this problem.

Problem: Opening sentence and main idea are vague or too narrow. Main idea is too broad to be recognizable. The opening statement does not inform the reader what the passage is all about.

Solution: The student should have a clear conception of what is meant by main idea, major detail, and minor detail. Trying to state the main idea in the opening sentence in unambiguous terms and relegating major and minor details to subsequent sections can minimize this problem.

Problem: Sentences too simple. Sentences are simple structurally and in terms of vocabulary.

Solution: Try to connect choppy sentences to make them into a longer sentence. Avoid redundancy in word usage but make sure the meaning is preserved while using synonyms.

Problem: Fragmented and run-on sentences. These sentences are the result of a lack of effort to read and comprehend the sentence that is written. It also reflects a lack of sensitivity to grammar or a lack of punctuation rule knowledge.

Solution: It is more desirable to write short and understandable sentences than long and incorrect sentences. If each clause is constructed to represent a unit of meaning, this problem can be minimized.

Problem: Errors of syntax and anaphora.

Solution: While reading the essay, look for suffix errors. Relate the subject to its verb and grammatical morphemes to their anaphoric representations, and make sure they agree with each other.

Problem: Overuse of certain words. This problem indicates that the student writes colloquially the way she/he speaks. It also indicates that sufficient attention is not given to the ideas represented by the essay. The conjunction *and* reflects agreement between two clauses or ideas and ignores other possibilities such as disagreement and conditional situations. Overuse of the term *rather* indicates uncertainty.

Solution: Examine carefully the relationship between ideas and explore the possibility of using other relationships and corresponding conjunctions such as *because, since, but,* and *although.*

Problem: Inappropriate use of personal pronouns you *and* I: This is one of the common mistakes committed by students in higher grades and reflects a colloquial style. An example: "They try to make things look bigger to trick *you,* But *I* think they should keep them like they are" (Scott, 1989, p. 311). This also indicates that the writer uses a conversational, colloquial style.

Solution: The writer should realize that he is not speaking to a person but is writing to someone who is removed in space and time.

Several books are available on the topic of teaching writing, and the following is a selection: *When Writers Read* (Hansen, 1987); *The Art of Teaching Writing,* (Calkins, 1986); *Writing: Teachers and Children at Work* (Graves, 1983).

Critiques of the written composition are essential for proper revision and improvement of writing skill. Objective assessment of the written work and students' writing skills is an essential component of teaching reading. Most students put their best efforts into their work and believe they have written the best essay they can; they also may believe that others share this opinion. An objective evaluation of the writing skill of students with reading disabilities, therefore, is important, but such feedback must be handled so as not to discourage the student or dampen his enthusiasm. This is particularly true of children who may feel insecure about their writing skills.

There are two ways of assessing the written work of students: quantitative and qualitative. Quantitative measures are provided by the number of sentences, words and clauses used in the written sample, and by the ratio indicating total number of words relative to the variety of words used. A relatively objective measure of this kind is provided by "readability formulas." Even though no perfect formula has been devised, several such formulas have been developed and standardized. Some of these are available for use with the computer, and are discussed in Chapter 7. However, there is no objective way to evaluate the quality of an essay for its originality, creativity, organization, and humor. This form of assessment, therefore, has to be done by the teacher.

STRATEGIES FOR IMPROVING METACOGNITIVE SKILLS

It was noted in Chapter 3 that metacognition involves the accurate appraisal of one's own ability and an awareness of the task requirements. These aspects of metacognition, therefore, involve *self-appraisal* and *task appraisal*. Self-appraisal includes two components: (1) the ability to monitor one's own comprehension process and to take corrective action when comprehension fails, and (2) self-perception about one's reading skill and cognitive style. Task appraisal refers to the knowledge the reader has about the requirements of the task at hand—whether it requires detailed reading, skimming, scanning, getting the main idea only, preparing for a multiple-choice test which requires attention to details, or preparing for an essay exam which requires that major concepts be identified and organized. Some studies show that children with poor reading skills consider accurate oral reading to be the ultimate goal of reading; some college students use the same strategies whether they prepare for multiple-choice tests or for essay exams.

Self-Appraisal

Comprehension monitoring is a very basic metacognitive process. If a child reads and comprehends poorly but is aware of this fact, she/he can take appropriate measures to remedy the comprehension failure. In contrast, a child who does not monitor his or her own comprehension will not take corrective action. A direct way to assess a child's comprehension monitoring skill is to ask him to read aloud a passage and see if he/she self-corrects oral reading errors committed. The child's perception about his reading skill can be assessed by asking direct questions such as "how many questions do you think you can answer correctly after you have read the story"? "how many words on this page do you think you can read"? etc. Any striking discrepancy between the child's estimate and performance is indicative of incorrect self-perception. If the child has unrealistic views about his own ability, he may be provided opportunities to correct those misperceptions.

Other aspects of self-appraisal include a knowledge about one's own reading speed and cognitive style. There is a great deal of variation in the speed with which students read. The average reading speed of a college student can vary from 300 to 500 words per minute. There is a much greater degree of variation in reading speed among children from junior high school and elementary grades. Reading speed, of course, depends a great deal on the type of material read and on the purpose of reading. Slow readers are handicapped because the amount of material to be read and comprehended in high school and college is quite vast. Improving the reading speed of students with reading disabilities can, therefore, be of tremendous help in improving their academic performance. There is, however, little evidence that the reading speed of those who are slow can be substantially increased by procedures other than reading practice. Claims have been made about the effectiveness of speed-reading training, but most of these appear to be extravagant. When excessive speed is achieved, it is done so at the expense of accuracy. The speed–accuracy trade-off is well demonstrated. After carefully comparing "speed-readers" with normal readers, Just and Carpenter (1987) concluded that speed readers had a comprehension advantage only on familiar topics; speed-reading skill is not perceptual but conceptual; and speed-readers do more top-down than bottom-up processing. In other words, one can read fast only the material she/he is already thoroughly familiar with. The value of speed-reading training is not established where comprehension of new and difficult material, such as textbooks, is required.

An awareness on the part of the student with reading disability that he is a slow reader is the metacognitive skill he needs to have. A majority of these students assume that they are reasonably fast readers simply because they have no way of assessing their own reading speed. The student's reading speed can be quickly assessed by asking him/her to read the lists of words provided in Appendix IV. Inspection of the number of questions attempted and correctly answered within the allotted 35 minutes in the passage comprehension subtest of the Stanford Diagnostic Reading test provides another reasonably accurate measure of reading speed. Once the student becomes aware of his slow rate of reading, she/he can invest more time in reading and cover the same amount of material that normal readers do in less time.

It was noted in earlier chapters that cognitive style is defined as a consistent pattern in the organizing and processing of information. The term "learning style" is sometimes used interchangeably with "cognitive style," even though some educators claim there are subtle distinctions between these two terms. Learning style includes an assortment of factors which range from physiological variables such as cerebral hemispheric dominance to personality characteristics such as the student's preference to work either alone or in groups. Many of these variables are beyond the control of the consultee. For instance, it is neither possible to reliably determine a child's "cerebral dominance" nor is it possible to change it. Similarly, it is not possible to allow a child to wander around the classroom because seat work is not compatible with his or her learning style. In contrast, cognitive styles are more widely researched and can be assessed with reasonable accuracy, if not altered.

The metacognitive aspect of cognitive style would involve recognizing one's own cognitive style and taking actions if modification were necessary. However, it has to be stressed that while it is possible to evaluate a student's cognitive style, it is uncertain as to what extent such styles could be modified.

The cognitive styles relevant to the reading process are: impulsivity–reflectivity; scanning–scrutinizing; and dysfluency–fluency. Even though, theoretically, within any given pair one style is not preferred over the other, in reality cognitive styles such as "reflectivity" and "fluency" are preferable to "impulsivity" and "dysfluency." Readers who are impulsive tend to respond quickly without considering all aspects of a problem. For this action they pay a penalty, particularly when they take multiple-choice tests. Students who are scanners also tend to overlook important details and take in information in huge chunks. Dysfluent readers are extremely slow in reading even though they do not have a reading disability. They tend to perform poorly on timed tests, not because they do not know the subject matter, but because they simply do not have sufficient time to complete the test.

It is thought that cognitive styles are enduring personality traits and are resistant to instructional change. Nevertheless, it is also claimed that techniques such as cognitive behavior modification can have a positive impact on children who are identified as having attention deficit and are impulsive (Kirby & Grimley, 1986). At the high school and college levels, a lack of awareness of one's own cognitive style can be detrimental to the student's reading performance. Dysfluent readers can be encouraged to ask their instructors for extra time to complete assignments and tests.

Task Appraisal

The nature of the reading task can vary from situation to situation; under some circumstances, the text may have only to be scanned for main ideas and not for details; at other times, careful reading of even minor details may be necessary. Reading disabled children generally lack this sensitivity. These children can be made to increase their sensitivity about the nature of the task by teaching them to frequently ask themselves what is the purpose of their reading.

The effectiveness of metacognition training on reading achievement has not been extensively studied. The few studies which have examined the benefits of metacognitive instruction have concluded that such training produces positive results. Paris, Cross, and Lipson (1984) taught 8- to 12-year-old children what comprehension strategies are, when they should be used, and why they are effective. This comprehension instruction was designed to stimulate children's awareness about reading procedures, the goals of reading, and how to evaluate, plan and regulate their own comprehension strategies. Paris et al. found that such training was beneficial to children of all ages and reading abilities. Duffy, Roehler, and Rackliffe (1986) also found that teachers who provide explicit descriptions of strategies to be used during reading and how to monitor them promote children's understanding of the lesson content.

A few general principles to be observed in metacognition training are presented here. The student may be encouraged to ask the following questions of himself: "When I read the textbook, how often do I go back to a passage or sentence and reread it so as to clarify things?" "How often do I ask a fellow student or the teacher for clarification of ideas?" "Do I remember to look for the main idea when I start reading a passage?" "Am I able to get the main idea of the passages that I have read?" "How often, after an exam, have I felt I had done well, only to find out when the exam was returned that I was in for a big disappointment?" Comprehension monitoring during reading can be improved by continuously asking oneself these questions.

A metacognitive strategy that endeavors to teach students to plan, implement, and evaluate strategic approaches to reading and reading comprehension has been described by Palincsar (1986). It is referred to as *reciprocal teaching*. In this training procedure, the concept of "strategy" is introduced by using a football game metaphor. Students are told that the successful team not only knows many strategies, but selects the one that best fits the play. This involves a clear idea about the nature of the opponents and a knowledge of their strengths and weaknesses. Furthermore, the team continually evaluates the effectiveness of its strategy and changes it if necessary. Similarly, the reader selects the appropriate strategy (e.g., reading for details, or skimming), continually evaluates his/her progress, and takes corrective action when necessary. Skills such as question generating, clarifying, predicting, or anticipating the next idea; summarizing the main idea and separating it from subordinate ideas; and deleting redundancies are explicitly taught.

Reciprocal teaching is carried out by implementing the following procedures. Before starting reading each day, students and their teacher review the skills necessary for successful reading, namely, strategy planning, self-monitoring of comprehension, and self-evaluation. Then, the title of the text is presented and the group is encouraged to make use of the background information they have regarding the topic at hand. Next, the classroom teacher models and provides instruction regarding these strategies. As the days progress, the teacher slowly transfers the responsibility to the students. At times, the roles of teacher and student are reversed and children pose questions to the teacher. Children particularly seem to enjoy this role reversal. Palincsar reports that this procedure was used to teach junior high school students who were adequate decoders but poor comprehenders. According to her, after a trial of 20 consecutive school days, the group which had ranked below the 20th percentile on comprehension tests before training earned scores that placed them in the 50th percentile and above following reciprocal teaching.

The following descriptions of strategies recommended for use in metacognition training are adopted from the instructional programs developed by Paris et al. (1984), Jacobs and Paris (1987), and from the *Index of Reading Awareness* measurement instrument used in these studies. Children are given the following instructions with demonstrations of the skills to be developed in seven steps.

1. *Set up your goal.* Realize that reading has different goals and purposes. Some materials are read for details, whereas others are read for the main idea. Some materials are read for information, and some materials are read for enjoyment.

2. *Know the purpose of reading.* The general purpose of reading is to understand the text content and not necessarily to read fast or to read without making mistakes.

3. *Plan your strategy.* If you read for details, you should read every sentence. If the purpose is to get the main idea, you can skim and leave out unimportant sentences. Look for redundancies. (Some useful suggestions for developing skimming skills are provided by Memory & Moore, 1981).

4. *Use comprehension strategies.* Focus on important points; you can underline the text if you wish. Constantly check yourself as to whether the material you read makes sense. If you do not understand a word, use the words and sentences around it and guess. If you do not understand

what you are reading, slow down. Figure out the most important sentences in a story by identifying the sentences that tell most about the characters or events in the story. Try to identify the unimportant sentences in the story; often they do not tell anything about the characters or events in the story. Pay special attention to sentences in the beginning of the story because they tell you what the story is about. If you do not understand a sentence and you think it is important, go back and reread it. If you still do not understand it, think about other sentences in that paragraph.

5. *Monitor your comprehension continuously.* As you read along, ask yourself these questions: Can I tell what happened up to now? Can I tell the main idea of the story? Do I remember what has happened thus far? Do the sentences I have read fit together? As you read along, ask "who," "what," "when," and "where" questions.

6. *Try to resolve comprehension failure.* If you cannot answer these questions satisfactorily, identify the sentence or sentences that are causing problems. Again, ask yourself why this sentence is hard: Is it because the words are difficult? Is it because the sentence is too long? Once the problem is identified you can solve it by taking appropriate steps such as rereading, asking the teacher, or consulting the dictionary.

7. *Evaluate your reading accomplishment.* Ask yourself the following questions: Can I tell the story in my own words? Can I summarize the passage? Can I identify the main idea?

In the program described above, as well as in *reciprocal teaching*, students are given explicit training, with the teacher illustrating and demonstrating each step. Once the students have mastered the skills described in each step, fewer direct instructions are given, and students assume more responsibility in guiding their own instruction.

INTERVENTION STRATEGIES: COLLEGE LEVEL

As more and more students with reading disabilities successfully complete high school education, more of them are admitted into postsecondary institutions. Many colleges have become aware of the increased influx of students with LD and have made special arrangements to meet the needs of these students. Some colleges and universities have developed programs specially intended for students with learning disabilities, whereas others have the reading disability program as part of the total disability program. It is estimated that across the nation, more than 200 colleges and universities have such programs. Some of these are prestigious institutions which are very selective in their admissions. We do not have firm figures about the number of college students who may have reading disabilities, but according to Sandoval (1988), even in a highly selective university such as the University of California, as many as 0.5% of the student body may have symptoms of reading disability. In a medium sized university of about 20,000 students, one can, therefore, expect to have more than 100 students with SRD. This figure will certainly be higher in community colleges. According to Anderson (1982), the number of students enrolled in developmental and remedial studies programs ranges from 10% to 50% of the total community college population. It appears, therefore, that organizing and administering a reading disability–learning skills program in postsecondary institutions is likely to become a subspecialty within school psychology. Because reading-related difficulties are the source of most of the learning problems, school psychologists have to possess the necessary consultative skills in dealing with reading problems at the college level.

Recognition of reading difficulties among college students is not an entirely new phenomenon. According to Smith (1965), between the years 1924 and 1935, a total of 654 studies on reading were conducted and reading disability was one of the most frequently investigated topics; among those studies that investigated reading disability, more were reported on college reading than either on elementary or high school reading. After a lull during the war years, interest in the teaching of reading skills at high schools and colleges was revived during the 40s and 50s. This is reflected in the title of the Forty-seventh Yearbook of the National Society for the Study of Education (1948): *Reading in High School and College*. The Yearbook recognized two different kinds of reading programs, a remedial program designed to improve the skills of students with reading problems and a developmental program that was geared to foster high levels of reading competence in students without specific problems.

In the 50s and 60s, many colleges initiated reading programs for students who experienced academic difficulties partly because of the awareness created by publications such as the yearbook and partly because of the realization that large numbers of college freshmen could not read well enough to succeed in academia. According to a survey conducted by Causey and Eller (1959), of the 418 colleges investigated, almost three-fourths had reading programs for their students, and these programs served about 57,000 students. These programs, however, were perceived by administrators as irksome encumbrances and were not systematically organized and executed. According to Smith (1965), "Because of lack of experience in developing reading programs at the secondary level, lack of training in reading for high school teachers, and in many cases, lack of guidance from a reading specialist, the programs are sometimes growing in lop-sided and irregular ways" (p. 370). Conditions have not changed dramatically since Smith made these remarks, and currently, there is much need for reading programs that are organized and executed in a systematic fashion.

The primary goal of reading disability programs in colleges is to enable students with reading disabilities to realize their potential in academic areas. It is not realistic to expect to remediate reading disabilities which students have had for a number of years. We do not have the techniques for the remediation of such chronic disabilities, nor do the students have time to undergo such remedial training. A modest but pragmatic goal is to teach these students certain management skills which will help them cope with academic problems. Such management techniques include providing the students help in written assignments, giving tutorial assistance, teaching them academic strategies such as how to listen to lectures, take notes, and tackle examinations, and advising students in the selection of proper courses and instructors.

Ideally, the management program should have two components: an academic support program and an academic skills program. Included in the academic support program are initial screening and assessment, providing guidance in the selection of courses, teachers, and academic major, as well as providing psychological counseling. Tutorial assistance given to students who need them is also a component of the support program. The academic skills program is designed to teach strategies of learning aimed at improving academic performance of the student with reading disability.

Academic Support Program

Initial screening of students at risk is based on their high school grades and SAT test scores. The criteria for requiring students to be enrolled in the reading disability management program, of course, will vary from school to school. The goal of reading assessment is to identify the type of reading problem the student has, and to determine whether a student is underprepared or has a reading disability. In the event the student has a reading disability, the assessment results are useful in determining the nature of reading disability, whether it is due to weak decoding skill, difficulties in comprehension, or a combination of the two. Students with comprehension deficits have a relatively poor prognosis as compared to those with decoding deficits only. The assessment results are also useful in helping the student choose courses and academic major. Reading diagnosis can be carried out following the same procedures described in Chapter 4. At a minimum, the reading comprehension subtest and word-attack skill subtest of the *Woodcock Reading Mastery Tests* (Form G) should be administered. In addition, the reading comprehension subtest, Form H, can also be administered as a listening comprehension test. College students with Specific Reading Disability often do well on the Woodcock reading comprehension subtest. This is because, these students have, over the years, developed adequate sight vocabulary, and given sufficient time can guess the answers correctly on untimed tests such as the *Woodcock Reading Mastery Test.* Taken at face value, reliance on a single untimed reading test can, in the long run, result in a number of false negatives. It is essential, therefore, to assess reading comprehension under timed conditions, with a second test such as the Stanford Diagnostic Reading Test. In addition to these, simple oral reading and spelling tests such as the one shown in Appendix IV can also be given. In all, these assessment procedures could be carried out by the consultee or his/her assistants within two hours. There is no need to administer time-consuming intelligence tests (which also require the services of a certified psychologist).

Academic Skills Program

Teaching the strategies necessary for success in academic courses is an important service rendered to students with reading disabilities. For optimal results, such strategies should be taught through a well-structured course. The extent to which any student utilizes the opportunities provided in such a course depends, to a large extent, on the motivation level of the student. Because of past failures, many students with reading disabilities lack the motivation needed for the maximum utilization of opportunities available at the college and high school. For this reason, basic academic skills are best imparted to students with reading disabilities through an Academic Skills course in a highly structured format. There is some disagreement as to whether a "remedial" course should be part of the regular college curriculum and offered on a credit basis because college students are expected to have mastered the basic academic skills before they enter college. This, however, is not too difficult an objection to meet because a course in study skills is not necessarily a remedial course. It is designed as a self-improvement course which is open to *all* students. Even though it is to be expected that a majority of students enrolled in an Academic Skills course have experienced learning difficulties in the past, it is not unusual for students with no previous history of reading disability to express a desire to enroll in such a course. As a matter of fact, students who are maintaining a C or B grade gain the most from such a course. A grade of C or B, of course, does not mean an absence of a reading disability. In fact, many students with SRD maintain a decent grade-point average. Our own impression of this has also been confirmed by research. For instance, Cordoni (1982) reports that of the 46 students enrolled in Project Achieve at Southern Illinois University during the years 1980 and 1981, a majority maintained a "B" average in their chosen field. Four of these students were able to make the Dean's list. Furthermore, when offered as a noncredit course, much of the seriousness that is associated with a regular course is lost, and this usually results in poor attendance. Eventually the objectives of the course are compromised.

It is desirable to offer the Academic Skills course as part of the General Education Curriculum for a 3-hour credit and not as an extracurricular activity. The course should be mandatory for students who are in the Reading Disability program and for those who are thought to be at risk. Optimal results can be expected from the Academic Skills course if it is taken at the time when students enter college or during the summer which, in the case of those who have graduated from high school, precedes college entry. Many colleges offer such a preparatory course and require students who are thought to be deficient in academic skills to take it.

In Indiana State University, the course is offered for 3 hours' credit under the title *The Psychology of Effective Study* by the Department of Educational and School Psychology. The skill level and needs of the students who enroll in this course vary a great deal. Upon entering the course, nearly one third of the students have a "B" grade; nevertheless, they wish to improve their grade-point averages. Almost all of them attain this goal.

The Academic skills course provides training in the use of several strategies required for success in the academic setting. These include providing training in note-taking and test-taking techniques, and teaching strategies to improve listening comprehension, reading comprehension, vocabulary, writing skills, and metacognition. The basic principles that underlie these skills are introduced in a lecture format and students are provided hands-on experience in the classroom to try out what they have learned from these lectures. The content of these lectures and the exercises that provide the hands-on experiences are shown in Table 6.1.

The class usually begins with the instructor introducing the basic techniques and strategies that are relevant to the topic under discussion in the form of a lecture. This is followed by students' completing exercises and reporting back to the entire class, at which point both the instructor and other students in the class react to the report. Several books on study skills improvement are available, and most of these books also contain exercises which can be used both in the classroom and given as take-home assignments. We have used the following books and found them to be satisfactory.

1. Cortina, J., Elder, J. & Gonnet, K. (1989). *Comprehending College Textbooks: Steps to Understanding and Remembering What You Read* (McGraw Hill).

TABLE 6.1. Syllabus for an Academic Skills Course

Ed. & School Psych. 200: THE PSYCHOLOGY OF EFFECTIVE STUDY
Credit: 3 Hours   Spring, 1990
Prerequisites: None   Mon. 6:15–9:00 P.M.

Date	Topic	Assignment
Jan. 15	Introduction; pretest; note-taking; listening comprehension.	Read Sotiriou Ch. 9 Assignment: Sotiriou, Ch. 9.1 & 9.2
Jan. 22	Lecture: The reading process; vocabulary & spelling Exercise: Fry, Unit 1 Software: Bearings (Spelling)	Read Sotiriou Ch. 10 & 11 Assignment: Sotiriou, Ch. 10 & 11
Jan. 29	Lecture: Reading comprehension (main idea, topic sentence) Exercise: Pauk, Units 48–50 Software: Grammar Gremlins	Read Sotiriou, Ch. 3 Assignment: Sotiriou, Ch. 3; Fry, Unit 2
Feb. 5	Lecture: Reading comprehension (major & minor details) Exercise: Pauk, 51–54 Software: Vocabulary Devt., (Hefte & Doody)	Read Sotiriou, Ch. 4 Assignment: Sotiriou, Ch. 4; Fry, Unit 3
Feb. 12	Lecture: Reading comprehension (inferential comprehension) Exercise: Pauk, 55–57 Software: Vocabulary Adventure	Read Sotiriou, Ch. 6 Assignment: Sotiriou, Ch. 6; Fry, Unit 4
Feb. 19	Lecture: Reading comprehension (organizational pattern of the text) Exercise: Fry Unit 4, Pauk, 56–60 Software: Skills Bank II	Read Sotiriou, Ch. 5 Read Cortina et al., Ch. 6 Assignment: Sotiriou, Ch. 5 & Cortina et al., Ch. 6.
Feb. 26	Lecture: Reading comprehension (summarizing & paraphrasing) Exercise: Fry, Unit 5; Pauk, 61–63 Software: Skills Bank II	Read Sotiriou, Ch. 8 and complete exercises
Mar. 5	Lecture: Cognitive Style, metacognition Exercise: Pauk, 64–70 Software: 88 Passages	Assignment: Fry, Units 6 & 7
Mar. 12	Lecture: Writing skills development Exercise: Pauk, 71–75; Fry, Unit 8; Software: 88 Passages	Assignment: Read Sotiriou, Ch. 12 and complete exercises

TABLE 6.1. *(continued)*

Date	Topic	Assignment
Mar. 19	Lecture: Writing skills development Exercise: Pauk, 76–80; Fry, Unit 9 Software: 88 Passages	Exercise: Analyze the organizational pattern of the article supplied to you and provide a summary Construct sentences using 20 words from the list provided
Mar. 26	Lecture: Writing skills Exercise: Discussion of the take-home assignment; Pauk, 81–85 Software: Bank Street Writer II	Write a 2-page article on the topic provided. Construct sentences using 20 words from the list provided.
Apr. 9	Lecture: Writing skills Exercise: Discussion of the take-home assignment; Pauk, 86–90 Software: Bank Street Writer II.	A 2-page article on the topic provided. Construct sentences using 20 words from the list provided Use the computer and compute the readability index of your essays
Apr. 16	Lecture: Writing skills. Exercise: Pauk, 91–95, discussion of the take-home assignment.	Complete the assignments missed
Apr. 23	Lecture: Test-taking strategies Exercise: Pauk, 96–100; Fry, Unit 10 Software: 88 Passages	Read Sotiriou, Ch. 14 & 15 Assignment: Construct a 50-item multiple choice and a 20-item T/F test from chapters in your subject matter textbooks; complete exercises in Sotiriou, Ch. 14 & 15
Apr. 30	Review of the course Posttest	

<ol start="2">
<li>Fry, E. (1986). Vocabulary Drills, Advanced Level (Jamestown Publishers).</li>
<li>Sotiriou, P. (1989). Integrating College Study Skills: Reasoning in Reading, Listening, and Writing (2nd Ed.) (Wadsworth).</li>
<li>Pauk, W. (1986). Six-way Paragraphs, Advanced Level (Jamestown Publishers).</li>
</ol>

The following books are recommended by Scheiber and Talpers (1987):

1. McWhorter, T. (1983). *College Reading and Study Skills* (Little Brown).
2. Fitzpatrick, E. M. (1982). *College Study Skills Program Level III* (Reston, VA: National Association of Secondary School Principals).

3. Pauk, W. (1983). *How to Study in College* (3rd ed.) Boston (Houghton Mifflin).
4. O'Brien, L. (1985). *S.O.S.: Strengthening of Skills* (Specific Diagnostics, Inc., 11600 Nebel Street, Suite 130, Rockville, MD).
5. Turkel–Kesselman and Peterson, F. (1981). *Study Smarts: How to Learn More in Less Time* (Contemporary Books, Inc., 180, N. Michigan Ave., Chicago, IL).

Additional exercises are given in the form of take-home assignments, and these are also reported to the class during subsequent meeting. Students are also required to complete lessons and assignments presented through the personal computer. Satisfactory execution of all these activities, including the lecture, requires more than 2 hours of class time. We have found that a class meeting of 3 hours' duration, once per week, is a satisfactory arrangement. The 3-hour meeting is not fatiguing to the students because the class time is filled with a variety of activities, and the students are kept busy most of the time. Because the instructor often has to interact on a one-to-one basis with the students, enrollment has to be kept within reasonable limits, not exceeding 15. The student's overall performance in the course is determined on the basis of attendance, completion of take-home assignments, and participation in the classroom activities.

A detailed description of this reading disability program and how to operate one is provided in the book, *Reading Disabilities in College and High School*, by P. G. Aaron and C. Baker (1991).

Another Book on this topic is *College Reading and Study Strategy Programs* (Flippo, R., & Caverly, D., 1991) published by the International Reading Association, 800, Barksdale Rd., P.O. Box. 8139, Newark, Delaware, 19714-8139.

Computers and the Reading Consultant

INTRODUCTION

Introduction of the computer in the field of education can be considered as the major technological change after the invention of the printed textbook. The eagerness with which the field of education adopted the computer is not surprising because the computer is a natural successor to the "teaching machine" that had been experimented with as an instructional aid in the 1950s and 1960s. Today, the computer is as much a part of the educational scene as the chalkboard and textbook. Within the field of education, reading, writing, and mathematics lend themselves more readily to instruction based on drill and practice than do other subject areas. For this reason, a large amount of software has been produced to teach reading and mathematics.

The computer, of course, is only a tool and not a surrogate teacher. The concern expressed by some educators about the potential hazards of computer instruction is perhaps due to a failure to appreciate this distinction. As Rude (1986) points out, educators have not been sufficiently instructed in the use of the microcomputer as an adjunct to their teaching efforts. The computer is not a panacea for all educational problems and, certainly, it cannot be considered as a method of remediation for reading disabilities; rather, it is a vehicle to deliver remedial methods in an efficient manner. As such, it should be integrated with the regular reading and language arts curriculum. In addition to integrating the computer into the remedial program, teachers are also often required to express expert opinions in matters regarding the selection of hardware, software, and the organization and administration of computer-assisted instruction. The quantity of software available, even within the field of reading instruction is overwhelming; there are also different "breeds" of computers that are often incompatible with each other. In addition, new products are introduced every day that make what is novel today become obsolete tomorrow. The short history of the computer industry, in combination with its phenomenal growth, leaves little time for teachers to keep up with technological developments. A knowledgeable consultant can be of great value to teachers if he/she can provide the needed information in the area of computer-assisted instruction.

In the field of education and psychology, computers are used for three different purposes: simulation, computer managed instruction (CMI), and computer-assisted instruction (CAI). Even though computer simulation, data analysis, and data maintenance are useful in the area of reading, by far the greatest use of the computer is in the area of instruction. This chapter is concerned mainly with computer-assisted instruction; computer simulation and data maintenance and analysis are only briefly discussed. A selective list of software, with brief descriptions, is provided at the end of the chapter.

COMPUTER SIMULATION IN READING

In the areas of reading research and reading instruction, we can identify three different ways in which computer simulation is used: (1) to test the validity of theories about psychological processes, (2) to simulate teaching/learning models and clinical cases, and to (3) simulate teaching/learning situations and events. When the computer is used to validate psychological theories, certain predictions based on available empirical data are made; these predictions are then verified or falsified by running simulations through the computer. If a concordance between computer behavior and the prediction made on the basis of preexisting empirical data is obtained, the theory is accepted. If not, the hypothesis is rejected and the theory is modified. One example of theory validation through computer simulation is the testing of the "cell assembly theory" forwarded by Hebb (1949) to explain neuronal learning. The proper testing of this theory had to wait until "neurocomputers" that operate on an analog design were developed. When such a computer is "taught," its learning pattern comes close to what has been predicted by the cell assembly theory. Even though Hebb's cell assembly theory will have to undergo substantial revision, the essential outline of the theory has turned out to be valid. The parallel distributed processing model of reading described in Chapter 3 draws heavily on Hebb's cell assembly theory.

Computer simulation is beginning to be used in reading research to test the validity of different theories of word recognition. A major theory of word recognition postulates that two different strategies are used for pronouncing written words, one for phonologically regular words and another for exception words. Regular words are pronounced by assembling their pronunciation through applying phoneme–grapheme rules, whereas exception words are pronounced by addressing their pronounciation as "wholes" (Patterson & Coltheart, 1987). In contrast, the parallel distributed processing theory proposes that both regular and exception words are pronounced by using the same mechanism (Seidenberg, 1990). Seidenberg and McClelland (1989) "trained" a neurocomputer to pronounce written words and found that the computer could pronounce both regular and exception words equally well, provided these two sets of words were matched for features such as frequency, and the computer software had enough built-in interconnections. This was taken as evidence to support the view that a single strategy is sufficient to pronounce regular as well as exception words.

Many studies carried out within the framework of Artificial Intelligence (AI) also fall into this category of simulation. AI studies attempt to determine what procedures are successful in programming computers to solve certain problems. The assumption is that the human brain also uses similar procedures in processing information. Progress in the field of AI had been less than satisfactory when simulation studies were carried out on digital computers using algorithms to solve problems. The recently developed neurocomputers, which use heuristic procedures based on analog designs, come closer to resembling human mental processing than do the digital computers. The neurocomputer, instead of following a preset program in a sequential manner, learns by trial and error and thereby can be "adaptive" in problem solving. The computer simulation study by Seidenberg and McClelland (1989), described earlier is an example of this kind. If computers can recognize words without using two different strategies, perhaps humans also use a single strategy for word recognition. Of course, the fact that a computer can solve a problem successfully does not ensure that human beings also solve the problem the same way as the computer does.

The second category of computer simulation starts with the development of models of the teaching/learning process and clinical cases. For example, computer simulations have been developed to imitate and model the interactive conversational protocols of experienced counselors. In the area of reading disabilities, the usefulness of simulating expert behavior has been demonstrated by Vinsonhaler, Weinshank, Wagner, and Polin (1987) in training diagnosticians. These investigators report the findings of two simulation studies. In one study, they tested the hypothesis that training based on simulated cases would improve diagnostic agreement among clinicians. They gave diagnostic training to 28 experienced teachers for 30 hours by using eight simulated cases of reading disabilities. The diagnostic procedure apparently was modeled after the expertise of the investigators. A comparison of pre- and posttraining performances showed that interclinician agreement regarding the diagnosis of disability showed a significantly higher correlation after training than before training. In their second study, Vinsonhaler et al. used 15 experienced classroom teachers. Two-thirds of the subjects were trained on simulated cases and one third on children referred to the clinic. As in the first study, training significantly improved agreement among clinicians from pretest to posttest even though there was no significant difference between the experimental and control groups regarding diagnostic conclusions. These studies suggest that by using simulated cases, much time can be saved in the training of school psychologists who eventually become reading consultants. Simulation also provides an opportunity to present unusual and perplexing cases of reading disabilities which may not be seen in psychology clinics during brief internship programs.

Third, the computer can be helpful in simulating teaching–learning situations and events and can be used for running "mock" experiments. A simulation study conducted by Atkinson (1972) is an example. In this study, a "research project" was carried out to see which method of studying German as a second language produced the best results. Three conditions of teaching/learning were simulated: random order study in which students studied lists of words randomly presented by the computer; a learner-controlled strategy in which students selected the words to be learned; and a response-sensitive strategy in which words were selected by the computer on the basis of the learner's previous success and failure. It was found that studying words selected by the computer based on the subject's past success and failure yielded the best result.

Computer simulation can be used also for instruction by creating simulations of situations and events that are far removed from the classroom in space and time and, therefore, are beyond the reach of the student. These simulations can be presented in the form of "problems" for which the student has to find answers. Examples of such problems are "cleaning up an oil spill in your neighborhood," and "crossing a river on the Oregon trail."

COMPUTER MAINTAINED INSTRUCTION

The computer can be a time-saving device when it is used by teachers to keep track of the data that pertain to students' performances in the classroom. The computer can also carry out the necessary statistical analyses of these data. Such information can be helpful in monitoring the progress of an entire class or of a single student. Many computer software packages come with such record-keeping options. Computers can be used for other purposes as well. In this section we discuss computer-maintained instruction (CMI) under four headings: collection and analysis of experimental data, analysis of students' written work, computation of readability level (level of difficulty) of passages, and data maintenance.

Collection and Analysis of Experimental Data

The computer has made a major contribution to the psychology of reading by making it possible to collect enormous amounts data with precision and to analyze them. The computer is particularly useful in the analysis of processes that are too fast to record by conventional means. Many "eye-movement" studies use the computer to study processes that occur in milliseconds.

McConkie and Zola (1987) report that the computer they use in their eye-movement studies can sample eye position 1,000 times per second, with each sample indicating where the eye is being directed in both horizontal and vertical dimensions, at that moment in time. This yields 4,000 bytes of information for every second of reading, resulting in a vast amount of data. Without the computer, neither the collection of data nor the analysis of this data would be possible. Several useful findings have come out of such eye-movement studies. To give one example, McConkie and Zola (1987) tested the hypothesis that when they read, skilled readers form predictions or have anticipations of what word they will encounter next in the text. Commonly referred to as "context effect," such anticipation is thought to facilitate word recognition. To test this hypothesis, these investigators programmed the computer in such a way that during the saccade (eye movement) it replaced certain words in the text with an "X." Thus, when the eyes came to rest during the fixation, no text was available. When readers were asked to guess the words, the responses showed that they were not aware of what the word might be. This indicates that under such circumstances, readers were not making predictions about what the next word would be. This study indicates that anticipations based on context may not play an important role in word recognition during normal reading.

Analysis of Students' Written Work

The computer has also come to be used in the quantitative analysis of certain features of written essays. Computer programs that can analyze written material for grammatical accuracy, vocabulary use, and the overall level of writing have been developed. For example, the program *English Microlab* (Houghton Mifflin) presents lessons which are taught in modules pertaining to learning goals. The computer keeps a record of the student's test performance and evaluates the work for punctuation and grammar and comes up with an individualized plan of instruction based on the student's performance. It identifies the student's errors and suggests supplemental work in writing. Many reading programs intended for children also give a pretest and posttest and display the results soon after the child has finished the lesson. Software packages that incorporate these features are described later in this chapter.

A closely related function that some software programs are designed to perform is text analysis. *Writer's Workbench* (AT&T Technologies), for example, can analyze an essay and provide information to the writer about sentence length, sentence structure, verb choice, and punctuation. Costanzo (1989) who tested *Writer's Workbench* with one paragraph of his own writing reports that the computer printed four pages of commentary which included comments on organization, use of verbs such as "to be," and vocabulary. It suggested that the phrase "in order to" could be shortened to one word, "to," and the word "changed" be used in place of the word "modified." It also pointed out that some of his sentences were more complex than what is usually found in good papers. Additionally, it listed all sentences longer than fifty words and offered tips for writing simpler sentences. Further analysis included verb choice, nominalizations, and passives. The computer noted that more than 2% of the words in the essay were abstract and pointed out that concrete text is easier to read and remember than abstract material. In addition to detecting spelling errors, it also gave readability estimates of the writing. While Costanzo admits that he was impressed with some of the computer's "insightful suggestions," such as the use of shorter sentences, he was not inclined to make changes such as replacing the word "modified" with the word "changed." However, he wonders whether under similar circumstances students lacking in confidence would defer to the authority of the machine. But one must remember that the computer is intended to carry out only structural, and not qualitative, analysis. Other composition aids available are *HBJ Writer* (Harcourt Brace Jovanovich) and *PWR: English Composition Software* (Macmillan). A program that can be used at junior and senior high school levels is *Ghost Writer* (Minnesota Educational Computing Consortium, MECC) which analyzes written material for readability, sentence length, and vocabulary redundancy. It also checks for grammatical accuracy by pointing out misuse of prepositions, voice, and conjunction.

Computation of Readability

Another form of text analysis is determining the ease with which a text can be read. This analysis is carried out by using a readability formula and expressing the result in the form of a readability index. Readability of a text is determined primarily on the basis of features such as sentence length and the level of vocabulary used in those sentences. It generally is assumed that longer sentences are more difficult to comprehend than shorter sentences, and that both multisyllabic and low-frequency words are of a higher level than monosyllabic ones. These variables are used in computing the readability index, often expressed in terms of grade level. Some of the criticisms raised in connnection with computer-based text analysis are also applicable to readability formulas. That is, readability formulas carry out a mechanical analysis of text and miss the most important aspect of an essay: its literary quality. Nevertheless, readability index can be a guide when the teacher prepares "home-made" texts for children to read or when books are selected for classroom use, particularly in elementary grades. In the words of Weaver and Kintsch (1991):

> The theoretical case against readability formulas has been argued many times . . . at best these formulas provide a scandalous oversimplification, more frequently a serious distorion. Nevertheless . . . they continue to be used. It is the only game in town, and as long as modern research . . . does not provide viable alternatives, there is not much else to do. (p. 242)

Several readability formulas are available. According to Chall (1984), more than 50 have been published, but the ones in wide use are by Dale–Chall (1948), Flesch (1948), Fry (1968), and Spache (1974). The software program *Ghost Writer* (MECC) can analyze output files written in several popular word-processing languages and give readability estimate based on the Fry formula. *School Utilities*, Volume 2, also by MECC gives readability estimates based on six different readability formulas.

Data Maintenance

Software packages intended to perform this function range widely in their capabilities, from simply storing the scores of individual students on a certain task, to noting the progress made by a student on several tasks, to interpreting the differences between pre- and posttests. The same functions can be carried out for a class as a whole. There is also software that can, on the basis of initial testing, construct a profile for each child in a special program and develop an individual educational plan based on the profile. *Apple Grade Book* (J & S Software) maintains class rosters, enters the grades for each student, and can compute test statistics for the entire class. Instructional software that comes along with capabilities for data maintenance can considerably reduce the record-keeping responsibilities of the teacher.

COMPUTER ASSISTED INSTRUCTION

In conformity with the componential nature of the reading process, computer programs that are designed to assist in the acquisition of reading skills can be classified into two groups: programs that help the learning of word recognition skills and programs that promote comprehension skills. Programs that assist the development of word recognition skills accomplish their goals through drill and practice and are easier to construct than programs intended to promote comprehension skills. It is not surprising, therefore, that many more programs designed to develop word recognition skills are available than are programs of comprehension development. In this section we will examine briefly computer-assisted instruction (CAI) that attempts to promote the acquisition of word recognition skills, vocabulary, and text comprehension. Because writing is an integral part of the school curriculum, CAI designed to promote writing skills is also examined.

Word-Recognition Skills Development

Prereading skills necessary for word recognition usually are taught to children during preschool years. These skills include the awareness that spoken language can be expressed in written form, that written language is in the form of symbols, and that written words can be related to spoken words. Many programs intended for preschool children are in game format and have color graphics of good quality. For example, in *Paint With Words* (MECC), when the child selects one word from the many on the computer screen, moves it to a background, and then presses the space bar, the word "magically" turns into the picture it represents. Many of these programs also introduce the alphabet. *Sticky Bear ABC* (Xerox Education Publications) is an interesting program intended to help children learn the alphabet by associating letters and pictures of objects and words that begin with those letters. Letter-recognitions skills development is also one of the goals of the software *Kindercomp* (Spinnaker Software Corporation). The program *Fun from A to Z* is part of MECC's Early Learning Series. It is a collection of three programs designed to give preschool and kindergarten children practice in a variety of early reading skills involving the alphabet. In this program, the child connects dots to produce letters and identifies correctly letters which enable a favorite animal to win a running race. The good graphics and the game format are helpful in holding the attention of children. IBM's *Bouncy Bee Learns Letters* is another example of a program designed to develop letter-recognition skills by using a game format. The program has an optional speech feature that allows the bee's voice to help students to learn the letters of the alphabet. The *Phonics Primetime Series* (MECC) provides practice with initial consonants, final consonants, vowels, blends, and digraphs. Another reading readiness and language development program that has received much publicity is IBM's *Writing to Read*. This is more fully described under the heading "Teaching Reading through Writing" later in this chapter. Other software programs that are suitable for beginning readers are *Letter Recognition* and *Word Families* (both from Hartley Courseware), and *Ready to Read and Add* (MECC).

Many of the programs that attempt to develop word-recognition skills are similar to *DISTAR* and the *Spalding Method of Teaching Reading* in philosophy and, therefore, can be used in combination with these teaching methods or modified to suit these methods in teaching children with reading disabilities. The color graphics and game format of these computer programs can make remedial reading more interesting than mere drill.

The format in which decoding skills should be presented to children with reading disabilities has not been extensively studied. What is the best way to teach word-recognition skills to children with reading disabilities? Is a whole word approach better than the phonics approach? If phonics appears to be more beneficial, should it be analytic or synthetic? Should the basic unit be the phoneme, the syllable, or some intrasyllabic unit? Olson and his associates have conducted a series of studies to answer some of these questions. In these studies, computer speech was utilized to teach word recognition skills.

According to Olson and Wise (1987) computer speech can be produced in two ways: by digitizing a model's recorded speech and retrieving it, or by synthesizing speech from speech codes. According to these investigators, the first method, digitizing speech, requires a great deal of computer memory and may not be a practical proposition as a teaching aid in most schools. Synthesized speech, on the other hand, is less expensive and can be quite readily adopted to classroom instruction. The technology of speech synthesis has advanced rapidly so that many of the present-day systems are capable of producing synthesized speech that approaches the intelligibility levels of the human voice. In their research, Olson and his associates used the text-to-speech synthesizer called *DECtalk* produced by Digital Equipment Corporation. They have classified their studies into short- and long-term studies (Olson & Wise, 1992). In one of the short-term studies, they compared the relative effectiveness of using four different orthographic units to teach word recognition skills to poor and average first and second grade readers. In this study, the computer was programmed to highlight and pronounce targeted words in four different ways: whole word, BOSS-syllabic (i.e., dividing the word on the basis of meaning as morphemic units, such as *act/or*), onset–rime, or as grapheme–phoneme units. They found that poor readers learned fewer multisyllabic words by onset-rime segmentation than by syllabic and whole word presentations. The long-term study attempted to see if onset–rime segmentation (which was effective with single-syllable words in the short-term study) would show a long-term advantage for the development of phonological coding skill. In this study, children from Grades 3 through 6 who were considered by their teachers to be at the bottom 10% of the class, were assigned to whole word, segmented feedback, or to an untreated control condition. As students read selected passages from the computer screen, they could target the word they did not know how to pronounce. The computer would then pronounce the word or the segments of the word, depending on which experimental group the child belonged to. The treatment sessions were presented for 4 days a week for 30 minutes a day, and lasted 10 weeks. At the beginning of the project, students were given several pretests; after the training, the same tests were administered as posttests. Analysis of the results showed that experimental students could read more than twice as many new words as the control groups. Wise and Olson (1992) also found that segmented feedback specifically improved phonological coding more than did nonsegmented feedback. This series of studies shows that the computer can be used as an aid in decoding training; it also shows that certain forms of decoding techniques are more effective than others. With the cost of high quality speech synthesizers coming down, it is possible that in the near future, speech-aided decoding training programs of this kind will become commercially available. Programs that are designed to teach structural analysis of words can also be expected to increase word-recognition skills. Identifying prefixes, suffixes, and plurals are included in structural analysis. *Vocabulary Skills: Prefixes, Suffixes, and Rootwords* (Milton Bradley) and *Word Division* (Ahead Designs) are representative of this software category.

Learning to spell words correctly has always been thought to improve decoding skills. The computer is well suited to present spelling tests and, if necessary, tutor the student in correct spelling. Maintaining student interest on the spelling task, however, is a great challenge to software designers. Almost every educational software producer has a program that teaches spelling.

Comprehension Skills Development

Programs that are designed to improve comprehension skills have approached the problem at the word level (i.e., vocabulary), sentence level, and text level. Vocabulary can be taught as a paired-associate learning task by associating a word with its meaning, even though this is not the best way to teach it. Because the meaning of a sentence depends on the context, sentence comprehension cannot be readily taught in a paired-associate way. For this reason, the teaching of vocabulary lends itself more readily to drill techniques than the teaching of sentence comprehension. Understandably, more computer software programs that teach vocabulary have been developed than those teaching sentence and text comprehension. In the following section, brief descriptions of the methods and materials that promote vocabulary and sentence comprehension are presented under separate headings.

Teaching Vocabulary

Many programs on vocabulary development have adopted a multiple-choice format. A sentence is presented with the target word missing, and the student has to select the one word from the options he/she thinks best fits the context. The computer gives feedback as to the correctness of the selection. If the answer is incorrect, the program may show the correct answer or it may give the student another chance. Some programs such as *Skills Bank II* (Soft Writers Development Corporation) give the meaning of all the four multiple-choice words. Program developers have demonstrated a considerable amount of ingenuity in making some of these lessons interesting by presenting them in some kind of game format. In the *Vocabulary Baseball Game* (J & S Software), for instance, every time the student guesses the correct meaning of a word, he/she get a "hit" and his/her player moves up one base. If the student misses four words in a row, he/she loses a player. *Word Blasters* (Random House) is in an arcade game format. Words from the multiple-choice question float around and the student has to "shoot down" the correct word.

Direct instruction in vocabulary also is presented in the form of antonyms, homonyms, and homophones. An example is *The Antonym Game* (J & S Software) in which the student tries to beat the auto race record established by another student in the classroom. Every time he/she gets the right answer, his/her car moves up 3 miles. If an error is made, it is explained and the correct answer is provided. *Word Attack* (Davidson) has four separate activities for vocabulary development in nine levels of difficulty. The four activities are: word display (definition), sentence completion (Cloze format), multiple-choice quiz, and word attack game in which the student "shoots" one of four words which matches a given definition.

While experts may disagree as to the extent of the value of direct instruction in vocabulary development through the computer, it is thought that such training cannot harm the student and that any approach is better than none (Strickland, Feeley, & Wepner, 1987).

A different approach which utilizes the "interactive" capability of the computer has been adopted by some software programs to teach vocabulary. In this format, the student reads the passage presented on the computer monitor screen, and as he/she encounters an unfamiliar word, targets the word and presses a key. The computer then presents the meaning of the word on the screen and illustrates it with sample sentences. The computer can also be programmed to sound out the word and its meaning, thus promoting decoding skills as well as word knowledge. This feature of the computer software is known as *hypertext.* According to Costanzo (1989), the hypertext is a combination of natural language text and the computer's capacity for interactive branching and the dynamic display of nonlinear text. When the student uses a lesson formatted as hypertext, he could access a word's definition, meaning, and a host of other concepts associated with it by targeting that word. Information displayed could be further targeted, leading to another layer of information, and so on. In a sense, the hypertext comes closer to mimicking the human brain in which information is organized in an associative or connectionist format. Most of the "hypertexts" available today are designed to retrieve information from literature or the sciences. Commercially developed interactive programs that are designed explicitly to develop vocabulary and sentence comprehension should become available soon.

Reinking and Rickmans (1990) developed interactive computer texts and found them to be effective. They investigated whether an intermediate-grade reader's vocabulary and comprehension would be improved by displaying texts on a computer screen that could display meanings of different words. These passages were taken from sixth grade basal readers and were presented on Radio Shack PC computers. Subjects were assigned to four treatment conditions. In two of the conditions, they read the passages on printed pages accompanied by either a standard dictionary or a glossary that contained the target words. In the two experimental conditions, students read the passages on a computer screen that provided either optional or mandatory assistance with the meanings of the target words. The results indicated that subjects who read passages with computer assistance scored significantly higher than the noncomputer groups on a vocabulary test that measured subjects' knowledge of the target words. Cutler and Truss (1989) describe a different but less expensive (about $2,500) interactive system. The apparatus these investigators used consists of a computer, a graphics tablet, a stylus, and a small speaker. The student places photocopied sheets of the text on the grid and when he/she encounters an unfamiliar word, he/she could, by touching a spot near the word with the stylus, hear the word pronounced along with its synonym. These authors tested the efficacy of this method on five teenage readers for a period of 5 weeks. They found in these subjects an increase both in their rate of reading and in the degree of their active reading involvement.

Teaching Sentence and Text Comprehension

A large number of vintage programs that were designed to promote comprehension are in the *Cloze format*. In this form of presentation, a passage is shown with every *n*th word deleted from each of the sentences in the passage. The student is required to supply the missing word. Depending upon the software, the student may be given the correct answer or asked to try again. The comprehension part of *Skills Bank II* uses the Cloze format. *Cloze Plus* (Milliken) also follows a Cloze format to develop vocabulary and comprehension by providing exercises in synonyms, definitions, and meanings. An interesting story-like format is used for answering Cloze questions in *Vocabulary Adventure* (Intellectual Software). In this program, the computer tells the student that he/she is going on a vocabulary adventure in a castle in the woods and that he/she has to answer the questions correctly in order to discover the hidden treasure. The computer then presents the information in a story format, and the student is taken through underground passages where he/she comes across several obstacles which can be overcome only by correctly completing the sentences presented. This program is meant for high school and college students. *Those Amazing Reading Machines* (MECC) is suitable for children from Grades 3 and up and uses animation in presenting the material. In this program, children are given the opportunity to edit incorrect sentences, to locate sentences that are out of place in short paragraphs, and to rearrange them in the right order.

Many programs follow the traditional style of presenting text and then requiring the student to answer questions. *Read to Comprehend,* which is part of the IBM educational software, teaches through drill and practice literal comprehension, and an appreciation of figurative language. It is intended for normally achieving readers from Grades 5 and 6, but can be used with children from higher grades as part of remedial reading instruction. *Tutorial Comprehension* (Random House) attempts to promote comprehension by developing skills in identifying main ideas, details, sequence, and in inference-making and critical thinking. Each of the five comprehension packages contains pretest, posttest, and practice lessons.

Many software programs are in a story or adventure format and are more interesting than formal lessons. Even though not primarily intended exclusively to teach reading, answering questions or solving the problems and puzzles posed by these stories requires word-recognition and comprehension skills. For example, *Snooper Troops* (Spinnaker) is a collection of mysteries which requires players to formulate hypotheses and test them. *Deadline* (Infocom) contains participatory stories in which the player solves a mystery by actively taking part in the story. The program is interactive in the sense that the student has several options available and the decisions made by him/her can alter the course and outcome of the story.

Writing Skills Development

Many computer programs that analyze written compositions (discussed earlier in this chapter under "Collection and Analysis of Experimental Data") also promote writing skills. Software geared to the development of writing skills ranges from packages that provide instruction in the mechanical aspects of computer use (such as keyboard training and word processing) to interactive programs that can be used in high school and college-level courses.

Examples of programs that teach typing techniques are *Primary Editor* (IBM), which can be used from Grade 3 and up, and *Keyboarding Primer* (MECC), intended for Grades 4 and above. Software programs designed to facilitate writing can be classified into four categories—those that (1) teach word processing skills, (2) help in planning the essay or story, (3) help in analyzing, editing, and composing the written text, and (4) teach reading skills through writing.

Teaching Word Processing Skills

In their book, *Using Computers in the Teaching of Reading*, published in 1987, Strickland et al. note that there are over 300 word processing programs. Consequently, the consultant and consultee have a wide selection to choose from. This also makes the selection process difficult. Even though many software programs are designed for use by professionals, programs that introduce word processing to children and are designed with this purpose in mind are available. The more widely known programs for elementary school children are *Bank Street Writer* (Scholastic Software), *MacWrite* (Apple), *Magic Slate* (Sunburst Communications), and *Primary Editor* and *Primary Editor Plus* (IBM). Books by Balajthy (1986), Daiute (1985), Rude (1986), and Strickland et al. (1987) contain lists of the most widely used programs as well as brief descriptions of these.

Is word processing a bane or boon for creative writing? Does it enhance the writing skills of its users by freeing them from the restraints imposed by spelling, grammar, and the editing process, or does it reduce the art of writing to a meaningless mechanical operation? This question can be debated, and certainly we can find experts on both sides of the issue. Undoubtedly, word processing has removed much of the resistive forces that stand in the way of free-flowing writing by eliminating much of the chore involved in copying, editing, and revising essays. Costanzo (1989) raises the following three questions and attempts to answer them on the basis of research findings as well as opinions expressed by more than 1,000 students who have used word processing:

1. How do the keyboard, editing commands, and other mechanical characteristics of the computer modify students' writing habits?
2. How does word processing influence the process of writing, which includes exploration and planning, development of the text, and the revision of the essay?
3. How does the word-processing experience affect different groups of learners—younger and older students, inexperienced and practiced writers, and students with or without learning disabilities?

Costanzo found that most of the students rated their word processing experience as "very positive" or "positive." Many students reported a change of attitude toward writing as a positive experience compared to pen-and-paper writing. Unencumbered by the constraints of spelling and grammar, and armed with the confidence that what is on the monitor is not final but could be changed quite easily, students tend to focus on substance rather than on form. This enhances their fluency, which, in turn, enables them to produce more. In a developmental study of writing skills, Daiute (1985) found that the computer also encourages children to write more. In addition, according to Costanzo (1989) the computer enables the writer to "decenter," that is, to step back and take a fresh look at his/her own writing. This makes writers look at what they have actually written instead of what they think they have written. Most students find the editing features of the word processor to be very useful when they write.

Finally, Costanzo (1989) cites a study conducted at LaGuardia Community College in New York City in which students who had previously failed the developmental writing course were taught collaborative writing and revising using computers for a semester. The study showed that word processing enabled these students to concentrate effectively on writing in sequential drafts and to experience a sense of accomplishment as their writing improved dramatically from draft to draft. Gallagher (cited in Costanzo, 1989, p. 122), who worked with writers having a variety of disabilities such as dyslexia, hyperactivity, and poor auditory memory, also found that those who were unable to concentrate on paperwork discovered that the screen was a more compelling focus for reading and writing than a sheet of paper. Gallagher concluded that word processing makes the writing of many drafts a practical possibility and provides disabled writers with key conditions for success.

Consultants who recommend the use of word processing as a means of improving writing skills in students with reading disability, however, should be aware of some criticisms levelled against the teaching of writing skills with the aid of the word processor. Collier (1983) analyzed college students' handwritten revisions and compared them with revisions done on the computer. He found that students made changes more frequently on the computer, but these changes were limited to words, phrases, and clauses. The handwritten changes, however, were made at a deeper level of idea clusters and paragraphs. Noting that revisions made on the computer were sometimes minimal and often trivial, he concluded that the use of a word processor for revising purposes did not enhance the quality of the students' written products. Collier's findings, however, were challenged by some investigators (e.g., Schwartz, 1985). Costanzo (1989), who has reviewed some of these studies, concludes that definitive judgments on this issue would be premature. Regarding this issue, our opinion is that it is unreasonable to expect the computer to enhance the quality of one's writing; the computer is a tool, and what it contributes to writing is that it removes some of the impediments that hamper free-flowing writing and makes the process less strenuous.

Planning the Essay or Story

Teachers of composition have come to realize that the process of writing an essay is as important as the final product. "Writing" includes planning, writing, and reviewing. Planning is just as important as writing and reviewing; without a good plan, good writing is impossible. As a result, in composition classes students are explicitly taught planning strategies before they start to write. Some authors call planning "prewriting" which implies that a student may develop an outline of what he/she is going to write later. Other terms used for describing this initial stage of writing are "free writing" and "brainstorming." Computer programs use more than one strategy to get the student get started with his/her plans about the writing. The computer may ask the student to write whatever comes to his/her mind. Some computer programs prompt the student into action by asking a series of questions. Once a sentence has been typed, the computer may elicit additional answers from the student by asking a series of "what," "why," "when," and "how" questions. Or the computer may ask the student what the main idea is and urge him/her to express it in more than one way. The computer may query the writer about the nature of the essay planned, for example, by asking questions such as "Is it expository (meant to persuade the reader to a certain point of view), or is it a cause–effect statement?" Subsequently, the computer may analyze the responses and present them in a reorganized fashion. Depending upon the nature of the project, the computer may furnish a list of words that can be used in writing the essay. This is expected to remove any mental block the student may have and induce him/her to look at the many options available. Once the actual writing has begun, it may ask the student to elaborate on what he/she has already written by asking questions such as "What do you mean by that?" or "Can you give me an example?" Such programs are interactive and engage the writer in a dialogue.

The software program *Writing a Narrative* (MECC) is meant for children from Grades 7 through 9 and contains three parts: "idea storming," "catch the moments," and "point of view"; each part has two components—brainstorming and drafting the story. "Idea storming" helps the student to start thinking of ideas for writing a story. It provides cues to generate words and then put them together in the form of a narrative. In addition, it asks open-ended questions; the student responds with a phrase, sentence, or short paragraph. "Catch the moment" asks the student to list some of the experiences he/she has had. Then it asks a series of questions about these experiences. "Point of view" explains the differences between first person and third person narratives and tries to teach differences in voice, actor, and observer. Another program, *Writing a Character Sketch,* also by MECC, is meant for Grades 9 through 12. The program titled *Composition Strategy: Your Creative Blockbuster* (Behavioral Engineering) uses key words and cues to shape the writer's thinking. It supplies key words such as "because," "before," or "while" after a sentence is written and prompts the student to incorporate key words into the writing and to continue along those lines.

Analyzing, Editing, and Composing

These three functions—analyzing, editing, and composing—go together and cannot be carried out independently of each other. Analysis of text was described in an earlier section of this chapter and examples of software useful for analyzing and editing written compositions were presented. Because children in early primary grades are still mastering reading and writing skills, what may be considered as "composing programs" are limited to activities such as sentence combining, proper use of adjectives, adverbs, prepositional and adverbial phrases, and correct use of subordinate clauses. IBM's *Combining Sentence Series* is an example of this genre of software. This software comes in three levels, starting from Grade 3 and extending into Grade 8. A series of programs collectively known as *Writer's Workbench* (AT&T Technologies) that is designed to provide mature writers with feedback about the quality of their work was developed at Bell Labs almost 20 years ago. That program was described earlier in this chapter. Another program similar to the *Workbench* is *RightWriter* (Decisionware, Inc.). This program analyzes the text for readability, vocabulary redundancies, and grammar. In addition, it also can make a qualitative analysis of phrases and mark certain phrases as clichés or weak. It inserts these comments in the text, but they can be removed at the time of revising. *Sensible Grammar* (Sensible Software, Inc.) is a program meant for the Apple Computer. From the pull-down menu the writer can select that aspect of writing he/she wants the computer to analyze. For example, the writer may wish to check sexist phrases or verbage. After highlighting what it thinks a potential error, the computer suggests alternative words and phrases. Milliken's *Writing Workshop* and Macmillan's *PWR* are two other composing systems that were already described. Many updated versions of popular word processing programs come with some of these capabilities.

The value of the computer as an aid in teaching composition skills has been a matter of controversy. Dobrin (1986), for example, argues that computers will never be good as text analyzers because they deal with symbols and not meaning.

> They can count and match but do not evaluate meaning. . . . These programs encourage false, silly, or limited ideas about language and give people new opportunities for petty tyranny, as they try to impose those ideas on others. At worst, the programs give users exactly the wrong ideas about language, that writing well is just satisfying some syntactic rules. (p. 24)

Not all educators share this extreme point of view. A reasoned argument is made by Costanzo (1989) who says that for those who are not used to thinking about their thinking, the computer offers a means for insight and self-control: "It is like having a copilot on board. Ideally, the copilot gives advice when you need it and takes over some of the controls in times of stress. But there is always a danger that the copilot may give the wrong advice" (p. 237). In view of these conflicting opinions, the consultant has to critically examine the appropriateness of "text-editing" programs before recommending them to the consultee as part of the instructional program.

Teaching Reading Through Writing

In Chapter 5, we saw that several remedial methods have emphasized the role of writing in reading and that the *Spalding method,* which uses writing as a starting point to teach reading, has been found to be quite successful in teaching word recognition skills to disabled readers. It is not surprising, therefore, that computer programmers have developed programs that emphasize the role of writing in the teaching of reading. One program that has received a considerable amount of publicity is IBM's *Writing to Read* system. Because it is very likely that the consultant's opinion is likely to be sought about this program, we will describe it in some detail. *Writing to Read* is a multicomponent system meant for children in kindergarten and first grade. The components include a computer-based instructional program, correlated student work journals, and supplemental language development activities. Used as a supplement to regular instruction, children work in pairs for about one hour every day with an IBM personal computer that "talks" to them. The computer station is housed separately from the classroom. When they use the computer program, children go through a period of pre-reading preparation by practicing the "alphabet song" and the letters of the alphabet. After this, they move to the automated part of the program. The "talking" computer pronounces a simple word and the letters in it and presents the standard and phonemic spellings (e.g., turtle and /t/ /ur/ /t/ /l/) of the word. Drawings that illustrate the word's meanings are also displayed on the monitor. This way, children learn to associate the word's sound, meaning, and spelling with each other. The second automated part of the program is the "syllable and segment program" in which letters and digraphs are presented on the computer screen. After they have finished the prescribed exercises on the computer, children move to the *Work Journal station* where they listen to a taped lesson about the sounds of the words they just learned at the computer station. They write those words in their journals, plus new words that use the same sounds. Subsequently children move to the *Listening Library station* in which they listen to tapes of award-winning stories. The next stop is the *Typing station.* In this station students write stories using *Primary Editor Plus.* At first, they practice writing the words they have just learned. Later, children write about anything they choose. Finally, children move to the *Make Words station* in which they form letters and words they have just learned by using clay, sand, pieces of fabric, cards, paper, and colored markers. Here they also play phoneme-based games such as "make words" and "writing to read bingo." All these "station activities" take about one hour and are carried out as an addition to the normal reading instruction. It should be noted that *Writing to Read* is not exclusively a computer program, nor does it focus only on decoding skills.

After two years in operation, the program was evaluated by the Educational Testing Service (Murphy & Appel, 1984). A brief report of the findings can be obtained by writing to IBM. The evaluation covered more than 10,000 kindergarten and first-grade children and, in the second year, concentrated on a core sample of 3,210 students who used *Writing to Read* and 2,379 comparison students from classes that did not use *Writing to Read.* In the first grade, standardized tests were used. Pre- and posttest score gains indicated that *Writing to Read* children in kindergarten have a significant advantage over comparison students. In the first grade, however, the groups did not differ from each other. In spelling, no differences emerged between the groups at both levels. Strickland et al. (1987) interviewed some of the teachers who have used the *Writing to Read* program. According to them, the reviews from these teachers were mixed. Some teachers complained that the division of learning into tiny fragments divorced from content fails to give the child a sense of reading purpose. Other teachers, however, noted that children's interest in reading increased and that they could read everything they wrote. It was also reported that "special needs" children were more attentive than usual in this program and were able to retain what they had learned.

We were able to get the impressions of some teachers and supervisors who have used this program. One of them is Debbie McKinnie, Computer Manager at the Rockville, Indiana, elementary school system, who has used the program for the last two years. According to her, *Writing to Read* is an excellent program primarily because it does not frighten children away from reading; third grade teachers who have the first batch of *Writing to Read* graduates in their classroom report that these children are better readers than the ones they have had in the past. Ms. McKinnie also felt that children from low-reading groups in the first grade benefit much from the program.

We also obtained information from Laura Coffey, School Psychologist/Consultant, who has interviewed several teachers in North Carolina, including Ms. Sandra Francis, Elementary Supervisor of the Burlington City Schools. The experience of these professionals is quite positive. All the 48 kindergarten and first grade teachers of the Burlington School system endorse *Writing to Read* and are pleased with the results. The strongest feature of the program, as seen by these teachers, is that children learn early to write anything they can say and can read what they write; they thus learn the interdependence of the two modes of communication. These teachers also observed some weaknesses of the program. The program is intensive, and they believe that some children are not developmentally ready for it. Such children are not mature enough to handle the testing aspect at the end of each of the 10 program segments. When "looped back" to previous segments, these children saw this as threatening and a sign of failure.

Another potential problem is *perceiving* children's "invented spelling," which is phonological in form, as faulty learning. Many parents can be alarmed when they see the written work their children bring home (e.g., "Mun cum aut on nit. Muns are yllo. Muns are brot."). Teachers may also become concerned and begin to overemphasize correct spelling. However, there is no need for such concern. Psychological studies, as well as observations by teachers, show that phonological spelling is one stage in the normal development of spelling acquisition, and most children learn to spell correctly by the time they are in the second grade. The transition from phonetic to standard spelling of a child enrolled in the *Writing to Read* program is shown in Fig. 7.1.

It should be noted that when the color monitor, speech attachment, networking options, and other accessories are added, *Writing to read* could become a very expensive program. Recently, IBM has introduced a program called *Writing to Write* intended for children in upper grades.

CRITERIA FOR SELECTING SOFTWARE PROGRAMS

In recent years, the computer has become a major instructional tool. Many school systems not only own computers but also have used them to organize "learning centers." Computer literacy, therefore, has become a required qualification for teachers. However, it is not the hardware, but the software, that is the heart of the computer-assisted instructional program. Acquiring a knowledge of what software is available, as well as choosing the right software to meet the educational needs, can be a major challenge for educators. Williams and Williams (1985) identify several problems usually encountered in courseware selection. Some of these are:

1. The hardware is purchased first, and then a hunt is made to locate the software that fits the computer. Software that is compatible with the computer, but does not meet the curricular needs, can be a waste.

2. There is a mismatch between those who promote and sell the educational software and the educator–consumer. Salespersons try to sell expensive nonreproducible software in large numbers, whereas educators would like to buy high quality reproducible software.

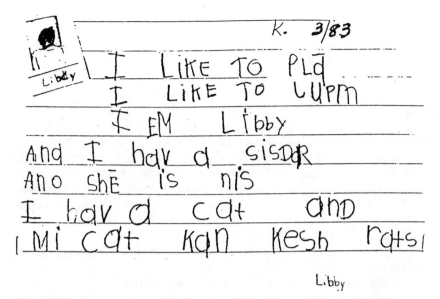

K. 3/83

Libby

I LIKE TO PLa
I LIKE TO LUPm
I EM LIbby
And I hav a SISDR
Ano ShE is niS
I hav a cat anD
MI cat Kan Kesh rats

Libby

3. 1985

I like to play. I like
to jump.

I am Libby   . And I have

a sister and she is nice.

I have a cat and my cat can

Catch rats.

FIGURE 7.1. Transition of a child's spelling from phonological to standard form.

3. Often the software selection decision is made by individuals who are not closely acquainted with the instructional needs of the classroom. Unless the classroom teacher feels that he/she has a say in the course-ware selection, the software is likely to be left unused on the shelf. The software will probably be put to good use when selection decisions are

made by the users rather than when made centrally by the administration. The consultant can play an important role in breaking down barriers that exist between teachers and administrators and can facilitate shared decision making.

4. Many teachers do not know the software options available on the market, how to find them, or how to evaluate them. They generally locate software by word of mouth or by reading advertisements in popular journals. The mostly advertised software need not necessarily be the best. The very few courseware evaluation studies published are in specialized journals. Here, too, the consultant can play a crucial role by collecting relevant information from journals and from teachers who have actually used different programs, and disseminating the results of his fact-finding efforts. The consultant also can arrange for meetings and workshops where information about the different programs and the effectiveness of these programs can be shared.

5. Curricular changes that are necessary to fit the CAI program may not be easy to make.

6. Administrators want software that meets broad curricular needs and software that will not become obsolete; teachers want software that is up-to-date and meets their immediate classroom needs.

7. Teachers prefer software that is self-administering and requires little personal attention to operate; children are less concerned about its value as an instructional tool and prefer programs that are in game format.

In the following section we present some guidelines for selecting software to assist reading instruction. Subsequently, we describe some of the software programs available for use in this regard.

There are five criteria to be considered in making decisions about software selection. These are instructional needs, appropriateness for the student's ability, interest level, ease of use and program characteristics, and cost of the program.

Instructional Needs

In the remedial reading program, we are primarily concerned with the improvement of reading and writing skills, and therefore, other subject matter areas such as math and science are not considered here. These principles, however, apply equally well to different content areas and to developmental education. Selection of the computer and its accessories should be based on the fact that they will be utilized by many teachers for teaching many different courses and for different purposes—reading instruction being one of them. Within the area of reading and writing, software programs are available for improving grammar, spelling, decoding skills, writing skills, development of vocabulary, and improving comprehension. As noted earlier, the remedial course may focus on the improvement of decoding skills, or it may be designed to improve comprehension skills, or both. Producers of software generally state whether their software is meant for improving decoding skills, writing skills, or comprehension. Major software producers such as MECC, Skills Bank Corporation, and IBM have single packages of software that cover several aspects of reading. The titles of some software, however, may not be self-revealing, and the name of a program can be misleading. For instance, the program *Word Attack* is not designed to improve phonics skill, but is meant to be used for vocabulary development. As noted earlier, some programs which are in a problem-solving and story format can also be used to teach reading skills, albeit indirectly. For these reasons, it is essential that the consultant examine the software before recommending it to the consultee.

Appropriateness

Software programs should be appropriate for the student's ability level and should fit the remedial approach that is planned. It is our experience that even though many software producers prescribe the grade level for which the program is intended, sometimes there can be a mismatch between the prescribed level and the grade level for which the program is actually suitable. This is true of many programs which are supposedly meant for high school and junior college. In reality, these programs may turn out to be appropriate only for the 9th- or 10th-grade levels. This, however, may not be a serious problem if the software is used for remedial reading instruction. But such programs may not be challenging to students who do not have reading disabilities and are enrolled in an academic skills improvement course for general enrichment. Thus, the anticipated composition of the class is a factor in program selection.

Interest Level

Closely related to the appropriateness criterion is the interest level of the student. One of the common criticisms of mechanized devices for teaching is that they are boring to the learner. This is true of many drill and practice exercises, and some tutorials presented through the computer. Software program developers are aware of this problem and have incorporated several motivating devices in their products. These include presenting the lessons in a game format or a problem-solving format. Generally, these software programs are able to hold the attention of students and challenge them and, therefore, are preferable to those which present information in a matter-of-fact format. Even though attention-getting gimmicks can be criticized as having the potential to distract the student from the main objective, it is a fact that if the student is not interested in using the computer software, no learning can take place.

A good software program should also be interactive with the student and not simply a one-way information source. Interactive programs create a feeling of control in the user and can be a good reinforcing agent. The interactive capability of the computer is perhaps the major feature that separates computer programs from worksheets. Computer programs that do not exploit this feature are not utilizing the advantages of the computer to the fullest extent. Nevertheless, teachers also report that reinforcers, such as "That is very good John; You are doing great," when they appear too often on the monitor, acquire a mechanical tone and lose their value.

Ease of Use and Program Characteristics

In spite of the fact that personal computers have become commonplace, some teachers are wary of them and express reservations about their effectiveness. Similar reactions can also be seen in students with reading disabilities. Software programs with instructions that are easy to follow are likely to alleviate the fears of the RD student. A software program which can be installed on a hard-disc drive is preferable to the one which comes on two floppy discs. Programs installed on the hard-disc drive eliminate the need for frequent swapping of the program and the data disc.

Software programs which provide immediate feedback and are able to summarize data regarding the performance of the learner enhance learning. In addition to providing information about the day-to-day progress of the student, this feature also makes record keeping easy for the teacher. Flexibility of the program which allows the teacher to introduce his/her own exercises in the program is a desirable feature. This is an important factor that is to be taken into consideration while deciding which program to use. Another important feature is the availability of a provision for skipping those sections which the student has already gone over or considers too simple. If a program does not have this feature, the student is forced to repeat the same steps before she/he reaches the point where the needed section begins. Programs that have this feature usually ask the student, when he/she logs out, to indicate whether he/she intends to start at the same point when he/she resumes the lesson. Some programs require complicated maneuvers for accessing a program. With the good intention of protecting data of individual students, some programs require a "password" before the lesson can be accessed. This can create unwanted problems.

Cost of the Program

There may always be a temptation to save money by purchasing the least expensive system available. In the long run, however, such a policy may turn out to be costly. While planning a computer-assisted instructional program, it is better to consider both hardware and software options together as a package and have a long-range plan. Computers with a large memory capacity are more expensive than those with less memory. Computers with small memory, however, may not allow for the addition of peripherals and other options at a later date. Thus, in a year or two, the computer may become obsolete. Major producers of educational software design their system to be used by a group of students simultaneously in one classroom. While planning the purchase of a system, such networking possibilities also should be considered. Most of the recently produced software packages use color graphics as a vehicle to teach. Usually these are in the form of animation and require high resolution color monitors. In the future, color monitors may be required to run almost all the reading-related materials designed for elementary grades. In summary, decisions have to be based on long-range goals rather than on immediate needs; instructional needs should be given precedence over fiscal matters.

A set of questions that can be helpful when software selection decisions are to be made is provided by Balajthy (1986). The following list includes some of these questions in a slightly modified form.

1. Can the same work be done just as well with nonelectronic media?
2. Will the skills learned have value to students in the classroom?
3. Does the program state instructional objectives, and does the program fulfil those?
4. Do the instructional techniques of the program mesh with current trends in education?
5. Is the student able to leave the program at any point and return to that point?
6. Is there a HELP command by which the student can return to the instruction?
7. Does the program allow input mistakes to be corrected?
8. Does the program provide a "second chance" to the student?
9. Are explanations of incorrect answers provided?
10. Does the program branch in some way to suit individual needs?

11. Is there a "management system" that keeps track of students' performances?
12. Is the "management system" easy to use? Does it perform diagnostic analyses of scores and provide useful statistics?

In their book *Computer Application in Reading,* Blanchard, Mason, and Daniel (1987) also present several criteria that should be taken into account in software selection and cite many articles that are pertinent to this issue. The book *Microcomputer Resource Book for Special Education* (Hagen, 1984) lists the names and addresses of software publishers and distributors, as well as selected software packages for special education. Brief descriptions of software classified according to instructional goal along with the names of publishers is provided also by Strickland, Feeley, and Wepner in their book *Using Computers in the Teaching of Reading* (1987). Other books that can be of value to the reading consultant are *Microcomputers in Reading and Language Arts* (Balajthy, 1986), *Teaching Reading Using Microcomputers* (Rude, 1986), and *Writing and Computers* (Daiute, 1985). A recent book by Howie (1989), titled *Reading, Writing, and Computers,* discusses both theoretical and practical aspects of using the computer as an aid in reading and writing instruction. Because the computer business moves so fast, books published a year or two ago may already be out of date. The consultant will have to look for updated editions of these books and other current publications in this area. Articles that appeared in *School Psychology Review* which may be helpful are those written by Heath, (1984); McCullough and Wench, (1984); and Moursund, (1984).

Articles that evaluate currently available software are peridocially published in the following Journals: *Classroom Computer Learning; Computers in the Schools; Computers, Reading and Language Arts; Creative Computing; Educational Computer Magazine; Educational Technology; The Computing Teacher; Electronic Education; Electronic Journal; Electronic Learning; Journal of Computer-based Instruction; Library Software Review; Personal Computing;* and *Teaching and Computers.*

A SELECTED LIST OF SOFTWARE

Prereading Instruction and Phonics

Paint with Words (MECC, 3490, Lexington Avenue North, St. Paul, MN 55126-8097). For K through 2. Children create colorful pictures which, upon pressing a key, turn into words.

Fun from A to Z (MECC). Part of the Early Learning Series, this is a collection of three programs designed to give preschool and kindergarten children individual practice in a variety of early reading skills involving the alphabet.

First Letter Fun (MECC). Also part of the Early Learning Series, this program gives young children practice in matching the initial sounds of words with the letters that make these sounds. Only short vowel sounds are introduced in this program.

Phonics Prime Time (MECC). This program includes five levels of instruction and introduces blends and digraphs, final and initial consonants, and vowels. The lessons are introduced in a game format and are intended for Grades 1 through 6.

Writing to Read (IBM). This program was described earlier in this chapter under the heading "Teaching Reading Through Writing."

Bouncy Bee Learns Letters and *Bouncy Bee Learns Words* are two programs from IBM. These programs use an animated bee to teach children the needed skills. An optional speech attachment is available. The words used in the program account for approximately 60% of the words found in basal readers, supplementary readers, and library books usually meant for Grades 1 through 6.

Grammar and Punctuation

Grammar Gremlins (Cambridge Developmental Laboratories, 214, Third Avenue, Waltham, MA 02154). This software program has a pretest and a posttest, and provides drill and practice in the use of plurals, possessives, subject–verb agreement, parts of speech, and capitalization. A printout option provides feedback to the student about his or her overall performance. The teacher can add additional grammar rules and questions. Even though intended for Grades 3 through 6, the information in this program can sensitize the older reading-disabled student to punctuation and grammar.

Essential Punctuation (Distributed by Cambridge Developmental Laboratories). This program provides instruction in the correct use of punctuation, capitalization, and quotation marks. Feedback is provided at the end of each lesson.

Skills Bank II, Reading and Language Series (Skills Bank Corporation, 825D Hammonds Ferry Road, Linticum, MD 21090-1301). The entire set of software programs in the reading and language series consists of 44 discs; one of the lessons in the language series contains lessons on grammar and punctuation. It also contains quizzes and tests.

Comma Cat (IBM). Lessons are reinforced by games that challenge children to insert appropriate punctuation marks in sentences. Meant for Grades 3 and up.

Punctuation Series (IBM). This comes in three levels meant for Grades 3 through 8. It is designed to help students develop the skills needed to correctly captitalize and punctuate sentences and short passages. In one of the lessons students practice editing short stories for a fictional newspaper.

Punctuation Skills (IBM). Meant for Grades 5 through 12, this program reviews the most important basic rules of punctuation.

Parts of Speech Series (IBM). This program comes in two levels, one for Grades 3 and 4 and the other for Grades 5 and 6. As a remedial program, it is recommended for Grades 5 through 12.

Spelling

Spelling Workout (MECC). This is meant for Grades 1 through 6. The program includes a pretest and a posttest.

The IBM Spelling Series (IBM). This comes in three levels, starting with Grade 1. It teaches spelling skills through exercises and is in a game format. Teachers can enter additional words from their own lists. Even though intended for Grades 1 through 6, it can be used for remedial instruction up to Grade 12.

Spelling (Skills Bank Language Series). This series is meant for Grades 5 through 12. Instruction is provided on plurals, suffixes, confusing sounds, and common misspellings.

Spell It (Davidson, 6069 Groveoak Place, 12, Rancho Palos Verdes, CA 90274). This program comes in five levels and teaches 1,000 commonly misspelled words. The lessons are in multiple-choice format and scrambled letters. An arcade game is included.

Vocabulary

Word Attack Plus (Davidson). This new version of *Word Attack* is intended to build vocabulary by introducing nearly 700 words through activities such as multiple-choice quizzes, sentence completion, word and meaning matching, and an arcade-style word-attack game. The program is flexible enough to allow the instructor to add his/her own list of words. It has 10 levels, with the highest being suitable for high school and college students with limited vocabularies.

Vocabulary Adventure II (Queue Inc., 5 Chapel Hill Drive, Fairfield, CT 06432). This program introduces nearly 750 words in context and is in a game format. It requires the reader to select the correct word from a choice of four words. Presentation of words in context is an advantage of this program which also makes it interesting. It is suitable for high school and college students with reading disabilities.

Vocabulary Development (Weekly Reader Family Software, 245 Long Hill Road, Middletown, CT 06457). This program contains exercises in the use of synonyms, antonyms, homophones, suffixes, and prefixes. The program does not provide feedback data and does not permit the skipping of exercises.

The Vocabulary Baseball Game (J & S Software, 140 Reid Avenue, Port Washington, NY 11050). Intended for high school, words are introduced in an interesting game format.

The Antonym Game (J & S Software). This program comes in three levels of difficulty. Antonyms are introduced in a game format in which students can compete with each other. The highest level is intended for high school students and can be used to prepare students for the SAT.

Words at Work (MECC). This series has four programs that teach prefixes, suffixes, and compound words. The series is intended for Grades 2 through 6. The graphics are good but the game is somewhat difficult to play.

Skills Bank II, Reading Series (Skills Bank Corporation). The entire series consists of 8 discs covering vocabulary and word knowledge. These include lessons on root words, prefixes, suffixes, homonyms, antonyms, and compound words.

Vocabulary Series (IBM). The three levels of this series are designed to teach students how to use correctly the words they already know and how to learn new words. Students are taught roots and affixes, and they practice combining them to make words. It is intended for Grades 3 through 8, but can be used for remedial instruction up to Grade 12.

Word Knowledge Skills (IBM). Intended for Grades 5 and up, this program is designed to improve students' communication skills by introducing homonyms, synonyms, antonyms, and idioms.

Vocabulary Building Skills (IBM). This program provides drill and practice in important basic rules for understanding how words are built. The program explores compound words, words that have a Greek heritage, word roots, prefixes, and suffixes.

Reading Comprehension

Cloze Plus (Milliken Publishing Company, 1100, Research Boulevard, St. Louis, MO 63132). This program comes in six levels. The presentation is in a multiple-choice format and introduces definitions, meanings of words, and compare–contrast relationships.

Comprehension Power (Milliken Publishing Company). This program, which is meant for Grades 4 through college, comes in a set of 12 discs. The program is intended to build inductive comprehension skills.

Skills Bank II, Reading Series (Skills Bank Corporation). This program is part of the reading series and comes in four discs. The topics covered are events and sequences, main ideas, cause and effect relationships, character analysis, author bias, techniques of persuasion, and figurative language. Presented in a matter-of-fact manner, the program is intended for Grades 5 and above.

Reading for Meaning Series (IBM). By reading stories and answering questions, students develop skills needed to predict story outcomes, infer meaning, and summarize information. It also teaches them how to use contextual clues to supply missing words. Color graphics and pictures are incorporated in some levels of the program. It comes in four levels and is intended for Grades 2 through 8.

Reading for Information Series (IBM). This series is intended for students from Grades 3 through 8 and comes in three levels. Students learn the following skills: drawing inferences, interpreting information on graphs and charts, locating facts and information, identifying main ideas, and recognizing cause–effect relationships.

88 Passages (College Skills Center, 320 West 29th Street, Baltimore, MD 21211). This program is intended for Grade 6 through college. Students choose an area that interests them, and after reading the passage presented by the computer, answer comprehension questions. If the answer is incorrect, the program explains why the answer is wrong, and the student is directed back to the text. The program also gives reasons why an answer is correct. Strickland, Feeley, and Wepner (1987) report that college instructors who have used this program are enthusiastic about it.

Many programs that are intended to promote reading comprehension at the high school and college levels do so by combining book-reading with computer-presented exercises. Some programs also attempt to increase the speed of reading.

Keyboarding, Word Processing, and Writing Skills

Keyboarding Primer (MECC). This introduces basic principles of learning the keyboard.

Primary Editor (IBM). This is described as a program that teaches students as young as 4 years how to write and edit. A separate "learning the keys" diskette uses graphics to introduce children to the keys for simple text editing. An optional speech attachment is available.

Primary Editor Plus (IBM). This is an extension of the *Primary Editor* and can be used by children as young as 5 years. This program also contains teacher management options and lets the teacher control children's use of the various options. Speech attachment is optional.

Many programs combine improvement of writing skill with the teaching of word processing. Many of these programs also have provisions for evaluating the quantitative aspects of the student's written work.

Kidwriter (Spinnaker). Children assemble pictures to create stories. Word processing includes printing. This is intended for children age 6 through 10.

Bank Street Writer (Scholastic Software, P. O. Box 7502, East McCarty Street, Jefferson City, MO 65102). This is a menu-driven word processor which is easy to use. It is intended for children from Grades 3 and up.

MECC Editor (MECC). Intended for Grades 7 through 12, this program analyzes students' written material for verb choice, vocabulary use, vague and overused words, wordy and redundant sentences, and certain aspects of grammar.

Ghost Writer (MECC). This program can analyze essays written in different popular word processors for readability, sentence length, clarity, and vocabulary. Intended for Grades 6 through college.

Writing a Narrative (MECC). This program encourages idea-storming and prewriting in students by providing prompts, before they write a draft. It supplies cues to generate words and narrows them down to a narrative. Students respond to open-ended questions with a phrase, sentence, or a short paragraph. It is intended for Grades 7 through 9.

Grammar and Writing (Scholastic Software, Inc.). Part 1 of the program provides instruction on parts of speech by challenging the student to use the various parts of speech correctly in context; Part 2 provides practice in forming basic sentences; Part 3 provides practice in the correct usage of verbs and pronouns; and Part 4 focuses on creating and editing paragraphs.

Success with Writing (Scholastic Inc.). This is described as a "complete writing composition course" by its creators. Students progress stage by stage from note-taking and developing ideas to editing and revising. The program also contains models devised to check the writing structure and the reading level of the written product. The completed text can be transferred to Word processing programs such as *The Bank Street Writer III, or Apple Works*.

Composition Strategy: Your Creative Blockbuster (Behavioral Engineering, 230 Mt. Herman Road, Suite 207, Scotts Valley, CA 95066). This program interacts with the student by providing prompts which direct the student's thought processes as she/he is engaged in writing. After a sentence is typed, the program presents a key word such as "because," "before," or "whenever" and requires the student to continue the writing by incorporating the prompt provided.

The Skills Bank II, Language Mechanics Series (Skills Bank Corporation). This series contains 16 discs and provides lessons on various topics such as errors in letters, use of nouns, verbs, tenses, patterns in sentences, fragments and run-on sentences, wordiness, unnecessary tense shifts, developing topic sentences, connecting ideas in a paragraph, paragraph logic and organization. It is intended for Grades 5 through college.

Programs Specially Designed for Students with Reading Disabilities

In a recent issue of *Electronic Learning,* Cowan and Jones (1991), reviewed three computer software programs that were specifically developed to help students who need remediation in reading. These are *Optimum Resource Reading Program* (ORRP; Optimum Resource, Inc., Norfolk, CT); *The Sentence Master* (SM; Laureate Learning Systems, Winooski VT); and *Autoskill Component Reading Subskills* (ACRS; Autoskill, Ottawa, Canada). The ORRP uses digitized computer speech and provides training in decoding and comprehension skills; the SM program uses a speech synthesizer and is aimed at improving automaticity in decoding function words and bound morphemes; and the ACRS program is designed to identify subtypes of word-recognition disability and provide training for automaticity which, however, has to be carried out on a one-to-one basis.

Readability Estimation

Even though originially intended for estimating the ease with which a passage in a textbook could be read, readability formulas can be used for evaluating certain quantitative aspects of written work. This can be particularly useful in classrooms where curriculum-based assessment is practiced. The two basic criteria for assessing readability are semantic difficulty, measured in terms of the quality of vocabulary used, and syntactic complexity, which is measured in terms of sentence length and embedded clauses. Several readability formulas are available, and they may differ from each other in the criteria they use for computing the readability index. The Dale–Chall formula (1948) is based on traditional methods and uses the number of uncommon words and average sentence length in a sample writing. The Fry formula (1977) counts the number of syllables and sentences per 100 words. Three written passages are sampled and the mean scores are checked against the table provided. The Raygor readability estimate (1977) is based on the number of words which have more than six letters from a sample of 100 words as well as the mean number of words in a sentence.

As noted earlier, readability formulas provide a quantitative measure which cannot be used to evaluate the quality of written material. For this reason, their value in grades above elementary school is limited. Another problem in using readability formulas is that estimating the readability indices for a large number of students is a tedious and time-consuming task. The enormity of this problem, however, has been minimized to a large extent by the personal computer. The computer also enables students to evaluate their own written work.

While selecting a program to calculate readability, caution should be exercised to see that the program is compatible with the word processor used. The following books and articles can be consulted for more detailed information regarding the use of computers for estimating the readability level of written essays.

Books and Articles on Readability Estimation

Blanchard, J. S., Mason, G. E., and Daniel, D. (1987). *Computer applications in reading (3rd Ed.)*, Newark, DE, International Reading Association.
Hague, S., and Mason, G. (1986). Using the computer's readability measure to teach students to revise their writing. *Journal of Reading, 1,* 14–17.

Kennedy, K. (1985). Determining readability with a microcomputer. *Curriculum Review, 25,* 40–42.

Strickland, D. S., Feeley, J. T. and Wepner, S. D. (1987). *Using Computers in the Teaching of Reading,* New York: Teachers College Press.

Standal, T. (1987). Computer-measured readability. *Computer in the Schools, 4,* 88–94.

Software

Ghost Writer. (MECC). This can analyze material written in different word-processing languages. Its estimate of readability is based on the Fry formula.

School Utilities, Vol. 2. (MECC). This program can provide estimates of readability based on six formulas, including the ones by Dale–Chall, Fry, and Raygor.

Readability Analysis. (Available from Cambridge Developmental Laboratories). In this program, the passage to be evaluated is typed in and the computer counts syllables, words, and sentences, calculating word and sentence length as well as word difficulty. It can provide estimates based on the Spache Primary Reading Formula, the Dale–Chall Readability Formula, and the Fry Reading Scale.

Success With Writing. (Scholastic Software). This program combines a word processor and a teaching guide for writing. Also included is a text analyzer module which estimates the level of a student's writing.

Some Leading Publishers and Their Software

Sometimes hardware and software incompatibility can be a problem in choosing the right kind of software. It is possible that some consultees may feel comfortable in purchasing all the needed software from a single publisher rather than having a potpourri of programs. With this possibility in mind, we are providing a selected list of software produced by three publishers.

The MECC Series

The MECC Reading Collection

Phonics Series: *Phonics Prime Time: Initial Consonants* (Kindergarten, Grade 1)

Phonics Prime Time: Final Consonants (K, 1, 2)

Phonics Prime Time: Vowels I (1, 2)

Phonics Prime Time: Blends and Digraphs (1, 2, 3)

Word-building Series: *Words at Work: Contraction Action* (2, 3, 4)

Words at Work: Prefix Power (3–6)

Words at Work: Suffix Sense (3–5)

Words at Work: Compound it (3–6)

Reading Comprehension: *Those Amazing Reading Machines I* (3)

Those Amazing Reading Machines II (4)

Those Amazing Reading Machines III (5)

Those Amazing Reading Machines IV (6)

Keyboarding Series: *Keyboarding Master* (4–9)
                    Keyboarding Master (5–9)
Composing Information Series: *MECC Writer*   (6–12)
                              MECC Speller   (6–10)
                              MECC Editor   (7–12)
                              MECC Write Start (6–10)

The IBM Series

Reading–Language Arts
Primary Series: *Bouncy Bee Learns Letters* (Prekindergarten through Grade 2)*
                Get Set for Writing to Read (PK, K, 1)
                Bouncy Bee Learns Words   (K–3)
                Writing to Read   (K–4)
                Primary Editor   (1–6)
                Primary Editor Plus   (K–6)
                Touch Typing for Beginners (3–12)
Reading for Meaning Series: Levels I, II, III, and IV (2–12)
Reading for Information Series: Levels II, III, IV (3–12)
Spelling Series: Levels I, II, III (K–12)
Vocabulary Series: Levels II, III, IV (3–12)
Parts of Speech Series: Levels II, III (3–12)
Punctuation Series: Levels II, III, IV (3–12)
Combining Sentences Series: Levels II, III, IV (7–12)
Private Tutor Series: *Reading Comprehension Skills* (7–12)
                      Capitalization Skills   (7–12)
                      Language Skills   (7–12)
                      Punctuation Skills   (7–12)
                      Spelling Skills   (7–12)
                      Vocabulary Building Skills   (7–12)
                      Word Knowledge Skills   (7–12)

*The higher grade shown in parentheses applies to remedial students. For instance, *Bouncy Bee Learns Letters* is intended for kindergarten but can be used for teaching poor readers in Grade 2.

The Skills Bank II Series

Skills Bank II is a complete set of programs designed to teach all aspects of reading and writing skills. Even though it is intended for use from Grades 5 through 12, many college students can benefit from it. The Language Mechanics and Language Usage, and Sentence Structure series can be used at regular college composition courses. Because of its graded nature, it can also be used for teaching students who are deficient in academic skills. The program covers approximately 300 concepts tested by many standardized achievement tests. It comes with well sequenced tests as well as management disks for maintaining records and producing reports. It has IBM and Apple versions available, along with network options. According to the publisher's report, 10th grade students who were considered as high risk from one school in Alabama gained 9 months in reading, 15 months in language, and 14 months in spelling after being tutored through the *Skills Bank* software. The software package also contains tutorial material for math skills development.

Reading Series (Range: Grade 5 through High School and above)

Reading Comprehension: Persons, Places, Events, and Sequences
Main Ideas
Causes and Effects, Conclusions
Character Analysis
Author Bias/Viewpoint
Techniques of Persuasion
Figurative Language
Vocabulary: Compound Words
Greek and Latin
Prefixes and Suffixes

Word Knowledge: Words with Multiple Meanings
Homonyms
Synonyms and Antonyms
Idioms

Language Series (Range: Grade 5 through High School and above)

Capitalization: First Words, Proper Nouns
Pronouns, Adjectives, Titles for People
Language Express: Nouns, Pronouns, Verbs
Adjectives and Adverbs
Simple Sentences
Punctuation: Commas, Apostrophes, Quotation marks
Letters, Colons and Semicolons
Spelling: Forming Plurals
Adding Suffixes
Confusing Sounds, Common Misspellings.

Language Mechanics and Language Usage (High School and College)

Letters: Personal and Business Letters, Errors in Business Letters
Language Mechanics for Quotations
Errors in Prose Passages: Clauses and Phrases, Nouns, and Pronouns
Verbs: Number and Form
Verbs: The Six Tenses
Use of Adjectives and Adverbs
Use of Prepositions

Sentence Structure (High School and College)
Grammatical Form: Predicates, Nominatives, Adjectives
Patterns in Sentences: Fragments and Run-on Sentences
                    Combining by Adding Ideas Together
                    Combining by Subordinating Ideas
Paragraphs: Misplaced Modifiers
           Dangling Modifiers, Unclear Pronouns
           Nonparallel Grammatical Forms, Wordiness,
           Tense Shifts, Double Negatives
           Identifying Topic Sentences
           Developing Topic Sentences, Connecting Ideas,
           Paragraph Logic and Organization

APPENDIX I
Review of Selected Basal Readers*

Currently, basal readers are used by more than 95% of the schools for teaching reading to young children from reading readiness classes through Grade 6; nearly 65% of the schools use them up to Grade 8. Even though about twelve companies are involved in the publication of basal reading programs, five publishers account for nearly 80% of the total sales. Most of the basal readers emphasize reading skills, comprehension, and literature; many of them list the different skills emphasized at different levels of the program.

Basal readers are sometimes criticized as being too skill-development oriented and lacking in literary quality. For this reason, some proponents of *whole language* would like to see basal readers banished from schools. This criticism is not entirely fair because most basal reader series emphasize the development of both word-recognition skills and comprehension. They also do not disregard literature and the development of literature-related skills. Research also shows that teaching reading through the basal series does not result in inferior reading achievement when compared to teaching through an approach such as *whole language,* which is almost entirely meaning-oriented (Stahl & Miller, 1989). It should also be noted that "advocates of whole language have yet to provide compelling research evidence demonstrating the effectiveness of such approaches in teaching children to read; indeed research over the past 70 years shows that structured systematic teaching in the early grades produces the better results" (Chall & Squire, 1991, p. 138). Basal readers are useful aids in making reading instruction structured and systematic. Resourceful teachers know how to use basal readers flexibly to make the program meet their instructional needs.

In the following section, brief descriptions of six basal reader series are provided.

OPEN COURT: READING AND WRITING PROGRAM (1989)

Authors: Ann Brown, Joseph Campione, Carl Bereiter, Marlene Scardamalia, Valerie Anderson, and Walter Kintsch.

*A comprehensive evaluation of the contents of the basal reading programs is published under the title: A *Guide to Selecting Basal Reading Programs* by The International Reading Association, 800 Barksdale Rd; Newark, DE, 19714-8139. (Price $50.00)

Grades Covered: Kindergarten through Grade 6. This series has 12 levels—two levels each at kindergarten, 2nd, and 3rd grades; three levels at 1st grade, and one level at the 4th, 5th, and 6th grades.

Basic Materials: This series includes student readers, reading skills workbook, wall–sound cards, flash cards, phonics techniques, practice and review masters, spelling charts, unit theme questions, vocabulary enrichment programs, work-shop activity sheets, teacher's guide, and teacher's resource book. Optional materials include "big books," phonics kit, phonics practice books, record cards, learning log, writing skills workbooks, individual cumulative record cards, test and management system, and in-service videos.

Skills Stressed: Reading instruction focuses on the development of decoding skills as well as comprehension, vocabulary, and literature-related skills. Phonics skills are developed by introducing consonant and vowel sounds, spelling, blending, sight reading, and structural analysis of words. Word meaning is taught through synonyms, antonyms, homophones, compound words, and words with multiple meanings. Comprehension and critical thinking are taught through teaching how to identify main idea, cause–effect relationships and conclusions, how to predict outcomes, and how to distinguish facts from opinion. Literature-related skills such as knowing an author's purpose and techniques, and identifying story elements and story structure are also introduced. Strategies such as setting up reading goals and expectations, clarifying, summarizing, predicting, and asking questions, which are meant to promote comprehension, are also intro-duced.

   The development of writing skills is also attended to. Writing exercises in-clude fiction, nonfiction, poetry, and plays. In addition, there are provisions for teaching skills such as developing writing goals, proofreading, evaluating and revising, and grammar usage. The series also contains a study and research skills component which makes provision for the teaching of skills such as note-taking, test-taking, library use, and the interpretation of graphics.

Comments: This series is designed with a view to building a strong foundation in reading skills and strategies that will lead to early independence in reading and writing for all children, including slow learners. It relies to some extent on the synthetic phonics approach, introducing sounds first, followed by words those sounds make. The series, reportedly, is based on 10 years' research and 3 years of field testing.

Address: Open Court Publishing Co., PO Box 599, Peru, IL 61354.

MACMILLAN/MCGRAW-HILL: CONNECTIONS AND READING EXPRESS (1991)

Connections and *Reading Express* can either be used separately or together.

Connections

Authors: Virginia Arnold, Carl Smith, James Flood, and Diane Lapp.

Grades Covered: Kindergarten through the 8th grade. There are 14 levels.

Basic Materials: Kindergarten kit, pupils' editions of hard-cover and soft-cover books for all levels, workbooks, skills practice materials, teachers' editions, placement tests, unit tests, mid-year and end-of-year tests, informal assessment tools, evaluation charts, and administrator's guides. In addition, the following supplementary materials are available: phonics workbooks, vocabulary and comprehension materials, parent–child activities, and in-service videotapes. The program also has computer software for instruction in phonics, comprehension, and composition writing. The program has additional materials for students with limited proficiency in English.

Skills Stressed: Decoding, phonics skills, comprehension and vocabulary skills, study skills, and language and literature skills are listed as the scope of the program. Relating reading to language arts is a special optional section in each lesson.

Comments: The purpose of *Connections* is to provide learning materials and instructional strategies that will enable teachers and students to achieve the important goals of literacy. Although the program says that literature is the core of *Connections,* decoding is taught through phonics, structural analysis, and context clues. It teaches language arts through practice in listening, speaking, reading, and writing. The literature-based curriculum includes classic and award-winning literature. The program also provides opportunities for direct teaching of vocabulary and comprehension.

The Reading Express

Authors: Virginia Arnold and Carl Smith.

Grades Covered: Kindergarten through 8. There are 14 levels, which include three preprimary levels.

Basic Materials: Kindergarten kit, pupils' books, practice materials including workbooks, reteaching skills practice books, readiness tests at the kindergarten level, placement tests from preschool on, unit tests for all levels, mid-year and end-year tests, phonics inventory for levels 4 through 8, and teacher's editions. The following supplementary materials are available: teaching charts, and parent–child activity materials for all levels. The following computer software is also available: *Reading Express Computer Management System* and *Reading Express Computer-Assisted Instruction.*

Comments: The series is based on the premise that success in reading depends on three steps. Step 1 is preparation for reading in which phonics, vocabulary, and comprehension skills are taught. In Step 2, comprehension and appreciation of the literal and interpretive versions of the material read receive attention. In Step 3, additional skill instructions are provided; this is followed by enrichment and maintenance activities. *Reading Express* also provides high-interest, low-vocabulary materials for the at-risk student. Consequently, the program can be used in remedial and special education classes.

Address: Information about both *Connections* and *Reading Express* can be obtained from Macmillan–McGraw Hill School Publishing Co., Font and Brown Street, Riverside, NJ 08075-1197.

D.C. HEATH: BASAL READING PROGRAM (1991)

Authors: Donna Alvermann, Connie Bridge, Scott Paris, Barbara Schmidt, Lyndon Searfoss, and Peter Winograd.

Grades Covered: Kindergarten through Grade 8. There are 14 levels.

Basic Materials: Pupils' books, workbooks from preprimer to Grade 8; Heath reading libraries from Grades 1 through 8, shared literature collections, writing portfolios for Grades 1 through 8, spelling workshops, handbooks for grammar, spelling, and handwriting, language enrichment program, skill pads to reinforce skills learned, and teacher's editions. Additional materials include "big story books," and audio–video cassettes designed to improve listening skills and stimulate discussions. "Home flyers" that can be useful in enlisting parental involvement are also included. The assessment materials include unit tests, placement tests which test oral and silent reading, criterion-referenced diagnostic tests, cumulative record folders, and class record forms. The series also includes *Heath Reading Creative Assessment* which is an informal assessment instrument. Included in the series are the software programs *Read, Write and Publish* and an achievement monitoring system. Reading inservice videos are available from readiness level to Grade 8.

Comments: The Heath series is designed to support a literate environment and help children go "beyond the basal." Writing is introduced along with reading as early as the first grade. The series has incorporated some of the recent trends in teaching reading such as *cooperative learning* and *flexible grouping.* An attempt is made to teach skills in the context of literature, not in isolation. Decoding is taught by introducing consonants, vowels, blends, digraphs, structural analysis, context clues, and syllable patterns. Some of the strategies that are taught with a view to developing comprehension skills are the following: identifying the main idea, recognizing cause–effect and compare–contrast relationships, drawing conclusions, predicting outcomes, and distinguishing between fact and opinion. The series also makes provision for the teaching of study skills.

Address: D.C. Heath Co., 125 Spring Street, Lexington, MA 02173.

SCOTT FORESMAN: BASAL READING PROGRAM (1989)

Authors: Richard Allington, Camile Blachowicz, Ronald Cramer, Patricia Cunningham, Sam Sebesta, and Robert Tierney. The instructional consultant is John Manning, and the program consultants are Jesus Cortez and Robert Slavin.

Grades Covered: Kindergarten through Grade 8. There are 13 levels.

Basic Materials: Pupils' books and independent practice books for all levels, language activity books, and an anthology of literature for Grades 1 through 6. In addition, there are teacher's editions and teacher's resource files which include tests, activity masters, and thinking-skills masters. The series has placement tests, quarter tests and end-of-the-book tests. The formal tests were field tested for a year to establish their validity and reliability. The series also includes placement tests, informal reading inventories, and student profile sheets. *Write Connection* is a word-processing software which can help children in writing, proofreading, and revising. The series also comes with a computer management system which can provide information on test results, students' current mastery levels, individual and class progress, and prescription for mastery of skills for individual students.

Skills Stressed: Some of the major skills this series aims to develop are as follows: the ability to comprehend through gathering information, construct meaning, evaluate and make judgments, think analytically and inferentially, and an ability to read content area texts. Appreciation and understanding of literature is also stressed. Vocabulary and word-recognition skills are developed through phonological awareness and structural analysis of words. The series also has provisions for promoting study skills such as locating information and interpreting graphic data.

Comments: The publishers of this series believe that reading is a process of constructing meaning from written text through an interaction between the reader's skills and the text. The Scott Foresman series regards their basal reading program to be an aid in accomplishing this goal. The publishers realize that language arts—reading, writing, listening, and speaking—is an integral part of the curriculum. Even though the program says that literature is the heart of the reading program, it realizes that children should develop appropriate skills and strategies.

Address: Scott, Foresman & Co., 1900, East Lake Avenue, Glenview, IL 60025.

HOUGHTON MIFFLIN: THE LITERATURE EXPERIENCE (1991)

Authors: The senior advisor for the series is Richard Anderson. Authors are John Pikulski, Kathryn Au, William Durr, Karen Wixson, Jana Mason, and William Nagy.

Grades Covered: Kindergarten through Grade 8. There are 16 levels.

Basic Materials: The series includes "big books" for children in kindergarten and Grade 1 and theme books for children in Grades 1 through 8. In addition, there are "read-along library" materials and "read-along tapes." The program also has video cassettes and related materials designed to improve spelling and vocabulary. Similar to other basal reader series, *Literature Experience* also has teachers' guide books, teachers' handbooks, and theme book plans. There is also a "journal" which contains theme projects. Additional materials include spelling lists, independent reading log, and student handbook. Assessment is done through formal and informal tests as well as by examining samples of students' work. There is also a teacher evaluation booklet.

Skills Stressed: The philosophy of beginning reading instruction of this series is that as children are read to repeatedly, they begin to develop independent reading skills. The orientation of the series as well as its title, "Literature Experience," brings it close to the *Whole Language* philosophy. However, beginning at the first grade, children are given practice in phonics, vocabulary development, and other skills that are necessary to learn how to read and write. Phonics is primarily taught through an analytic approach.

Comments: As just mentioned, this series comes closer to *whole language* than the other basal reader series we have discussed so far. Nevertheless, it does cover phonics and other skills. It takes a wholistic approach to the teaching of reading and, as such, does not stress the sequence in which skills are to be taught.

Address: Houghton Mifflin Co., One Beacon Street, Boston, MA 02108.

SILVER BURDETT & GINN: THE WORLD OF READING (1991)

Authors: Theodore Clymer, David Pearson, Dale Johnson, Elfrieda Hiebert, Roselmina Indrisano, Richard Venezky, James Baumann, and Carl Grant.

Grades Covered: Kindergarten through Grade 8. There are 14 levels.

Basic Materials: The *World of Reading* contains student books and student texts. These texts contain stories selected from classical and contemporary literature. There is also a set of books that comes in a "trunk," which consists of paperback books, trade books, bookshelf activity cards, lit box, game cards, and a teacher handbook with instructions for using the "trunk." A magazine called *Reading Journal* which contains activities designed to promote creative and critical thinking is also included in the series. A unique feature of the series is the *Interactive Teaching Kit,* which contains videos of drama and author interviews, audios of music and poetry, and posters of art and photography. Additional materials include workbooks which consist of interest inventory, book logs, and checkpoints which can be used for informal assessment. Teacher editions have unit lesson organizers and resource kits which could be used to develop activities that promote motivation and creativity. These kits provide suggestions for integrating the language arts curriculum and meeting individual needs. Realizing the importance of parental involvement in reading, the series has "Home connection letters," which are sample letters that show how to make contact with families.

This series has provisions for both formal and informal assessment. Formal testing is done by using placement tests, unit process tests, and unit skills tests. The series also provides management tools to track students' progress. The software program *School Curriculum Manager,* can score tests, maintain results, generate reports on student, class, or school performance and recommend activities to address the needs of slow learners.

Skills Stressed: The publishers have three beliefs about reading: (1) reading is the freedom to explore the ideas of all people and the freedom to participate fully in our society; (2) reading is a conversation between the reader and the author, and (3) teaching of reading begins with the child, the child's language, and his/her own experience. This series makes provision for phonics instruction during the early years. Word-recognition skills are developed through letter formation, invented spelling, decoding activities and by means of practice in structural analysis of words. According to the authors, phonics lessons are structured in a reliable, systematic pattern and are imparted through direct instruction. Vocabulary is developed through direct methods as well as through the use of context, concepts, and techniques such as semantic mapping.

Writing about Reading incorporates the writing component. It emphasizes content, clarity, accuracy, style, and the mechanics of writing. The series also incorporates oral language activities as well as integrated language arts activities. These are in the form of language study, oral rereading, writing, and understanding and appreciating literature. Provisions are available for incorporating recently developed comprehension strategies such as *reciprocal teaching, cooperative learning,* and *peer tutoring.* The series also suggests instructional strategies that can be of help to at-risk students.

Comments: The *World of Reading* series draws on current research in teaching reading and stresses both word recognition skills and comprehension skills.

Address: Silver Burdett & Ginn, P.O. Box 2649, 4343 Equity Drive, Columbus, OK 43216.

APPENDIX II

Review of Selected Reading Tests

There is a large number of tests that are designed to assess reading ability. In spite of their large number, or perhaps because of it, these tests differ from each other in many respects and no two tests are alike. Tests differ from each other in many respects: the rigor with which they have been standardized, the kind of information they provide, and the manner by which this information is obtained. All these factors are to be kept in mind while interpreting the obtained test scores. The school psychologist–consultant may keep the following questions in mind when interpreting test results.

1. Is the test a standardized instrument or is it an informal inventory? If it is standardized,
   a. how valid is it?
   b. how reliable is it?
   c. does it give age norms, grade norms, and different norms for boys and girls? does it provide standard scores and percentiles?
   d. how long does it take to administer and score the test?
   e. what is the price of the test?
   f. does it have computer software backing?

If it is an informal inventory, is there any information about its face validity and reliability?

2. Is the test norm-referenced or criterion referenced, or both?
3. Is the test individually administered, or group-administered?
4. Is it a reading achievement, diagnostic, or aptitude test?
5. If it is a reading test,
   a. is it a silent reading test, or an oral reading test?
   b. does it assess word recognition skills and comprehension skills?
   c. does it assess both literal and inferential comprehension?
   d. is it a timed or an untimed test?

ACHIEVEMENT TESTS

There are several achievement tests which have, as part of the battery, a test of reading skill. Since most of the achievement tests are administered as group tests, they can assess only silent reading skills. Some of the commonly adminis-tered standardized achievement tests that have a reading component are the following: *California Achievement Test, Stanford Achievement Test, Metropolitan Achievement Test,* and *Iowa Test of Basic Skills.* Most of these tests could be considered as both norm-referenced and criterion-referenced. Many of these tests could be administered from first grade on. As noted earlier, reading skills of children in the first grade cannot be evaluated with precision; even if quantitative data are obtained, they cannot be interpreted objectively.

The above-mentioned tests are fairly widely used and have good reputation. In addition to these tests, school practitioners also use two other achievement tests: *Peabody Individual Achievement Test* (Revised) (PIAT-R) and *Wide Range Achievement Test* (Revised) (WRAT-R). PIAT-R (Markwardt, 1989) could be administered to children from kindergarten through 12th grade and is a norm-referenced test. It has the following six subtests: mathematics, reading recognition, reading comprehension, spelling, general information and written expression. We think it is a fairly well standardized test. The 1989 revised version has not been reviewed in the *Buros Mental Measurement Yearbook.* On the other hand, *Wide Range Achievement Test* (Revised) (WRAT-R; Jastak & Wilkinson, 1984) should be used cautiously. It has two levels: Level I, for ages 5-0 to 11-11, and Level II for 12-0 to 14. It measures reading, spelling, and arithmetic. Reading scores are obtained by asking the individual to read a list of words in isolation. Reading is much more than pronouncing words in isolation; comprehension is not measured by this test. Further, we could not find much information about the selection of the test materials. For instance, in the section of spelling tests, there is no information on the orthographic nature of words, whether the words follow regular grapheme–phoneme conversion rules or not (regular, exception or strange words), the frequency of words (high frequency or low frequency), grapheme–phoneme rules (hard /c/ vs. soft /c/, hard /g/ vs. soft /g/, etc.). *WRAT-R* is reviewed in the *Ninth Mental Measurement Yearbook,* by Elaine Clark and by Patti Harrison. We concur with Harrison's statement about this test: "Using the *WRAT-R* for screening may result in a great disservice to students" (p. 244).

SILENT READING TESTS

Gates–MacGinitie Reading Tests (1989)

Authors: Walter H. MacGinitie and Ruth K. MacGinitie.

Age/Grades Covered: Kindergarten to 12; there are two forms, K & L.

Publishers: Riverside Publishing Company.

Time Required: Generally, about 20 minutes for vocabulary and 35 minutes for comprehension.

Description: Silent reading achievement is measured through vocabulary and comprehension. There are about 45 questions on each of the vocabulary and comprehension portions, which are presented in a multiple-choice format.

Comments: The *Gates–MacGinitie* test is a fairly well-standardized test and easy to use. The 1989 edition is too new to be reviewed in the *Buros Mental Measurement Yearbook*. The 1978 edition of this test is reviewed in the *Ninth Mental Measurement Yearbook* by Robert Calfee and William Rupley. Both reviewers say that it is quite useful as a survey test of reading achievement.

Silent reading achievement can be measured with many of the school achievement tests. For the school practitioner, however, we would recommend the *Gates–MacGinitie Reading Tests*.

ORAL READING TESTS

Slossan Oral Reading Test (SORT) (1981)

For a quick survey of reading level, the *Slossan Oral Reading Test* could be used. It has 10 lists ranging from primer to high school level and each list has twenty words. The pupil is asked to read the list orally, and when he/she takes more than 5 seconds to pronounce the word, it is considered "incorrect" or that the word is not in his/her sight vocabulary. Again, it should be noted that this is a survey test which estimates the approximate grade level and should be used and interpreted accordingly. It has the same problem the *WRAT*-R has; that is, both tests do not measure reading comprehension.

Probably, the two most widely used oral reading achievement tests are the *Gray Oral Reading* and *Gilmore Oral Reading* tests. Since they measure oral reading, they have to be administered individually. When the pupil reads the passages, errors (also called miscues or deviations from print) such as mispronunciations, substitutions (reading "house" for "home"), additions, reversals (reading "was" for "saw"), and omissions, are noted.

Gray Oral Reading Test (Revised) (GORT-R) (1986)

Authors: J. Lee Wiederholt and Brian R. Bryant.

Ages Covered: 6 years and 6 months to 17 years and 11 months.

Time Required: Approximately 15 to 30 minutes to administer and score.

Description: GORT-R Consists of 13 increasingly difficult passages followed by five comprehension questions in each passage; it has two equivalent forms—A and B. The test measures oral reading rate and accuracy, oral reading comprehension, and oral reading ability. Errors such as substitutions, omissions, reversals, and insertions are also scored.

The *GORT-R* is reviewed in the *Tenth Mental Measurement Yearbook* (1989) by Julia Hickman and Robert Tierney. While Hickman supports the use of this test for diagnosing reading difficulties despite some minor limitations, Tierney questions the use of the test due to the fact that the test constructors have not taken into consideration the recent reading research findings.

Gilmore Oral Reading Test (1968)

Authors: John V. Gilmore and Eunice C. Gilmore.

Ages/Grades Covered: Grades 1 through 8.

Publishers: Harcourt Brace Jovanovich.

Time Required: 15 to 30 minutes for administration and scoring.

Description: The format and scoring of the *Gilmore Oral Reading Test* are very similar to the revised *Gray Oral Reading Test*. Students answer comprehension questions after reading the passages orally. Similar to *Gray Oral Reading Test*, errors such as omissions, substitutions, and reversals are scored.

The *Gilmore Oral Reading Test* was reviewed in the *Seventh Mental Measurement Yearbook* by Albert J. Harris and Kenneth J. Smith. Even though both reviewers question the validity of this test, Harris says that this is the "best standardized test of accuracy in oral reading" (p. 737).

So far, we have seen reading achievement tests which tell us how much the students have learned from previous experience. However, to find out the strengths and weaknesses of individual students, diagnostic tests should be used. Diagnostic tests measure various reading skills and hence take longer to administer and score. Three diagnostic tests are reviewed here.

DIAGNOSTIC READING TESTS

Woodcock Reading Mastery Tests (Revised) (1987)

Authors: Richard W. Woodcock.

Age/Grade Covered: Kindergarten to college level, and adults up to 75 years of age.

Publishers: American Guidance Services.

Time Required: About 60 to 90 minutes for administration and scoring.

Description: WRMT-R is an individually administered test and has six subtests that measure three components: the readiness component is measured by means of Letter Identification and Visual-Auditory learning; decoding is measured through Word Identification and Word-Attack Tests; comprehension is measured through Word Comprehension and Passage Comprehension. It has two forms, G and H. Several types of scores can be obtained such as grade equivalents, relative performance indices (RPI), age equivalents, percentile ranks, instructional ranges, and standard scores. Additionally, several profiles portraying strengths and weaknesses can be developed through this test. They are percentile rank profile, instructional level profile (to help develop instructional materials ranging from easy to difficult), and separate diagnostic profiles for readiness, basic skills, and comprehension. The attractive features of this test are the computer program called ASSIST for scoring, and detailed explanations for interpreting the performance of individuals.

Comments: WRMT-R is reviewed in the *Tenth Mental Measurement Yearbook* (1989) by Robert Cooter and Richard Jaeger. Both reviewers suggest this test be used with caution. In fact, this should be true for all of the tests. However, considering the fact that there are not too many diagnostic reading tests, we recommend WRMT-R highly for diagnosing reading problems.

Stanford Diagnostic Reading Test (SDRT) (1984)

Authors: B. Karlsen & E. Gardner.

Ages/Grades Covered: There are four levels, with two forms (G and H) in each level:

   Red level—end of Grade 1 to low achievers in Grade 3
   Green level—Grades 3, 4, and low achievers in Grade 5
   Brown level—grades 5 to 8 and low achieving high school students
   Blue level—end of eighth grade through college level

Publishers: The Psychological Corporation, San Antonio, Texas

Time Required: About 90 minutes for administration and scoring.

Description: SDRT is a group-administered, norm- and criterion-referenced test. Three important components of reading skills, namely, decoding, vocabulary, and comprehension, are included in all the levels: In the Brown and Blue levels, the fourth component, rate of reading is also included. Generally, decoding skills are measured through phonetic analysis and structural analysis of words. Vocabulary skills are measured by asking students to select words that best fit the context. (At the Red level, pictures have to be selected instead of the words.) Comprehension skills are measured through several means: sentence reading, paragraph comprehension, and both literal and inferential comprehension. Textual reading, functional reading, and recreational reading are used as part of comprehension skills at the Brown and Blue levels. Rate of reading is measured through "scanning and skimming" and through "fast reading" at the Blue level.

Five different statistics could be computed indirectly from obtained scores. These are percentile ranks, scaled scores, grade equivalents, stanines and progress indicators, which are criterion scores to show whether the student has mastered a specific skill or not. The manual also presents some instructional recommendations based on test performance.

Comments: According to Salvia and Ysseldyke (1991), this test is "exceptionally well standardized and is reliable enough to be used in pinpointing specific domains of reading in which pupils demonstrate skill-development strengths and weaknesses" (p. 405). We support this statement, even though, *Woodcock Reading Mastery Test* (Revised) could also be used as a diagnostic tool, since it is more recently standardized and can provide a reading–comprehension measure which is not confounded by time constraints.

Gates–McKillop–Horowitz Reading Diagnostic Test (1981)

Authors: Authur I. Gates, Anne S. McKillop, and Elizabeth Cliff Horowitz.

Ages/Grades Covered: Grades 1 through 6.

Publishers: Teachers College Press.

Time to Administer: Depends, as the examiner has to decide which subtests to administer.

Description: This is an individually administered test consisting of 14 subtests, and it provides 23 scores. Some of the subtests are Oral Reading; Auditory Blending; Auditory Discrimination. Word-attack skills are measured through syllabication, and blending. Written expression is measured through spelling and informal writing samples. Similar to *Gray Oral Reading Test* and *Gilmore Oral Reading Test*, errors in oral reading, such as omissions, repetitions, insertions, substitutions, reversals, and mispronunciations, are also noted. The individual is evaluated by means of grade scores as well as examiner's opinion.

Comments: Salvia and Ysseldyke (1991) mention that this test is a widely used diagnostic instrument despite serious limitations. It is reviewed by Priscilla A. Drum, and by P. David Pearson and Patricia Herman (1988) in the *Ninth Mental Measurement Yearbook*. We agree with the reviewers that the information about the validity, reliability, norms, and item selection are unsatisfactory. This is further confounded by the informal evaluation of some of the subskills by the examiner. This could be very subjective.

Other commonly available diagnostic tests are *Durrell Analysis of Reading Difficulty* (Durrell & Catterson, 1980) and *Diagnostic Reading Scales (Spache,* 1981). Even though the school practitioner has to use standardized tests, many times he/she will have to supplement this information from diagnostic tests with informal diagnosis. This is what we will turn to next.

INFORMAL TESTS

Informal tests in reading are generally referred to as *Informal Reading Inventories* or *IRIs*. They have only face validity (i.e., the reading materials are generally taken at face value and lack measures of validity, reliability and norms). The IRIs should be used for screening purposes only, not for placement. Generally, IRIs provide independent, instructional, and frustration reading measures on word recognition, comprehension, and hearing capacity/listening comprehension. (Independent level is the level at which the child can read without outside help; instructional level is that at which the child can read only with outside help; and frustration level is the level at which the child cannot read even with outside help.) Although there are several IRIs available, we will review two that are commonly used.

Classroom Reading Inventory (Fifth Edition) (1986)

Author: Nicholas J. Silvaroli.

Ages/Grades Covered: Grade 1 to Adult.

Publisher: William C. Brown.

Time Required: There is no fixed time limit.

Description: CLI consists of graded word lists and graded passages that measure word recognition and comprehension, respectively. Comprehension questions are both factual and inferential. Instructional level is indicated when the individual scores at least 95% on word recognition and 75% on comprehension. Both silent reading and oral reading skills are measured, and an optional spelling test is also included.

Comments: The fourth edition (1982) is reviewed by Ira Aaron and Sylvia Carter, and by Janet Norris, in the *Ninth Mental Measurement Yearbook*. All reviewers cautiously recommend the use of this test. For instance, Aaron and Carter say that "overall, the CRI is a useful tool in the hands of knowledgeable teachers" (p. 38), while Norris mentions that "as a quick inventory, it can provide the teacher with information about an individual child that is not available from achievement test scores or group reading activities" (p. 40).

Informal Reading Inventory (1989)

Authors: Paul C. Burns Betty D. Roe.

Ages/Grades Covered: Preprimer to 12th Grade.

Publisher: Houghton-Mifflin.

Time Required: There is no fixed time limit.

Description: Similar to CRI, this test has graded word lists and graded passages to measure word recognition and comprehension. Since oral reading is measured, this is an individually administered test. Silent reading and listening comprehension scores can also be obtained from this test, although they are optional. Instructional level is indicated if the pupil scores 85–95% on word recognition, at the Grade 1 and 2 levels, and 95–98% at Grades 3 through 12, and 75–89% on comprehension.

Comments: The second edition published in 1985 is reviewed in the *Tenth Mental Measurement Yearbook* (1989) by Carolyn Murphy & Roger Bruning, and by Edward Shapiro. All reviewers suggest this IRI be used with caution. For instance, Murphy and Bruning say that it provides "a relatively quick source of information about problems students may be experiencing with reading" (p. 16), while Shapiro says the information from this IRI "would be particularly valuable as an adjunct assessment measure for reading specialists or classroom teachers" (p. 118).

Other informal reading inventories available are the following: *Analytical Reading Inventory* (Woods & Moe, 1989), *Basic Reading Inventory* (Johns, 1988), and *Ekwall Reading Inventory* (Ekwall, 1986). Generally, all of them use graded word lists and graded passages to measure vocabulary and comprehension. Since the emphasis is on oral reading, they all have to be individually administered. Additionally, silent reading and spelling tests are included as optional measures. These IRIs provide measures of independent, instructional and frustration levels of reading ability that can help the teacher select appropriate reading levels.

APPENDIX III

Phonological Awareness Test I

The Phonological Awareness Test I (adapted from Stanovich, Cunningham, & Cramer, 1984) can be useful with preschool children and those in elementary grades suspected of having reading disability.

Note to Examiner: When needed, use the phoneme value (sound) of the letter and not the letter name. For example, the first phoneme in *cat* is /k/ and not "c."

1. Final phoneme same:

Instruction: Can you repeat the word *meat?* With what sound does the word end? /t/, right? What does the word *bean* end with? The sound /n/. Let's try again. What does the word *meat* end with? Now, if I say three words, can you say which of the words ends with the sound /t/?: *fin, coat, glass.* The word *coat* ends with the sound /t/. Now if I say *meat* and then *fin, coat, glass,* which word would you say has the same ending sound as *meat?* If I say *ball* and then say *book, doll,* and *run,* which word ends like *ball?*

1. WORM: warm, wall, ball   2. CUP: car, cap, can
3. PAN: pat, run, gum   4. BEAT: boy, girl, wet
5. LEAF: deaf, love, seed   6. BUD: red, blue, green
7. HOUSE: home, school, base   8. HOOK: rock, pencil, note
9. NAIL: wood, not, tall   10. BUG: but, hut, leg

2. Substitute initial phoneme:

Instruction: If I say the word *go,* and then change the first sound to /n/ the new word will be *no.* If I said the word *tall,* can you change the word by changing the first sound? *(ball).* If I say *man* what will you say? (ran). Now try these words.

1. TOP   2. BELL   3. LIP   4. FED   5. GUN
6. SICK   7. PIN   8. CAT   9. SAP   10. CUT

3. Initial phoneme not same:

(This test is similar to No. 7 except for the instructions).

Instruction: I am going to say a word aloud followed by three more words. Your task is to tell me which word does not begin with the same sound as the first word. I will say the word *mud* and then say the words *mice, dig,* and *mouth.* Can you tell me which word did not have the same beginning sound as *mud?* *(dig).* Now I say the word *run;* and then say, *rain, gun, ran,* and *rat.* Which word starts with a different sound?. Now, try these.

1. BOY: ball, bun, barn, girl
2. DOLL: tall, drum, dance, drink
3. SUN: sat, fan, sit, sing
4. KITE: kiss, kent, kill, neat
5. MAN: mean, men, boy, much
6. NEST: bell, neat, not, nine
7. FISH: fine, far, dog, five
8. TRAIN: trash, horse, trip, tram
9. PIE: fine, paper, pot, pepper
10. LAMP: luck, dump, lake, love

4. Supply initial phoneme:

Instruction: You will be hearing two words that are the same except for the beginning sound. You have to tell what sound is missing from the second word. If I say *cat*, and *at* what sound is missing from the second word that is in *cat*? (/K/). If I say *bat* and *at* what is missing in the second word? (/b/). If I say *ran* and *an* what is missing? (/r/). Now try these.

1. MEAL—EEL   2. FILL—ILL   3. SIT—IT
4. LAND—AND   5. DATE—ATE   6. NEAR—EAR
7. PAIR—AIR   8. BEND—END   9. TASK—ASK
10. CAN'T—ANT

$\bar{X}$ for beginning 2nd grade = 33.08
SD for beginning 2nd grade = 1.72

The above four tests constitute the test battery. The following phoneme awareness tests can be used for additional testing or for training purposes.

5. Rhyme supply:

Instruction: I will say a word and you will say a word that sound like it. If I say *fish* you are supposed to say *dish*. If I say *gun* what will you say? [If the S does not say a rhyming word, tell him *run* rhymes with *gun*.] Let's try again. If I say *silk* what will you say? *(milk).* I am going to say some words and you are going to say words that rhyme with them. O.K.?

1. Nose   2. Pup   3. Tie   4. Toy   5. Hill   6. Wing   7. Mouse   8. Tip
9. Note   10. Look

6. Rhyme choice:

Instruction: I am going to say one word first and then say three more words. You have to say which of the three words rhymes with the first word. For example, I say first *pet;* then I say *barn, net, hand.* Which word rhymes with *pet?* (If the child fails to understand, repeat the example; then give another example; *cat: ball, milk, rat*).

1. STAR: car, run, sun
2. MOP: milk, top, gun
3. GREEN: screen, play, house
4. PLANE: prime, dream, crane
5. CROWN: brown, green, yellow
6. FLASH: Irish, trash, flush
7. CAKE: ran, rake, rash
8. JUMP: pump, tall, dip
9. BOX: fix, mix, fox
10. JEEP: boy, deep, bell

7. Initial phoneme same:

Instruction: I am going to say a word. Listen to the first sound of the word. If I say *ball*, what is the first sound you hear? /ba/, that is right. If I say *foot*, what sound do you hear? Now, I will say a word and then say three more words. You will have to say which of the three words starts with the same sound as the first one. Here are some examples. Run: ball, gun, rat. What is the answer? *rat;* because *run* and *rat* begin with the sound /r/. Now let's try again. BELL: well, ball, tell; *ball* is the right answer. Let's try one more. CALL: yell, caught, tall, ball.

1. MILK: mix, click, drink   2. PEAR: pat, rat, rare   3. FAN: ran, man, fat
4. BONE: boat, home, done 5. SOAP: rope, sole, real 6. TENT: tell, call, mint
7. LEG: peg, let, got   8. DUCK: luck, bird, dull   9. NEST: best, yell, neat
10. KEY: lock, kiss, love

8. Strip initial phoneme:

Instruction: Listen to the word I say. The word is *task*. If you take away the /t/ sound, what word is left? *(ask)*. If the word is *ball* and you take away the first sound, what word is left? *(all)*. Now let us try these words.

1. PINK	2. TOLD	3. MAN	4. NICE	5. WIN
6. BUS	7. PITCH	8. CAR	9. FIT	10. POUT

9. Initial phoneme different.

Instruction: Listen to these four words: *bag, nine, beach, bike.* Can you tell me which one of the following words has a different beginning sound—*bag, nine, beach, bike? (Nine).* Now listen to these words: *ran, man, rat,* and *rain: (Man).* Now try these words.

1. EAR: den, eat, elm, end
2. POP: pup, pulp, cap, pen
3. HILL: hen, hat, house, ball
4. BAND: bend, bike, hind, but
5. ARM: germ, all, aunt, autumn
6. GIVE: gun, dive, get, gather
7. VAN: very, vary, run, varnish
8. CART: call, calm, cat, doll
9. RICE: roll, wheat, ring, rich
10. TEETH: teacher, tall, tree, mouth

10. Final phoneme different:

Instruction: I am going to say four words. One of them ends with a different sound than the other three words. For example, *rat, dime, boat,* and *mitt.* Can you tell me which word has a different sound at its end? *(Dime).* Let's try some more: *can, pan, man, boy.* Can you tell me which word ends with a different sound?; *(boy).* One more trial: *log, pen, bag, dig.* Can you say which word ends with a different sound?; *(pen).* Now we have some more.

1. HAM: gum, rim, dim, sun
2. CUP: dip, dog, lap, flip
3. LEAF: deaf, lean, puff, roof
4. FLAG: flat, rug, big, mug
5. DRESS: mess, dream, miss, bus
6. WRIST: twist, ring, best, last
7. BALL: hill, fell, bell, band
8. HAND: ham, end, mind, wind
9. RAIN: sun, tan, moon, raid
10. DESK: best, back, rack, clock

APPENDIX IV

Reading and Spelling Tests

READING TEST: WORDS

Name_____ **Grade**_____

Instruction: "Read aloud these 38 words as carefully as you can."

1. dog	11. changes	21. strong	30. became
2. cat	12. discover	22. cold	31. green
3. pages	13. edge	23. bring	32. children
4. chance	14. fact	24. center	33. gone
5. larger	15. large	25. eggs	34. cannot
6. special	16. cells	26. certain	35. begin
7. region	17. city	27. sing	36. game
8. decide	18. page	28. coming	37. moving
9. girl	19. having	29. songs	38. audible
10. uncle	20. exceptb3		

READING TEST: NONWORDS

Name_____ **Grade**_____

Instruction: "These are not real words, but read them aloud as best as you can."

1. gare	10. chape	19. gend	28. cilly
2. duncle	11. skar	20. cend	29. cept
3. ract	12. kute	21. grone	30. colp
4. gar	13. gite	22. chind	31. kar
5. bace	14. fedge	23. gen	32. pare
6. recide	15. git	24. pice	33. sute
7. kaces	16. bage	25. tite	34. kare
8. gade	17. ling	26. cad	35. par
9. skare	18. gog	27. dit	36. sut

READING TEST: FUNCTION WORDS

Name_____ **Grade**_____

Note to examiner: The subject is asked to read aloud either List 1 or List 2 (down columns from left to right) depending on his age. Children from Grades 1 to 3 are asked to read List 1. Older children are asked to read List 2.

List 1			List 2		
let	nor	once	every	which	during
has	will	soon	never	since	almost
ago	much	ever	could	ahead	before
off	also	upon	along	should	without
why	must	else	while	except	perhaps
any	even	thus	might	behind	although
yet	such		often	though	

READING TEST: CONTENT WORDS

Name_____ **Grade**_____

Note to examiner: The subject is asked to read aloud either List 1 or List 2 (down columns from left to right) depending on which list of function words he/she read previously.

List 1			List 2		
cat	man	name	water	story	number
run	bird	page	words	place	school
men	gold	work	house	force	things
boy	book	come	world	figure	picture
say	feet	look	three	letter	morning
dog	back	time	sound	family	distance
she	room		think	father	

SPELLING TEST

Note to examiner: Say the target word aloud. Read the corresponding sentence to the subject. Repeat the target word. Then ask the subject to write it down. Only those words the subject had read correctly but misspelled are counted as errors.

1. dog   The dog makes a good pet.   dog
2. cat   The cat is also a pet.   cat
3. pages   There are many pages in the book.   pages
4. chance   He has a chance of winning the game.   chance
5. larger   Jane's house is larger than Bill's.   larger
6. special   Christmas is a very special day.   special
7. region   They live in the northern region of the country.   region
8. decide   You must decide by tomorrow if you can come or not.   decide
9. girl   She is a pretty girl.   girl
10. uncle   You would like my uncle, but not my aunt.   uncle
11. changes   When Bill goes swimming he changes his clothes.   changes
12. discover   Did Columbus discover America?   discover
13. edge   They live on the edge of the town.   edge
14. fact   That is an interesting fact.   fact
15. large   That is a large house, not a small one.   large
16. cells   There are many cells in our body; you have to use a microscope to see them.   cells
17. city   We live in the city, not in a village.   city
18. page   Please turn to the first page of your book.   page
19. having   Jim was having a good time.   having
20. except   I like all kinds of food except spinach.   except
21. strong   Bill is very strong. He is not weak.   strong
22. cold   It is cold outside, but hot inside.   cold
23. bring   Will you bring me my plate?   bring
24. center   He hit it in the center, not outside.   center
25. eggs   I had eggs for breakfast.   eggs
26. certain   Are you certain of that, or are you not sure?   certain
27. sing   I like to sing but not dance.   sing
28. coming   John is coming home tomorrow.   coming
29. songs   He knows many songs and he sings them.   songs
30. became   Jill became a school teacher.   became
31. green   The grass is green.   green
32. children   Parents have children.   children
33. gone   He must have gone home.   gone
34. cannot   I cannot answer that question.   cannot
35. begin   We will begin a new lesson tomorrow.   begin
36. game   Basketball is a fun game.   game
37. moving   They are moving to their new house.   moving
38. audible   If the speech is audible you can hear it.   audible

TEST LESSONS IN READING*

Note to examiner: Ask the child to read aloud the two lists of words that corresponds to the grade he is in.

Next day ask the child to read aloud the two corresponding
passages. For example, a second grader reads lists of words
2A and 2B; the next day, he reads passages 2A and 2B. For
higher levels, see reference below.[†]

List 2A

home	to	walk	did	were
every	was	went	father	wanted
help	Betty	his	day	he
fed	birds	very	boy	what
happy	mother	brothers	dog	going
at	house	night	good	the
she	sun	Jimmy		

List 2B

crack	it	hear	called
stop	friends	to	do
just	day	something	his
thank	he	up	have
wagon	very	every	with
away	ride	asked	what
birthday	mother	too	happy
all	surprise	man	is
then	did	you	went
go	fast	this	was
man	wanted	Billy	here
please	not	for	

Passage 2A

Jimmy was a good boy at home. He wanted to help every day. Jimmy fed his dog.
Jimmy was very, very happy at home.

Betty was a good girl at home. She wanted to help every day. She fed the birds.
Betty was very happy at home.

Jimmy's mother was a friend at home. Jimmy's father was a friend at home.
They wanted to help every day. This was what they did. They were very happy at
home.

*From *Standard Test Lessons in Reading* by W. McCall and L. Crabbs, 1926, New York:
Bureau of Publications, Teachers College Press. Copyright 1926 by Teachers College,
Columbia University. Reprinted by permission.
[†]Miller, G. R., & Coleman, E. B. (1967). A set of thirty-six passages calibrated for complex-
ity. *Journal of Verbal Learning and Verbal Behavior, 6*:851–854.

Betty's mother and father were good friends at home. They wanted to help every day. This was what they did. They were very happy at home.

Jimmy's father was going home for the night. Jimmy's brothers were going home for the night. Jimmy went to the house for the night. Mother was very happy to see them. The sun was going down.

Walk, walk, Betty's father was going home for the night.

Passage 2B
Billy was very happy every day. This was Billy's birthday. He was very, very happy. His mother called him and said, "Billy, I have a surprise for you."

"A surprise, Mother! What is it?" asked Billy. "What is it?" "Here it is," said Billy's mother, "a wagon. Do not go away from home. Do not go too fast with it."

Billy was very, very happy. He did not hear his mother. He did not stop to thank her. Away he went to find his friends.

Billy's friends all wanted to ride. Away they went very fast. Just then a man called, "Stop! Please do not go too fast!" Billy did not hear the man. He went on and on.

Then Billy went away, very fast. He went so fast he could not stop. Just then something went, "Crack, crack, crack, crack, crack." Billy went down. His friends went up, up, up.

APPENDIX V

A Parent's Guide to Dyslexia

"My son has dyslexia; can I have him tested?" This is one of the most common requests school psychology clinics receive. The very nature of the question shows that many parents (as well as teachers) have misconceptions about dyslexia. If the parent already knows that the child has dyslexia, what is the need for diagnostic testing? The answer is that these parents interpret any sign of reading difficulty as dyslexia and fail to realize that dyslexia represents but one of the several varieties of reading problems. Moreover, they want some form of assurance from the psychologist to confirm the belief that their child is quite intelligent. This shows that parents, in addition to having misconceptions about dyslexia, may also have a "hidden agenda" when they approach the psychology clinic. In the following section, we provide, in nontechnical language, answers to questions the consultant can anticipate from parents and teachers.

1. What is developmental dyslexia?

Developmental dyslexia refers to a condition in which an individual encounters a great deal of difficulty in assigning proper sounds to the written or printed word. This means, the dyslexic individual is not able to decode the written word easily. The inability to assign, quickly and effortlessly, proper pronunciation to a word hampers the reading process. In addition, whenever the dyslexic reader encounters an unfamiliar word, he/she must invest a great deal of effort in deciphering that word. This makes the dyslexic reader forget that part of the sentence he/she had already read. As a result, comprehension is also affected. Poor reading comprehension is, therefore, secondary to poor decoding ability. Dyslexic children can, invariably, comprehend the text much better than their oral reading would indicate. In fact, their listening comprehension for ordinary spoken language is almost always normal. A child who fails to comprehend well both written and spoken language is *not* dyslexic.

The term *Specific Reading Disability*, which is often used as a synonym of dyslexia, captures the essence of the dyslexia syndrome. It implies that the dyslexic child's difficulty is specific or limited to the written language and does not involve spoken language to the same extent.

2. What is the cause of dyslexia?

Dyslexia is caused by a difficulty in converting, either overtly or covertly, the written word into the corresponding spoken form. The ability to convert written language into its spoken equivalent is sometimes referred to as "decoding" skill. It is important to remember that decoding is only a skill and that it is independent of general intelligence. Dyslexic children can, therefore, have normal intelligence; not infrequently they have high IQs.

But why do some children experience decoding difficulty? While we do not have all the answers to this question, cognitive psychology can provide a reasonable explanation. We understand and comprehend the world in two different ways by using two different strategies. These two strategies are labeled as *sequential* and *simultaneous*. When a sequential strategy is used, items are processed one after another. This takes time. Reading a sentence or listening to someone speak involves processing one word at a time, starting at the beginning of the sentence until one reaches the end. Beginning readers are not familiar with many words in their written form. They, therefore, have to analyze unfamiliar words sequentially as letters, digraphs, trigraphs, or syllables. In contrast to sequential processing, the simultaneous strategy is space dependent, and the information is processed all at once, as a single unit. For instance, when we look at a person's face and know who he/she is, we utilize a simultaneous strategy. It is believed, that once a certain level of reading proficiency is reached, written words are recognized by using a simultaneous strategy. Words that can be recognized as single units make up an individual's sight vocabulary. While most people can use these two strategies flexibly and equally well, some individuals tend to depend more on one than the other. When it comes to reading, dyslexic individuals appear to depend more on simultaneous strategy than on sequential strategy. They try to sight-read written words as though they are pictures. While this may work well with familiar words, such a strategy can fail with uncommon words.

This leads us to an important conclusion: dyslexia need not be viewed as a deficit; nor as a dysfunction. It is the result of looking at written language in a particular way and an overuse of the *simultaneous cognitive style,* which may not work well with the written alphabet, but can be effective with nonlinguistic material.

3. What are the symptoms of dyslexia?

The difficulty in converting the printed word into its phonological equivalent manifests itself in more than one symptom. There are four major symptoms which constitute the *syndrome of dyslexia*. These are: slow reading, poor written spelling, omission and substitution of grammar words and suffixes in oral reading, and omission and substitution of grammar words and suffixes in writing.

Contrary to what one may think, spelling a word correctly depends more on pronunciation skill than on visual memory. Similarly, because grammar words lack meaning, an ability to pronounce them helps much in reading, writing, and remembering them. It is not surprising, therefore, that dyslexic children also tend to be poor in spelling; they also use grammar incorrectly.

4. Is it true that dyslexic children see things in reverse?

This is not true; they see things the same way everyone else does.

5. Do dyslexic children have visual–perceptual problems? Can vision training improve their reading skill?

Even though a visual–perceptual hypothesis was popular at one time, a substantial body of research shows that dyslexia is not caused by visual–perceptual problems. Many studies show that, on the contrary, many dyslexic individuals have good or superior visual memory. Faulty eye movements and related visual defects also are not the cause of dyslexia. Vision training and eye-movement training can, therefore, be of little help in dealing with dyslexia. If vision is the problem, dyslexics will have difficulty seeing everything, not just the printed word.

6. Are reversals in writing an indication of dyslexia?

Not necessarily. Studies show that many children reverse letters when they are very young (5, 6, or 7 years of age). Research also shows that many children who reverse letters are good readers and that many children who show no signs of reversals may still be poor readers. In other words, reversals in writing and reading is not a *marker* for dyslexia. When a young child writes letters, words, and numbers in a reversed form, this should cause no alarm.

7. Are left-handed children more likely to be dyslexic than right-handed children?

First, it has to be pointed out that "handedness" is a somewhat elusive concept. Psychologists use terms such as "left-handedness," "mixed-handedness" and "ambidexterity" to describe different forms of hand preference. Since it is often difficult to separate unambiguously left-handed individuals from right-handed individuals, psychologists also use the term "nonright-handedness."

There is more than a casual association between left-handedness and reading difficulty. This relationship, however, lacks predictive ability. That is, we cannot say that a child will experience difficulty in learning to read because he/she is left-handed; nor can it be ensured that a child will learn to read with ease because he/she is right-handed.

8. Is it true that dyslexia runs in families?

Even though the answer to this question is "yes," it has to be qualified. Many research studies show that some families have an unusually high number of members with reading difficulties. The actual pattern of genetic inheritance, however, is not reliably established. It is, therefore, difficult to say whether it is a dominant or recessive trait. We do know, however, that it is not a sex-linked trait. It is also important to remember that familial history of reading problems could also be the result of environmental factors.

9. Why is it that only boys seem to have dyslexia?

The implication of this question (that girls do not have dyslexia) is not quite accurate. More boys reportedly have dyslexia than girls. Nevertheless, there are girls who have dyslexia. The reason for the preponderance of males probably lies with the organization pattern of the brain. The male brain, being exposed to large amounts of testosterone, perhaps becomes adapted to readily utilize the simultaneous strategy. When this tendency is carried to an extreme, the result may be developmental dyslexia. The female brain, not being exposed to a similar amount of testosterone, may become more balanced as far as the two strategies are concerned. A similar explanation is also advanced to explain the unequal ratio seen between the sexes in regard to spatial and language abilities.

10. Is the brain somehow involved in developmental dyslexia?

Of course, the brain is involved in everything we do. Reading is no exception. If the question is whether some form of brain damage is associated with dyslexia, the answer is NO. While it is expected that a structural abnormality in the brain can interfere with learning to read, the reverse need not be true. Some dyslexic individuals are too intelligent for the idea that they have a structurally abnormal brain to be entertained.

A more viable possibility is that dyslexic individuals tend to depend on their right cerebral hemisphere to recognize written words. This neurological explanation is in accordance with the view that dyslexia may be the result of an excessive reliance on the simultaneous information-processing strategy. Interesting even though it might be, this neuropsychological hypothesis has little educational relevance because we do not know how to change cerebral dominance.

11. Do dyslexic children outgrow dyslexia? What is the prognosis?

With proper instruction, all dyslexic children improve in their reading. Dyslexia is not an "all or none phenomenon" (i.e., it is not that you have it or don't have it) but is present in various degrees. For this reason, and because there is a great deal of variation in the intensity and type of remediation utilized, and the amount of reading done by the children, prognostic statements cannot be made with a high degree of accuracy. With proper training, many children improve their decoding skills. Even those who may not make appreciable progress in decoding, can improve their word-recognition skills with a continuous practice of reading. In fact, there is evidence that some historically famous individuals who might have had developmental dyslexia turned out to be avid readers and even accomplished writers (Aaron, Phillips, & Larsen, 1988; Aaron & Guillemard, 1992). Poor spelling, however, almost invariably persists as a residual problem.

12. How can we, as parents, help our dyslexic child?

The only known way for a dyslexic child to progress in learning to read is to read extensively. Even when intense phonics training fails, dyslexic children can become adequate readers, provided they have a substantial sight vocabulary. The size of the sight vocabulary is linked to the amount of reading done by the child. For this reason, parents should give the highest priority to the child's *interest in reading*. Parents, therefore, have to observe certain "do"s and "don't"s. Parents should first recognize that decoding is a skill, and if the child is not proficient in it, it may not be for want of effort. Often dyslexic children have talents in some other areas. Parents can use such "evidence" to bolster the self-image of the child. Parents themselves, by showing interest in reading, can be good role models for their children. Children can be taken to the library and allowed to borrow and read freely the books they like. If the child is tutored, teaching efforts should focus on the improvement of word-recognition skill. But care should be taken to see that it is taught in an interesting and meaningful way. Children should also be encouraged to do much spontaneous writing. They can write stories about their experiences. These stories should *not* be used as a means of improving the child's spelling and grammar. Rather, the child should be applauded for his/her efforts and the thematic value of the story.

Among the "don't"s are practices and policies that can ruin the interest of the child and turn him/her away from reading. While phonics and spelling drills can be expected to produce positive results, carrying them to extremes can alienate the child from reading once and for all. Do not overemphasize the importance of spelling. Do not be surprised if the child has much difficulty in learning to read "little words" such as "was," "the," and "why."

The International Reading Association has published a series of *Parent Brochures* which focus on concerns of parents and on ways to help their children develop reading skills. Even though not aimed specifically at dyslexic children, these brochures contain suggestions that can be of much help to parents of children with reading disabilities. Some of the titles are:

> *Good Books Make Reading Fun for Your Child;*
> *Studying, a Key to Success—Ways Parents Can Help;*
> *You Can Encourage Your Child to Read;*
> *You Can Help Your Child Connect Reading to Writing;*
> *You Can Use Television to Stimulate Your Child's Reading Habits;* and
> *Your Home Is Your Child's First School.*

Single copies of each brochure are available free upon request with a #10 self-addressed, stamped envelope. Write to:
International Reading Association,
800, Barksdale Rd., Box 8139
Newark, Delaware 19714-8139.

References

Aaron, I., & Carter, S. (1989). Review of Classroom Reading Inventory (4th ed.) In J. C. Conoley & J. J. Kramer (Eds.), *The tenth mental measurements yearbook.* Lincoln, NE: University of Nebraska Press.

Aaron, P. G. (1978). Dyslexia: An imbalance in cerebral information processing strategies. *Perceptual and Motor Skills, 47,* 699–706.

Aaron, P. G. (1982). The neuropsychology of developmental dyslexia. In R. N. Malatesha & P. G. Aaron (Eds.), *Reading disorders: Varieties and treatments.* New York: Academic Press.

Aaron, P. G. (1987). Developmental dyslexia: Is it different from other forms of reading disability? *Annals of Dyslexia, 37,* 109–125.

Aaron, P. G. (1989). *Dyslexia and hyperlexia.* Boston, MA: Kluwer Academics.

Aaron, P. G. (1991). Can reading disabilities be diagnosed without using intelligence tests? *Journal of Learning Disabilities, 24*(3), 178–186.

Aaron, P. G., Bommarito, T., & Baker, C. (1984). The three phases of developmental dyslexia. In R. N. Malatesha & H. A. Whitaker (Eds.), *Dyslexia: A global issue.* The Hague: Martinus Nijhoff.

Aaron, P. G., Olsen, J., & Baker, C. (1985). The dyslexic college student: Is he also dysphasic? *Cognitive Neuropsychology, 2*(2), 115–147.

Aaron, P. G., & Phillips, S. (1986). A decade of research with dyslexic college students: A summary of findings. *Annals of Dyslexia, 36,* 44–66.

Aaron, P. G., Larsen, S., & Phillips, S. (1988). Specific reading disability in historically famous persons. *Journal of Learning Disabilities, 12,* 523–538.

Aaron, P. G. & Joshi, R. M. (Eds.). (1989). *Reading and writing disorders in different orthographic systems.* Boston, MA: Kluwer Academics.

Aaron, P. G. & Simurdak, J. (1989). *Differential diagnosis of reading disabilities without using IQ tests.* Unpublished manuscript, Indiana State University, Blumberg Center for Interdisciplinary Studies in Special Education, Terre Haute.

Aaron, P. G., Franz, S., & Manges, A. (1990). Dissociation between pronunciation and comprehension in reading disabilities. *Reading and Writing: An Interdisciplinary Journal, 3,* 1–22.

Aaron, P. G., & Whitefield, J. (1990). Dysfluency–fluency: Implications for a new cognitive style for reading consultation. *Journal of Reading, Writing, and Learning Disabilities, International, 6*(4), 395–411.

Aaron, P. G., & Baker, C. (1991). *Reading disabilities in college and high school: Diagnosis and management.* Parkton, MD: York Press.

Aaron, P. G., & Simurdak, J. (1991). Reading disorders: Their nature and diagnosis. In J. Obrzut & G. Hynd (Eds.), *Neuropsychological foundations of learning disabilities.* New York: Academic Press.

251

Aaron, P. G. & Guillemard, J. (in press). Artists as dyslexics. In D. Willows, R. Kruk, & G. Corcos (Eds.), *Visual processes in reading and reading disabilities.* Hillsdale, NJ: Erlbaum.

Aaron, P. G., Wleklinski, M., & Wills, C. (in press). Dyslexia as a cognitive style. In R. M. Joshi & C. K. Leong (Eds.). *Differential diagnosis and treatments of reading and writing disorders.* Boston: Kluwer Academics.

Abrams, J. E., & Kaslow, F. (1977). Family stress and the learning disabled child: Intervention and treatment. *Journal of Learning Disabilities, 10,* 86–90.

Adams, M. J. (1990). *Beginning to read: Thinking and learning about print.* Urbana–Champaign, IL: Center for the Study of Reading.

Aitchison, J. (1987). *Words in the mind: An introduction to mental lexicon.* New York: Blackwell.

Alegria, J., Pignot, E., & Morais, J. (1982). Phonetic analysis of speech and memory codes in beginning readers. *Memory and Cognition, 10,* 451–456.

Alexander, J. E. (1988). Developing a meaning vocabulary. In J. Alexander (Ed.), *Teaching reading* (3rd ed.). Glenview, IL: Scott Foresman.

Allen, R., & Allen, C. (1982). *Learning experience activities* (2nd ed.). Boston, MA: Houghton Mifflin.

Allington, M., & McGill–Franzen, A. (1989). School response to reading failure: Chapter I and special education students in Grades 2, 4, and 8. *Elementary School Journal, 89,* 529–542.

Alpert, J. L. (1981). Conceptual bases of mental health consultation in the schools. In M. J. Curtis & J. E. Zins (Eds.), *The theory and practice of school consultation.* Springfield, IL: Thomas.

Altwerger, B., Edelsky, B., & Flores, B. (1987). Whole language: What's new? *The Reading Teacher, 41,* 144–154.

Anderson, J. R. (1990). *Cognitive psychology and its implications.* (3rd ed.). New York: Freeman.

Anderson, R. C., Hiebert, E. H., Scott, J. A., & Wilkinson, A. G. (1985). *On becoming a nation of readers.* Washington, DC: National Institute of Education.

Anderson, T. W. (1982). Functions for school psychologists in community colleges. *Psychology in the Schools, 19,* 221–225.

Anserello, C., & Sweet, T. (1990). Integrating consultation into school psychological service. In E. Cole & J. Siegel (Eds.), *Effective consultation in school psychology.* Toronto: Hoegrefe & Huber.

Aquino, M. R. (1969). The validity of the Miller–Coleman Readability Scale. *Reading Research Quarterly, 4,* 342–357.

Atkinson, R. C. (1972). Ingredients for a theory of instruction. *American Psychologist, 27,* 921–931.

Aukerman, R. C. (1984). *Approaches to reading.* New York: Wiley.

Babcock, N. L., & Pryzwansky, W. B. (1983). Models of consultation: Preferences of educational professionals at five stages of service. *Journal of School Psychology, 21,* 239–246.

Baddeley, A. D. (1966a). The influence of acoustic and semantic similarity on long-term memory for word sequences. *Quarterly Journal of Experimental Psychology, 18,* 302–309.

Baddeley, A. D. (1966b). Short-term memory for word sequences as a function of acoustic, semantic, and form similarity. *Quarterly Journal of Experimental Psychology, 18,* 362–365.

Baker, C. (1984). *Effects of comparison/contrast writing instruction on the reading comprehension of tenth-grade students.* Unpublished doctoral dissertation, Indiana State University, Terre Haute.

Baker, L., & Brown, A. (1984). Metacognitive skills and reading. In P. D. Pearson (Ed.), *Handbook of reading research* (Vol. 1). New York: Longman.

Balajthy, E. (1986). *Microcomputers in reading and language arts.* Engelwood Cliffs, NJ: Prentice Hall.

Beck, I., & McKeown, M. (1991). Conditions of vocabulary acquisition. In R. Barr, M. Kamil, P. Mosenthal, & D. Pearson, (Eds.), *Handbook of Reading Research* (Vol. 2). New York: Longman.

Becker, W. C. (1977). Teaching reading and language to the disadvantaged: What we have learned from field research? *Harvard Educational Review, 47,* 518–543.

Beers, J. (1980). Developmental Strategies of Spelling Competence in Primary School Children. In E. H. Henderson & J. W. Beers (Eds.). *Developmental and cognitive aspects of learning to spell.* Newark, DE: International Reading Association.

Begab, M. J. (1988). Childhood learning disabilities and family stress. In J. I. Arena (Ed.), *Management of the child with learning disabilities.* San Rafael, CA: Academic Therapy.

Benbow, C. (1986). Physiological correlates of extreme intellectual precocity. *Neuropsychologia, 24*(5), 719–725.

Benton, A. L. (1980). Dyslexia: Evolution of a concept. *Bulletin of the Orton Society, 30,* 10–26.

Bereiter, C., & Scarmadalia, M. (1987). Learning about writing from reading. In C. Bereiter & M. Scarmadalia (Eds.), *The psychology of written composition.* Hillsdale, NJ: Erlbaum.

Bergan, J. R. (1977). *Behavioral consultation.* Columbus, OH: Merrill.

Berger, M., & Kennedy, H. (1975). Pseudo-backwardness in children. In R. Eissler (Ed.), *The psychoanalytic study of the child.* New Haven: Yale University Press.

Berger, N. (1978). Why can't Johnny read? Perhaps he is not a good listener. *Journal of Learning Disabilities, 11,* 633–638.

Bergeron, B. (1990). What does the term whole language mean? Constructing a definition from literature. *Journal of Reading Behavior, 22*(4), 301–329.

Berninger, V. W. (1990). Multiple orthographic codes: Key to alternative instructional methodologies for developing the orthographic–phonological connections underlying word identification. *School Psychology Review, 19*(4), 518–533.

Bertelson, P. (1987). *The onset of literacy: Cognitive processes in reading acquisition.* Cambridge, MA: MIT Press.

Bettelheim, B., & Zelan, K. (1982). *On learning to read: The child's fascination with meaning.* New York: Knopf.

Biloine, Y. W. (1968). A new approach to Headstart. *Phi Delta Kappan, XLX*(7), 386–388.

Blachman, B. (1984). Relationship between rapid naming ability and language analysis skills to kindergarten and first-grade achievement. *Journal of Educational Psychology, 76,* 610–622.

Blachman, B. (1988). An alternative classroom reading program for learning-disabled and other low-achieving children. In W. Ellis (Ed.), *Intimacy with language.* Baltimore, MD: The Orton Dyslexia Society.

Blanchard, J. S., Mason, G. E., & Daniel, D. (1987). *Computer application in reading.* Newark, DE: International Reading Association.

Bloomfield, L., & Barnhart, C. (1961). *Let's read: A linguistic approach.* Detroit, MI: Wayne State University Press.

Boder, E. (1973). A diagnostic approach based on three atypical reading–spelling patterns. *Developmental Medicine and Child Neurology, 15,* 663–687.

Boder, E., & Jarrico, S. (1982). *Boder Reading and Spelling Pattern test: A diagnostic screening test for developmental dyslexia.* New York: Grune & Stratton.

Bond, G., & Dykstra, R. (1967). The cooperative research program in first grade reading instruction. *Reading Research Quarterly, 2,* 5–142.

Bos, C. S., & Flip, C. (1982). Comprehension monitoring skills in learning-disabled and average students. In B. Y. Wong (Ed.), *Metacognition and learning disabilities.* Rockville, MD: Aspen Systems.

Bowden, J. H. (1911). Learning to read. *The Elementary School Journal, 12*(1), 21–33.

Bower, G., & Hilgard, E. (1986). *Theories of learning.* Engelwood Cliffs, NJ: Prentice Hall.

Bradley, L. & Bryant, P. (1983). Categorizing sounds and learning to read—A causal connection. *Nature, 301,* 419–421.

Bradley, L., & Bryant, P. (1985). *Rhyme and reason in reading and spelling.* Ann Arbor, MI: University of Michigan Press.

Bradley, L. & Bryant, P. (1987). *Children's reading problems.* Oxford, UK: Blackwell.

Bransford, J., Vye, N., & Stein, B. (1984). A comparison of successful and less successful learners: Can we enhance comprehension and mastery skills? In J. Flood (Ed.), *Promoting reading comprehension.* Newark, DE: International Reading Association.

Bricklin, P. M., & Gallicon, R. (1987). Emotional disturbance. In K. Kavale, B. Forness, & M. Bender (Eds.), *Handbook of learning disabilities.* Boston, MA: Little Brown.

Bronner, A. F. (1917). *The psychology of special abilities and disabilities.* Boston, MA: Little Brown.

Brown, D., Pryzwansky, W. B., & Schulte, A. C. (1987). *Psychological consultation.* Boston, MA: Allyn & Bacon.

Bruck, M., & Waters, G. (1988). An analysis of spelling errors of children who differ in their reading and spelling skills. *Applied Psycholinguistics, 9,* 77–92.

Bryden, M. P. (1982). *Laterality: Functional asymmetry in the intact brain.* New York: Academic Press.

Burns, P., & Roe, B. (1989). *Informal Reading Inventory.* Boston, MA: Houghton Mifflin.

Butler, K. A. (1988). How kids learn: What theorists say. *Learning, 17,* 28–43.

Buxbaum, E. (1964). The parents' role in the etiology of learning disabilities. In R. Eissler (Ed.), *The psychoanalytic study of the child.* New York: International Universities Press.

Byrne, B., & Ledez, J. (1983). Phonological awareness in reading disabled adults. *Australian Journal of Psychology, 35,* 185–197.

Calfee, R. C., Venezky, R. L., & Chapman, R. S. (1969). Pronunciation of synthetic words with predictable and unpredictable letter–sound correspondences (Tech. Rep. No. 11). Research and Development Center, University of Wisconsin, Madison.

Calfee, R. (1985). Review of Gates–MacGinitie Reading Tests. In Mitchell, J. (Ed.), *The ninth mental measurements yearbook.* Lincoln, NE: University of Nebraska Press.

Calkins, L. M. (1986). *The art of teaching writing.* Portsmouth, NH: Heinemann.

Caplan, G. (1970). *The theory and practice of mental health consultation.* New York: Basic Books.

Carbo, M. (1988). The evidence supporting reading style: A response to Stahl. *Phi Delta Kappan, 70,* 323–327.

Carnine, D., & Silbert, J. (1978). *Direct instruction reading.* Columbus, OH: Merrill.

Carr, T. H., Brown, T. L., Vavrus, L. G., & Evans, M. A. (1990). Cognitive skill maps and cognitive skill profiles: Componential Analysis of individual differences in children's reading efficiency. In T. H. Carr & B. A. Levy (Eds.). *Reading and its development.* New York: Academic Press.

Carroll, J. B. (1977). Developmental parameters in reading comprehension. In J. T. Guthrie (Ed.), *Cognition, curriculum, and comprehension.* Newark, DE: International Reading Association.

Carroll, J. B., Davies, P., & Richman, B. (1971). *Word frequency book.* New York: Houghton Mifflin.

Causey, O. S., & Eller, W. (1959). Starting and improving college reading programs. *Eighth Yearbook of the National Reading Conference,* Fort Worth, TX: Christian University Press.

Cazden, C. B. (1988). Interaction between Maori children and Pakeha teachers. Auckland, New Zealand: *Bulletin of the Auckland Reading Association.*

Chafe, W. (1985). Linguistic differences produced by differences between speaking and writing. In D. R. Olson, N. Torrance, & A. Hildyard (Eds.), *Literacy, language, and learning: The nature and consequences of reading and writing.* New York: Cambridge University Press.

Chall, J. S. (1967, 1983). *Learning to read: The great debate.* New York: McGraw Hill.

Chall, J. S. (1984). Readability and prose comprehension: Continuities and discontinuities. In J. Flood (Ed.), *Understanding reading comprehension.* Newark, DE: International Reading Association.

Chall, J. S., & Squire, J. R. (1991). The publishing industry and textbooks. In R. Barr, M. Kamil, P. Mosenthal, & D. Pearson (Eds.), *Handbook of reading research* (Vol. 2). New York: Longman.

Chomsky, N., & Halle, M. (1968). *The sound patterns of English.* New York: Harper & Row.

Cirilo, R. K., & Foss, D. J. (1980). Text structure and reading time for sentences. *Journal of Verbal Learning and Verbal Behavior, 19,* 96–109.

Clairborne, J. H. (1906). Types of congenital amblyopia. *Journal of American Medical Association, 47,* 1813–1816.

Clark, D. (1988). *Dyslexia: Theory & practice of remedial instruction.* Parkton, MD: York Press.

Clark, E. (1989). Review of Wide Range Achievement Test (Revised). In J. C Conoley & J. J. Kramer (Eds.), *The tenth mental measurements yearbook.* Lincoln, NE: University of Nebraska Press.

Clay, M. (1982). *Observing young readers.* Portsmouth, NH: Heinemann.

Cole, E., & Siegel, J. (1990). *Effective consultation in school psychology.* Toronto: Hoegfre & Huber.

Collier, R. M. (1983). Revision strategies. *College Composition and Communication, 5,* 149–155.

Conners, F. A., & Olson, R. (1990). Reading comprehension in dyslexic and normal readers: A component skills analysis. In D. A. Balota, G. B. Flores d'Arcais, & K. Rayner (Eds.), *Comprehension processes in reading.* Hillsdale, NJ: Erlbaum.

Conoley, J. C., & Conoley, C. W. (1982). *School consultation: A guide to practice and training.* New York: Pergamon.

Cooter, R. B. & Jaeger, R. (1989). Review of Woodcock Reading Mastery Tests (Revised). In J. L. Conoley & J. J. Kramer (Eds.), *The tenth mental measurements yearbook.* Lincoln, NE: University of Nebraska Press.

Cordoni, B. (1982). Services for college dyslexics. In R. N. Malatesha & P. G. Aaron (Eds.), *Reading disorders: Varieties and treatments*. New York: Academic Press.

Cortina, J., Elder, J., & Gonnet, K. (1989). *Comprehending college textbooks: Steps to understanding and remembering what you read*. New York: McGraw Hill.

Cossu, G., Shankweiler, D., Liberman, I. Y., Tola, G., & Katz, L. (1988). Awareness of phonological segments and reading ability in Italian children. *Applied Psychology, 9*, 1–16.

Costanzo, W. (1989). *The electronic text: Learning to write, read, and reason*. Englewood Cliffs, NJ: Educational Technology.

Cowan, H., & Jones, B. (1991). Software review: Reaching students with reading problems. *Electronic Learning, 11*(1), 36–38.

Crain, S. (1989). Why poor readers misunderstand spoken sentences. In D. Shankweiler & I. Y. Liberman (Eds.), *Phonology and reading disability: Solving the reading puzzle*. Ann Arbor, MI: University of Michigan Press.

Cronbach, L. J., & Snow, R. E. (1977). *Aptitudes and instructional methods*. New York: Irvington.

Curtis, M. E. (1980). Development of components of reading skill. *Journal of Educational Psychology, 72*(5), 656–669.

Curtis, M., & Zins, J. E. (1981). Consultative effectiveness as perceived by experts in consultation and classroom teachers. In M. Curtis & J. Zins (Eds.), *Theory and practice of school consultation*. Springfield, IL: Thomas.

Cutler, R., & Truss, C. (1989). Computer-aided instruction as a reading motivator. *Reading Improvement, 26*(2), 103–109.

Daiute, C. (1985). *Writing and computers*. Reading, MA: Addison–Wesley.

Dale, E., & Chall, J. (1948). *A formula for predicting readability*. Columbus, OH: Bureau of Educational Research, Ohio State University.

Daneman, M. (1991). Individual differences in reading skills. In R. Barr, M. Kamil, P. Mosenthal & D. Pearson (Eds.), *Handbook of reading research* (Vol. 2). New York: Longman.

Danks, J. (1980). Comprehension in listening and reading: Same or different? In J. Danks & K. Pezdek (Eds.), *Reading and understanding*. Newark, DE: International Reading Association.

Dearborn, W. F. (1925). The etiology of word-blindness. In E. Lord, L. Carmichael, & W. F. Dearborn (Eds.), *Special disabilities in learning to read and write*. Harvard Monographs in Education, Vol. 2, No. 1.

Deaton, F. K. (1975). A comparison of the effects of reinforcing accuracy and on-task responses in a programmed remedial program. *Dissertation Abstracts International, 35*, 6067–6968.

DeFries, J., Fulker, D., & LaBuda, C. (1987). Evidence for a genetic aetiology in reading disability of twins. *Nature, 329*, 537–539.

Dejerine, J. C. (1891). Sur un cas de cecite verbale avec agraphie, suivi d'autopsie. *Memoirs Societe Biologie, 3*, 197–201.

Dejerine, J. C. (1892). Des differentes varietes de cecite verbale. *Memoirs Societe Biologie, 4*, 1–30.

de Manrique, A. M., & Gramigna, S. (1984). La segmentacion fonologica y' silabica en ninos de preescolar y' primer grado. *Lect. y' Vida, 5*, 4–13.

Denckla, M., & Rudel, R. (1976). Rapid automatized naming: Dyslexia differentiated from other learning disabilities. *Neuropsychologia, 14*, 471–479.

Derry, S. J., & Murphy, D. (1986). Designing systems that train learning ability: From theory to practice. *Review of Educational Research, 56*, 1–39.

Dobrin, D. (1986). Style analyzers once more. *Computers and composition, 3*(3), 22–32.

Dougherty, A. M. (1990). *Consultation: Practice and perspectives*. Pacific Grove, CA: Brooks/Cole.

Drum, P. A. (1985). Review of Gates–McKillop–Horowitz Reading Diagnostic Tests. In J. V. Mitchell (Ed.), *The ninth mental measurements yearbook*. Lincoln, NE: University of Nebraska Press.

Duffy, F. H., Roehler, L., & Rackliffe, G. (1986). How teachers' instructional task influences students' understanding of lesson content. *Elementary School Journal, 87*, 3–16.

Duker, S. (1965). Listening and reading. *Elementary School Journal, 65*, 321–324.

Dunn, R. (1988). Teaching students through their perceptual strengths and preferences. *Journal of Reading, 31*, 304–309.

Durrell, D., & Catterson, J. (1980). *Durrell Analysis of Reading Ability*. San Antonio, TX: Psychological Corporation.

Durrell, D. D., & Hayes, M. (1969). *Durrell listening–reading series: Manual for listening and reading tests*. New York: Psychological Corporation.

Dykman, R. A., & Ackerman, P. A. (1991). Attention deficit disorder and specific reading disability: Separate but often overlapping disorders. *Journal of Learning Disabilities, 24*(2), 96–103.

Dykstra, R. (1974). Phonics and beginning reading instruction. In C. C. Walcutt, J. Lamport, & G. McCracken (Eds.), *Teaching reading: A phonic/linguistic approach to developmental reading*. New York: Macmillan.

Edwards, M., & Shriberg, L. D. (1983). *Phonology: Applications in communicative disorders*. San Diego, CA: College Hill Press.

Ehri, L. C., & Wilce, L. S. (1980). The influence of orthography on readers' conceptualization of the phonemic structure of words. *Applied Psycholinguistics, 1*, 371–385.

Ekwall, E. (1986). *Ekwall Reading Inventory* (2nd ed.). Boston, MA: Allyn & Bacon.

Elkonin, D. B. (1973). Reading in U. S. S. R. In J. Downing (Ed.), *Comparative reading*. New York: MacMillan.

Ellis, N., & Hennely, R. (1980). A bilingual word-length effect: Implications for intelligence testing and the relative ease of calculation in Welsh and English. *British Journal of Psychology, 71*, 43–51.

Englemann, S., & Bruner, E. C. (1983). *Reading mastery I and II: DISTAR reading*. Chicago, IL: Science Research Associates.

Fedner, M., Bianchi, A., & Duffey, J. (1979). Priorities of special education teachers regarding consultative strategies. *Psychological Reports, 44*, 1181–1182.

Fenichel, O. (1945). *The psychoanalytic theory of neurosis*. New York: Norton.

Fernald, G., & Keller, H. (1921). The effects of kinesthetic factors in development of word recognition in the case of nonreaders. *Journal of Educational Research, 4*, 357–377.

Fildes, L. G. (1922). A psychological inquiry into the nature of the condition known as congenital word-blindness. *Brain, 44*, 286–304.

Fisher, H. (1910). Congenital word-blindness. *Transactions of the Ophthalmological Society, 30*, 216–222.

Fisher, P. F., & Frankfurter, A. (1977). Normal and disabled readers can locate and identify letters. Where is the perceptual deficit? *Journal of Reading Behavior, 9*, 31–43.

Flesch, R. (1948). A new readability yardstick. *Journal of Applied Psychology, 32*, 221.

Flesch, R. (1955). *Why Johnny can't read*. New York: Harper & Row.

Fox, B., & Routh, D. (1980). Phonemic analysis and severe reading disability in children. *Journal of Psycholinguistic Research, 9*, 115–119.

Frederiksen, J. R. (1982). Componential models of reading and their interrelation. In R. J. Sternberg (Ed.), *Advances in the Psychology of Human Intelligence.* Hillsdale, NJ: Erlbaum.

Fries, C. C. (1963). *Linguistics and reading.* New York: Holt, Rinehart & Winston.

Frith, U. (1980). Unexpected spelling problems. In U. Frith (Ed.), *Cognitive processes in spelling.* London: Academic Press.

Frith, U. (1985). Beneath the surface of developmental dyslexia. In K. E. Patterson, J. C. Marshall, & M. Coltheart (Eds.), *Surface dyslexia.* London: Routledge & Kegan Paul.

Frith, U., & Snowling, M. (1983). Reading for meaning and reading for sound in autistic and dyslexic children. *British Journal of Developmental Psychology, 1,* 320–342.

Fry, E. (1968). A readability formula that saves time. *Journal of Reading, 11,* 513–516.

Fry, E. (1986). *Vocabulary drills.* Providence, RI: Jamestown.

Fry, E., Fountoukidis, C., & Polk, J. (1985). *The new reading teacher's book of lists.* Englewood Cliffs, NJ: Prentice Hall.

Funnell, E. (1983). Phonological processes in reading: New evidence from acquired dyslexia. *British Journal of Psychology, 74,* 159–180.

Garner, R. (1987). *Metacognition and reading comprehension.* Norwood, NJ: Ablex.

Garner, R., & Kraus, C. (1982). Good and poor comprehender differences in knowing and regulating reading behaviors. *Educational Research Quarterly, 6,* 5–12.

Gates, A. I. (1922). The psychology of reading and spelling with special reference to disability. *Teachers College Contributions to Education* (No. 129). New York: Columbia University.

Gates, A. I. (1929). *The improvement of reading.* New York: MacMillan.

Gates, A. I., McKillop, A. S., & Horowitz, E. C. (1981). *Gates–McKillop–Horowitz Reading Diagnostic Tests.* New York: Teachers College Press.

Geschwind, N. (1974). The alexias. In N. Geschwind (Ed.), *Selected papers on language and the brain.* Dordrecht, Netherlands: Reidel.

Geschwind, N., & Behan, P. (1982). Left-handedness: Association with immune disease, migraine, and developmental learning disorder. *Science, 79,* 5097–5100.

Geschwind, N., & Galaburda, A. (1985a). Cerebral lateralization, biological mechanisms, associations, and pathology: A hypothesis and a program of research. *Archives of Neurology, 42,* 428–459.

Geschwind, N., & Galaburda, A. (1985b). Cerebral lateralization, biological mechanisms, associations, and pathology: A hypothesis and a program of research. *Archives of Neurology, 42,* 521–552.

Geschwind, N., & Galaburda, A. (1985c). Cerebral lateralization, biological mechanisms, associations, and pathology: A hypothesis and a program of research. *Archives of Neurology, 42,* 634–654.

Gillingham, A., & Stillman, B. W. (1979). *Remedial training for children with specific disability in reading, spelling, and penmanship.* Cambridge, MA: Educators Publishing Service.

Gilmore, J. V., & Gilmore, E. C. (1968). *Gilmore Oral Reading Test.* San Antonio, TX: Psychological Corporation.

Gjessing, H. J., & Karlsen, B. (1989). *A longitudinal study of dyslexia.* New York: Springer–Verlag.

Glass, G. G., & Glass, E. W. (1976). *Glass analysis for decoding only: A Teachers Guide.* Garden City, NY: Easier to Learn.

Glavach, M., & Stoner, D. (1970). Breaking the failure pattern. *Journal of Learning Disabilities, 3,* 103–105.

Glushko, R. J. (1979). The organization and activation of orthographic knowledge in reading aloud. *Journal of Experimental Psychology: Human Perception and Performance, 5,* 674–691.

Goodman, K. (1986). *What's whole in whole language?* Portsmouth, NH: Heinemann.

Goody, J. (1968). *Literacy in traditional societies.* London: Cambridge University Press.

Goswami, U., & Bryant, P. (1990). *Phonological skills and learning to read.* Hove, E. Sussex, UK: Erlbaum.

Gough, P. (1981). A comment on Kenneth Goodman. In M. L. Kamil (Ed.), *Directions in reading: Research and instruction.* Washington, DC: National Reading Conference.

Gough, P., Alford, J., & Holley-Wilcox, P. (1981). Words and contexts. In O. Tzeng & H. Singer (Eds.), *Perception of print: Reading research in experimental psychology.* Hillsdale, NJ: Erlbaum.

Gough, P. B., & Tunmer, W. (1986). Decoding, reading, and reading disability. *Remedial and Special Education, 7*(1), 6–10.

Graves, D. H. (1983). *Writing: Teachers and children at work.* Portsmouth, NH:

Gray, C. T. (1922). *Deficiencies in reading ability: Their diagnosis and remedies.* Boston, MA: Heath.

Gray, W. S. (1922). Remedial cases in reading: Their diagnosis and treatment. *Educational Monographs Supplementary* (No. 221). Chicago, IL: University of Chicago Press.

Gutkin, T. B., & Curtis, M. J. (1990). School-based consultation: Theory, techniques, and research. In T. B. Gutkin and C. R. Reynolds (Eds.), *The handbook of school psychology.* New York: Wiley.

Hagen, D. (1984). *Microcomputer resource book for special education.* Reston, VA: Council for Exceptional Children.

Hall, M. (1978). *The language experience approach for teaching reading.* Newark, DE: International Reading Association.

Hammill, D. D. (1974). Assessing and training perceptual-motor processes. In D. D. Hammil & N. R. Bartell (Eds.). *Teaching children with learning and behavioral problems.* Boston, MA: Allyn & Bacon.

Hansen, J. (1987). *When writers read.* Portsmouth, NH: Heinemann.

Hansen, J., Himes, S., & Meier, S. (1990). *Consultation: Concepts and processes.* Englewood Cliffs, NJ: Prentice Hall.

Harris, A. J. (1975). Review of Gilmore Oral Reading Test. In O. K. Buros (Ed.), *The seventh mental measurements yearbook.* Highland Park, NJ: Gryphon Press.

Harris, A. J., & Sipay, E. R. (1975, 1980, 1985, & 1990). *How to increase reading ability.* New York: Longman.

Harris, J. (1987). *A writer's introduction to word processing.* Belmont, CA: Wadsworth.

Harrison, P. L. (1989). Review of Wide Range Achievement Test (Revised). In J. L. Conoley & J. J. Kramer (Eds.), *The tenth mental measurements yearbook.* Lincoln, NE: University of Nebraska Press.

Hauserman, N., & McIntire, R. (1969). Training elementary reading skills through reinforcement and fading techniques. *Proceedings of the 77th Annual Convention of the American Psychological Association,* Part 2, (4), 669–670.

Healy, J. (1982). The enigma of hyperlexia. *Reading Research Quarterly, 17,* 319–338.

Hebb, O. (1949). *The organization of behavior*. New York: Wiley.

Heimlich, J. E., & Pittelman, D. S. (1986). *Semantic mapping: Classroom applications*. Newark, DE: International Reading Association.

Heitzman, A. J. (1970). Effects of token reinforcement systems on reading and arithmetic skills of migrant primary school pupils. *Journal of Educational Research, 63*, 455–458.

Henderson, E. H. (1980). Word knowledge and reading disability. In E. H. Henderson & J. W. Beers (Eds.). *Developmental and Cognitive Aspects of Learning to Spell*. Newark, DE: International Reading Association.

Henderson, L. (1984). Writing systems and reading processes. In L. Henderson (Ed.). *Orthographies and reading*. Hillsdale, NJ: Lawrence Erlbaum.

Henry, M. (1990). *Words, Tutor I and Tutor II*, Los Gatos, CA: Lex Press.

Henry, M., & Redding, N. (1990). *Structured, sequential, multisensory lessons based on the Orton–Gillingham approach*. Los Gatos, CA: Lex Press.

Herman, P. A. (1988). Two approaches for helping poor readers become more strategic. *The Reading Teacher, 42*, 24–28.

Hickman, J. A. (1989). Review of Gray Oral Reading Tests (Revised). In J. L. Conoley & J. J. Kramer (Eds.), *The tenth mental measurements yearbook*. Lincoln, NE: University of Nebraska Press.

Hinshelwood, J. (1895). Word-blindness and visual memory. *The Lancet, 21*, 1564–1570.

Hinshelwood, J. (1907). Four cases of congenital word-blindness occurring in the same family. *The British Medical Journal, 2*, 1229–1231.

Hinshelwood, J. (1917). *Congenital word-blindness*. London: Lewis.

Howie, H. (1989). *Reading, writing, and computers: Planning for integration*. Needham Heights, MA: Allyn & Bacon.

Huey, E. (1908). *The psychology and pedagogy of reading*. New York: Macmillan. (Republished in 1968 by MIT Press, Cambridge, MA.)

Hughes, J. S. (1909). *Teaching to read*. New York: Barnes.

Hunt, E. (1986). The next word on verbal ability. In P. E. Vernon (Ed.), *Reaction time and intelligence*. New York: Ablex.

Hunt, E., Lunneborg, C., & Lewis, J. (1975). What does it mean to be high verbal? *Cognitive Psychology, 7*, 194–227.

Hynd, G., & Clikeman, M. S. (1989). Dyslexia and brain morphology. *Psychological Bulletin, 106*(3), 447–482.

Idol-Maestas, L., Nevin, A., & Paolucci-Whitcomb, P. (1984). *Facilitator's manual for collaborative consultation: Principles and techniques*. Reston, VA: National RETOOL Center, Council for Exceptional Children.

Idol-Maestas, L., Nevin, A., & Paolucci-Whitcomb, P. (1986). *Practices in Curriculum-based assessment*. Rockville, MD: Aspen Publishers.

Idol-Maestas, L., Whitcomb, P., & Nevin, A. (1987). *Collaborative consultation*. Austin, TX: Pro Ed.

Jacobs, J. E., & Paris, S. G. (1987). Children's metacognition about reading: Issues in definition, measurement, and instruction. *Educational Psychologist, 22*, 255–278.

Jackson, E. (1906). Developmental alexia (congenital word-blindness). *American Journal of Medical Science, 131*, 843–849.

Jackson, M. D., & McClelland, J. L. (1973). Visual factors in word perception. *Perception and Psychophysics, 14*, 365–370.

Jackson, M. D., & McClelland, J. L. (1979). Processing determinants of reading speed. *Journal of Experimental Psychology (General), 108*(2), 151–181.

Jaeger, R. M. (1989). Review of Woodcock Reading Mastery Tests (Revised). In

J. L. Conoley & J. J. Kramer (Eds.), *The tenth mental measurements yearbook.* Lincoln, NE: The University of Nebraska Press.

Jansky, J., & de Hirsch, K. (1972). *Preventing reading failure: Prediction, diagnosis, and intervention.* New York: Harper & Row.

Jason, L., & Ferone, L. (1978). Behavioral versus process consultation intervention in school settings. *American Journal of Community Psychology, 6,* 531–543.

Jason, L., Ferone, L., & Anderegg, T. (1979). Evaluating ecological, behavioral and process consultation interventions. *Journal of School Psychology, 17*(2), 104–115.

Jastak, S., & Wilkinson, G. (1984). *Wide Range Achievement Test (Revised).* Wilmington, DE: Jastak Assessment Systems.

Johns, J. L. (1988). *Basic reading inventory.* Dubuque, IA: Kendall Hunt.

Johnson, D., & Myklebust, M. (1967). *Learning disabilities.* New York: Grune & Stratton.

Johnson, D. E., & Pearson, P. D. (1984). *Teaching reading vocabulary.* New York: Holt, Rinehart, & Winston.

Johnston, P., & Allington, R. (1991). Remediation. In R. Barr, M. Kamil, P. Mosenthal, & D. Pearson (Eds.), *Handbook of reading research* (Vol. 2), New York: Longman.

Joshi, R. M., & Aaron, P. G. (1991). Developmental reading and spelling disabilities: Are these dissociable? In R. M. Joshi (Ed.), *Written language disorders.* Boston, MA: Kluwer Academics.

Just, M. A., & Carpenter, P. A. (1987). *The psychology of reading and language comprehension.* Boston, MA: Allyn & Bacon.

Karlsen, B., Madden, R., & Gardner, E. (1984). *Stanford Diagnostic Reading Test.* New York: Harcourt Brace Jovanovich.

Katz, R., Shankweiler, D., & Liberman, I. Y. (1981). Memory for item order and phonetic recoding in the beginning reader. *Journal of Experimental Child Psychology, 32,* 474–484.

Kavale, K. A., & Forness, S. R. (1987). Substance over style: Assessing the efficacy of modality testing and teaching. *Exceptional Children, 54,* 228–239.

Kaye, S. (1982). Psychoanalytic perspectives on learning disability. *Journal of Contemporary Psychotherapy, 13*(1), 83–93.

Kennedy, D. K. (1971). *Training with the Cloze procedure visually and auditorially to improve the reading and listening comprehension of third grade underachieving readers.* Unpublished doctoral dissertation, Penn State University, College Park, PA.

Keogh, B., & Donlon, G. M. (1972). Field dependence, impulsivity and learning disabilities. *Journal of Learning Disabilities, 5,* 531–536.

Kershner, J. R. (1977). Cerebral dominance in disabled readers, good readers, and gifted children: Search for a valid model. *Child Development, 48,* 61–78.

Kintsch, W. (1977). On comprehending stories. In M. A. Just & P. A. Carpenter (Eds.), *Cognitive processes in comprehension.* Hillsdale, NJ: Erlbaum.

Kintsch, W., & Kozminsky, E. (1977). Summarizing stories after reading and listening. *Journal of Educational Psychology, 69,* 491–499.

Kirby, E., & Grimley, L. (1986). *Understanding and treating attention deficit disorder.* New York: Pergamon Press.

Kirby, J. R., & Robinson, L. W. (1987). Simultaneous and successive processing in reading disabled children. *Journal of Learning Disabilities, 20*(4), 243–252.

Kitz, W. R., & Tarver, S. G. (1989). Comparison of dyslexic and nondyslexic adults on decoding and phonemic awareness tests. *Annals of Dyslexia, 35,* 196–205.

Kleiman, G. M. (1975). Speech recoding in reading. *Journal of Verbal Learning and Verbal Behavior, 14*, 323–339.

Klesius, J. P., Griffith, P. L., & Zielonks, P. (1991). A whole language and traditional instruction comparison: Overall effectiveness and development of the alphabetic principle. *Reading Research and Instruction, 30*, 47–61.

Kline, C., & Kline, C. (1978). Follow-up study of 216 dyslexic children. *Bulletin of the Orton Society, 25*, 127–144.

Kratochwill, T. R., Van Someren, K. R., & Sheridan, S. M. (1989). Training behavioral consultants: A competency-based model to teach interview skills. *Professional School Psychology, 4*(1), 41–58.

Ladd, E. M. (1970). More than scores from tests. *The Reading Teacher, 24*(4), 305–311.

Lehr, F. (1981). Integrating reading and writing instruction. *The Reading Teacher, 34*(8), 958–961.

Leong, C. K. (1987). *Children with specific reading disabilities.* The Netherlands: Swetz & Zeitlinger.

Leong, C. K. (1988). A componential approach to understanding reading and its difficulties in preadolescent readers. *Annals of Dyslexia, 38*, 95–119.

Levy, B. A., & Carr, T. H. (1990). Component process analysis: Conclusions and challenges. In T. H. Carr & B. A. Levy (Eds.), *Reading and its development: Component skills approaches.* New York: Academic Press.

Lewkowicz, N. (1980). Phonemic awareness training: What to teach and how to teach it. *Journal of Educational Psychology, 72*, 686–700.

Liberman, A. M. (1989). Reading is hard because listening is easy. In C. von Euler, I. Lundberg, & G. Lennerstrand (Eds.), *Brain and reading.* London: Macmillan.

Liberman, I. Y., Shankweiler, D., Fischer, F. W., & Carter, B. (1974). Explicit syllable and phoneme segmentation in young children. *Journal of Experimental Child Psychology, 18*, 201–212.

Liberman, I. Y., Liberman, A. M., Mattingly, I. G., and Shankweiler, D. (1980). Orthography and the beginning reader. In J. Kavanagh & R. Venezky (Eds.), *Orthography, reading, and dyslexia.* Baltimore, MD: University Park Press.

Liberman, I. Y., Mann, V., Shankweiler, D., & Werfelman, M. (1982). Children's memory for recurring linguistic and nonlinguistic material in relation to reading ability. *Cortex, 18*, 367–375.

Liberman, I. Y., Rubin, H., Duques, S., & Carlisle, J. (1985). Linguistic abilities and spelling proficiency in kindergartners and adult poor spellers. In J. Kavanagh & D. Gray (Eds.), *Biobehavioral measures of dyslexia.* Parkton, MD: York Press.

Liberman, I. Y., & Liberman, A. M. (1990). Whole language versus code emphasis: Underlying assumptions and their implications for reading instruction. *Annals of Dyslexia, 40*, 51–78.

Lord, E. E. (1925). The study and training of a child who was word-blind. In E. Lord, L. Carmichael, & W. Dearborn (Eds.), *Special disabilities in learning to read and write.* Harvard Monographs in Education, Vol. 2, Series 2, No. 1.

Lundberg, I. (1988). Lack of phonological awareness—A critical factor in developmental dyslexia. In C. von Euler, I. Lundberg, & G. Lennerstrand (Eds.), *Brain and reading.* London: Macmillan.

Lundberg, I., Olofsson, A., & Wall, S. (1980). Reading and spelling skills in first school years predicted from phonemic awareness skills in kindergarten. *Scandinavian Journal of Psychology, 21*, 159–173.

Lundberg, I., Frost, J., & Petersen, O. (1988). Effects of an extensive program for stimulating phonological awareness in preschool children. *Reading Research Quarterly, 23*(3), 263–284.

Lytton, W. W., & Brust, C. M. (1989). Direct dyslexia. *Brain, 112,* 583–594.

MacGinitie, W. H., & MacGinitie, R. K. (1989). *Gates–MacGinite Reading Tests.* Chicago, IL: Riverside.

Mann, V. A. (1986). Why some children encounter learning problems: The contribution of difficulties with language processing and phonological sophistication in early reading disability. In J. K. Torgesen & B. L. Young (Eds.), *Psychological and educational perspectives on learning disabilities.* Orlando, FL: Academic Press.

Markwardt, F. C. (1989). *Peabody Individual Achievement Test (Revised),* Circle Pines, MN: American Guidance Service.

Marshall, J. C., & Newcombe, F. (1966). Syntactic and semantic errors in paralexia. *Neuropsychologia, 4,* 169–176.

Marshall, J. C., & Newcombe, F. (1973). Patterns of paralexia. *Journal of Psycholinguistic Research, 2,* 179–199.

Marshall, J. C., & Newcombe, F. (1980). The conceptual status of deep dyslexia: An historical perspective. In M. Coltheart, K. Patterson, & J. C. Marshall (Eds.), *Deep dyslexia.* London: Routledge & Kegan Paul.

Marshall, N., & Glock, M. D. (1978). Comprehension of connected discourse. A study into the relationship between the structure of text and information recalled. *Reading Research Quarterly, 14,* 10–56.

Marslen-Wilson, W. (1989). Access and integration: Projecting sound onto meaning. In W. Marslen-Wilson (Ed.), *Lexical presentation and process.* Cambridge, MA: MIT Press.

Martin, R. & Meyers, J. (1980). School psychologists and the practice of consultation. *Psychology in the schools, 17*(4), 478–484.

Marzano, R. J., & Marzano, J. S. (1988). *A cluster approach to elementary vocabulary instruction.* Newark, DE: International Reading Association.

Mattis, S., French, J. H., & Rapin, I. (1975). Dyslexia in children and young adults: Three independent neuropsychological syndromes. *Developmental Medicine and Child Neurology, 17,* 150–163.

McConkie, G. W., & Zola, D. (1987). Two examples of computer-based research on reading: Eye movement monitoring and computer-aided reading. In D. Reinking (Ed.), *Reading and computers: Issues for theory and practice.* New York: Teachers College Press.

McCracken, R. A. (1971). Initiating sustained silent reading. *Journal of Reading, 14,* 521–522.

Meacham, M. L., & Peckham, P. D. (1978). School psychologists at three quarters century: Congruence between training, practice, and preferred role. *Journal of School Psychology, 16,* 195–206.

Medway, F. J. (1979). How effective is school consultation: A review of recent research. *Journal of School Psychology, 17,* 275–282.

Memory, D., & Moore, D. (1981). Selecting sources in library research: An activity in skimming and critical reading. *Journal of Reading, 24,* 469–474.

Memory, D. (1983). Main idea prequestions as adjunct aid with good and low-average middle grade readers. *Journal of Reading Behavior, 15*(2), 37–48.

Memory, D. (1986). Guiding students to independent decoding in content area classes. In E. Dishner, W. Bean, J. Readence, & D. Moore (Eds.), *Reading in the content areas* (2nd ed.). Dubuque, IA: Kendall Hunt.

Messic, S. (1976). *Individuality in learning.* San Francisco, CA: Jossey Bass.

Meyer, L. A. (1984). Long-term academic effects on the direct instruction project follow through. *Elementary School Journal, 84,* 380–394.

Meyer, L. A., Gersten, R. M., & Gutkin, J. (1983). Direct instruction: A project follow through success story in an inner-city school. *Elementary School Journal, 84,* 241–252.

Meyers, J. (1975). Consultee-centered consultation with a teaching technique in behavioral management. *American Journal of Community Psychology, 3*(2), 111–121.

Meyers, J. (1981). Mental health consultation. In J. C. Conoley (Ed.), *Consultation in schools: Theory, research and procedures.* New York: Academic Press.

Miller, G. R., & Coleman, E. B. (1967). A set of thirty-six passages calibrated for complexity. *Journal of Verbal Learning and Verbal Behavior, 6,* 851–854.

Mitchell, D. C. (1982). *The process of reading.* New York: Wiley.

Mitford, M. (1966). *Teaching to read: Historically considered.* Chicago, IL: University of Chicago Press.

Monroe, M. (1932). *Children who cannot read.* Chicago: University of Chicago Press.

Morgan, W. P. (1896). A case of congenital word-blindness. *British Medical Journal, 2,* 1368.

Morton, J., & Patterson, K. (1980). A new attempt at an interpretation and an attempt at a new interpretation. In M. Coltheart, K. Patterson, & J. C. Marshall (Eds.), *Deep dyslexia.* London: Routledge & Kegan Paul.

Murphy, R. T., & Appel, L. B. (1984). *Evaluation of the Writing to read instructional system 1982–1984: A presentation from the second year report.* Princeton, NJ: Educational Testing Service.

Murphy, C. C., & Bruning, R. H. (1989). Review of the Burns–Roe Informal Reading Inventory: Preprimer to twelfth grade. In J. L. Conoley & J. J. Kramer (Eds.), *The tenth mental measurements yearbook,* Lincoln, NE: University of Nebraska Press.

Nagy, W. E., & Anderson, R. C. (1984). How many words are there in the printed school English? *Reading Research Quarterly, 19,* 304–330.

Nessel, D. D., & Jones, M. (1981). *The language experience approach to reading.* New York: Teachers College Press.

Newman, A. P. (1980). *Adult basic education.* Boston, MA: Allyn & Bacon.

Newman, J. M., & Church, S. M. (1990). Myths of whole language. *The Reading Teacher, 44*(1), 20–26.

Nist, S. L., & Kirby, K. (1986). Teaching comprehension and study strategies through modeling and thinking aloud. *Reading Research and Instruction, 25,* 254–264.

Norris, J. A. (1989). Review of Classroom Reading Inventory (4th ed.). In J. L. Conoley & J. J. Kramer (Eds.), *The tenth mental measurements yearbook,* Lincoln, NE: University of Nebraska Press.

Oakhill, J., & Garnham, A. (1988). *Becoming a skilled reader.* Oxford: Blackwell.

Olson, R. K., & Wise, B. (1992). Reading on the computer with orthographic and speech feedback: An overview of the Colorado Remediation Project. *Reading and Writing, 4* (in press).

Olson, R. K., Wise, B. W., & Rack, J. P. (1989a). Dyslexia: Deficits, genetic etiology, and computer-based remediation. *The Irish Journal of Psychology 10*(4), 494–508.

Olson, R. K., Wise, B. W., Conners, F. A., Rack, J. P., & Fulker, D. (1989b). Specific deficits in component reading and language skills: Genetic and environmental influences. *Journal of Learning Disabilities, 22,* 339–348.

Olson, R. K., & Wise, B. (1987). Computer speech in reading instruction. In D. Reinking (Ed.). *Computers and reading: Issues for theory and practice.* New York: Teachers College Press.

Orton, S. (1925). Word-blindness in school children. *Archives of Neurological Psychiatry, 14*, 518–615.

Orton, S. (1937). *Reading, writing, and speech problems in children.* New York: Norton.

Palincsar, A. S. (1986). Metacognitive strategy instruction. *Exceptional Children, 53*(2), 118–124.

Palmer, J., McCleod, C., Hunt, E., & Davidson, J. (1985). Information processing correlates of reading. *Journal of Memory and Language, 24,* 59–88.

Paris, S. G., & Myers, M. (1981). Comprehension monitoring, memory, and study strategies of good and poor readers. *Journal of Reading Behavior, 13,* 5–22.

Paris, S. G., Cross, D. R., & Lipson, M. Y. (1984). Informed strategies for learning: A program to improve children's reading awareness and comprehension. *Journal of Educational Psychology, 76,* 1239–1252.

Paris, S. G., McCleod, C. M., Hunt, E., & Davidson, J. (1985). Comprehension monitoring, memory, and study strategies of good and poor readers. *Journal of Reading Behavior, 13,* 5–22.

Patterson, K. E., Marshall, J. C., & Coltheart, M. (1985). *Surface dyslexia.* Hillsdale, NJ: Erlbaum.

Patterson, K. E., & Coltheart, M. (1987). Phonological process in reading: A tutorial review. In M. Coltheart (Ed.), *Attention and performance: The psychology of reading* (Vol. 12). Hillsdale, NJ: Erlbaum.

Pauk, W. (1986). *Six-way paragraphs.* Providence, RI: Jamestown.

Pearson, D. (1984). A context for instructional research on reading comprehension. In J. Flood (Ed.), *Promoting reading comprehension.* Newark, DE: International Reading Association.

Pearson, P. D., & Herman, P. (1985). Review of Gates–McKillop–Horowitz Reading Diagnostic Test. In J. V. Mitchell (Ed.), *The ninth mental measurements yearbook.* Lincoln, NE: University of Nebraska Press.

Pelosi, P. L. (1977). The roots of reading diagnosis. In H. A. Robinson (Ed.), *Reading and writing instruction in the United States: Historical trends.* Newark, DE: International Reading Association.

Pennington, B. F. (1990). The genetics of dyslexia. *Journal of Child Psychology and Psychiatry, 31*(2), 193–201.

Pennington, B. F., Lefly, D., Van Orden, G., Bookman, M., & Smith, S. (1987). Is phonology bypassed in normal or dyslexic development? *Annals of Dyslexia, 37,* 62–89.

Pennington, B. F., & Smith, S. D. (1988). Genetic influences on learning disabilities: An update. *Journal of Consulting and Clinical Psychology, 56,* 817–826.

Perfetti, C. A. (1985). *Reading ability.* New York: Oxford University Press.

Perfetti, C. A. (1991). The psychology, pedagogy, and politics of reading. *Psychological Science, 2*(2), 70–76.

Perfetti, C. A., Finger, E., & Hogaboam, T. W. (1978). Sources of vocalization latency differences between skilled and less skilled young readers. *Journal of Educational Psychology, 70*(5), 730–739.

Petrauskas, R. S., & Rourke, B. (1979). Identification of subtypes of retarded readers: A neuropsychological multivariate approach. *Journal of Clinical Neuropsychology, 1,* 17–37.

Phillips, B. (1990). *School psychology at a turning point: Ensuring a bright future for the profession.* San Francisco: Jossey Bass.

Phillips, S., Taylor, B., & Aaron, P. G. (1985). *Developmental dyslexia: Subtypes or substages?* Paper presented at the *annual convention, Indiana Psychological Association,* Indianapolis, IN.

Pichert, J., & Anderson, R. C. (1977). Taking different perspectives on a story. *Journal of Educational Psychology, 69,* 309–315.

Piersal, W. C., & Gutkin, T. B. (1983). Resistance to school-based consultation: A behavioral analysis of the problem. *Psychology in the Schools, 20,* 311–320.

Pikulski, J. J. (1971). Candy, word recognition, and the disadvantaged. *The Reading Teacher, 25,* 246–247.

Pipes, R. B. (1981). Consulting in organizations: The entry problem. In J. C. Conoley (Ed.), *Consultation in schools: Theory, research, and procedures.* New York: Academic Press.

Pollard, R. S. (1889). *Pollard's synthetic method: A complete manual.* Chicago, IL: Western.

Poostay, E. J., & Aaron, I. E. (1982). Reading problems of children: The perspectives of reading specialists. *School Psychology Review, 11*(3), 251–255.

Raygor, A. (1977). The Raygor Readability Estimate: A quick and easy way to determine difficulty. In P. D. Pearson & J. Hansen (Eds.), *Reading: Theory, research, and practice.* Clemson, SC: National Reading Conference.

Rayner, K., & Bertera, J. H. (1979). Reading without a fovea. *Science, 206,* 468–469.

Rayner, K., & Pollatsek, A. (1989). *The psychology of reading.* Englewood Cliffs, NJ: Prentice Hall.

Reinking, D., & Rickmans, S. (1990). The effects of computer-mediated text on the vocabulary learning and comprehension of intermediate-grade readers. *Journal of Reading Behavior, 22*(4), 395–408.

Reinking, D., & Brickwell-Bowles, L. (1991). Computers in reading and writing. In R. Barr, M. Kamil, P. Mosenthal, & D. Pearson (Eds.), *Handbook of reading research* (Vol. 2). New York: Longman.

Reynolds, C. R., Gutkin, T., Elliott, S., & Witt, J. (1984). *School Psychology: Essentials of theory and practice.* New York: Wiley.

Rice, J. M. (1897). The futility of spelling grind. *The Forum, 23* April, 163–172; June, 409–419.

Richardson, S. O. (Spring, 1989). Response to CBS *60 minutes* issues. *Newsletter,* Indiana Branch of the American Council of Learning Disabilities.

Robinson, A., Faraone, V., Hittleman, D., & Unruh, E. (1990). *Reading comprehension instruction, 1783–1987.* Newark, DE: International Reading Association.

Rohl, M., & Tunmer, W. (1988). Phonemic segmentation skill and spelling acquisition. *Applied Psycholinguistics, 9,* 335–350.

Rosenfield, S. A. (1987). *Instructional consultation.* Hillsdale, NJ: Erlbaum.

Royer, J. M., Kulhavy, R. W., Lee, J. B., & Peterson, S. E. (1986). The sentence verification technique as a measure of listening comprehension. *Educational and Psychological Research, 6,* 299–313.

Rozin, P., & Gleitman, L. R. (1977). The structure and acquisition of reading: The reading process and the acquisition of the alphabetic principle. In A. S. Reber & D. L. Scarborough (Eds.), *Toward a psychology of reading.* Hillsdale, NJ: Erlbaum.

Rude, R. T. (1986). *Teaching reading using microcomputers.* Englewood Cliffs, NJ: Prentice Hall.

Rudel, R. G. (1985). The definition of dyslexia: Language and motor defects. In F. H. Duffy & N. Geschwind (Eds.), *Dyslexia: A neuroscientific approach to clinical evaluation.* Boston, MA: Little Brown.

Runyon, K. (1991). The effect of extra time on reading comprehension scores for university students with and without learning disabilities. *Journal of Learning Disabilities, 24*(2), 104–108.

Rupley, W. H. (1985). Review of Gates–MacGinitie Reading Tests. In J. V. Mitchell (Ed.), *The ninth mental measurements yearbook.* Lincoln, NE: University of Nebraska Press.

Salvia, J., & Ysseldyke, J. E. (1991). *Assessment* (5th ed.). Boston, MA: Houghton Mifflin.

Sandoval, J. (1988). The school-psychologist in higher education. *School Psychology Review, 17*(3), 391–396.

Sanford, A. J., & Garrod, S. C. (1981). *Understanding written language: Explorations in comprehension beyond the sentence.* New York: Wiley.

Scheiber, B., & Talpers, J. (1987). *Unlocking potential: College and other choices for learning disabled people.* Bethesda, MD: Adler & Adler.

Schein, E. H. (1978). The role of the consultant: Content, expert, or process facilitator. *Personnel and Guidance Journal, 56,* 22–27.

Schmitt, C. (1918). Developmental alexia: Congenital word-blindness or inability to read. *Elementary School Journal, 18,* 680–700.

Schwartz, H. (1985). *Interactive writing: Composing with a word processor.* New York: Holt, Rinehart & Winston.

Scott, C. M. (1989). Problem writer: Nature, assessment, and intervention. In A. G. Kamhi & H. W. Cats (Eds.), *Reading disabilities.* Boston, MA: Little Brown.

Seidenberg, M. S. (1990). Lexical access: Another theoretical soupstone? In D. A. Balota, G. B. Flores d'Arcais, & K. Rayner (Eds.), *Comprehension processes in reading.* Hillsdale, NJ: Erlbaum.

Seidenberg, M. S., & Tanenhaus, M. K. (1979). Orthographic effects on rhyme monitoring. *Journal of Experimental Psychology: Human Learning and Memory 5*(6), 546–554.

Seidenberg, M. S., & McClelland, J. L. (1989). A distributed, developmental model of visual word recognition and naming. *Psychological Review, 96,* 523–568.

Shankweiler, D., & Liberman, I. Y. (1989). *Phonology and reading disability.* Ann Arbor, MI: University of Michigan Press.

Shapiro, E. S. (1989). Review of the Burns–Roe Informal Reading Inventory: Preprimer to twelfth grade (2nd ed.). In J. L. Conoley & J. J. Kramer (Eds.), *The tenth mental measurements yearbook.* Lincoln, NE: University of Nebraska Press.

Shepherd, M. J., & Marmalejo, A. (1991). *Vocabulary instruction and reading disabilities.* Paper presented at the NATO Advanced Study Institute, Bonas, France.

Shinn, M. (1989). *Curriculum-based measurement: Assessing special children.* New York: Guilford.

Siegel, L. S. (1989). IQ is irrelevant to the definition of learning disabilities. *Journal of Learning Disabilities, 22*(8), 469–479.

Siegel, E., & Cole, E. (1990). Role expansion for school psychologists: Challenges and future directions. In E. Cole & J. Siegel (Eds.), *Effective consultation in school psychology.* Toronto: Hoegrefe & Huber.

Silberberg, N., & Silberberg, M. (1967). Hyperlexia: Specific word recognition skills in young children. *Exceptional Children, 34,* 41–42.

Silver, A. A., & Hagin, R. (1960). Specific reading disability: Delineation of the syndrome and relationship to cerebral dominance. *Comparative Psychiatry, 1*(2), 126–134.

Silvaroli, N. J. (1986). *Classroom Reading Inventory* (4th ed.). Boston, MA: Allyn & Bacon.

Singer, E., & Pittman, M. (1968). A Sullivan approach to the problem of reading disability: Theoretical considerations and empirical data. In G. Natchez (Ed.), *Children with reading problems.* New York: Basic Books.

Slingerland, B. (1974). *Screening tests for identifying children with specific language disabilities.* Cambridge, MA: Educators Publishing Service.

Slingerland, B. (1977). *A multi-sensory approach to language arts for specific language disability children.* Cambridge, MA: Educators Publishing Service.

Slossan, R. L. (1981). *Slossan Oral Reading Test.* Circle Pines, MN: American Guidance Services. (Revised in 1990)

Smith, D. K., & Lyon, M. A. (1985). Consultation in school psychology: Changes from 1981–1984. *Psychology in the Schools, 22,* 404–409.

Smith, F. (1979). *Understanding reading.* Hillsdale, NJ: Erlbaum.

Smith, K. J. (1975). Review of Gilmore Oral Reading Test. In O.K. Buros (Ed.), *The seventh mental measurements yearbook.* Highland Park, NJ: Gryphon Press.

Smith, N. B. (1965, 1986). *American reading instruction.* Newark, DE: International Reading Association.

Smith, S. L. (1989). The masks students wear. *Instructor, 98*(8), 27–32.

Sotiriou, P. (1989). *Integrating college study skills: Reasoning in reading, listening, and writing.* Belmont CA: Wadsworth.

Spache, G. D. (1974). The Spache readability formula. In G. D. Spache (Ed.), *Good reading for poor readers.* Champaign, IL: Garrard.

Spache, G. D. (1981). *Diagnostic Reading Scales.* Monterey, CA: CTB/McGraw Hill.

Spalding, R. B., & Spalding, W. T. (1986). *The writing road to reading.* New York: Morrow.

Sperling, G. (1960). The information available in brief visual presentations. *Psychological Monographs, 74,* No. 498.

Spillich, G., Vesonder, G., Chiesi, H., & Voss, J. (1979). Text processing of domain-related information for individuals with high and low domain knowledge. *Journal of Verbal Learning and Verbal Behavior, 18,* 275–290.

Spring, C., & French, L. (1991). Identifying children with specific reading disabilities from listening and reading discrepancy scores. *Journal of Learning Disabilities, 23*(1), 53–58.

Stahl, S. (1988). Is there evidence to support matching reading styles and remedial reading methods? *Phi Delta Kappan, 70,* 317–322.

Stahl, S., & Fairbanks, M. (1986). The effects of vocabulary instruction: A model-based meta-analysis. *Review of Educational Research, 56,* 72–110.

Stahl, S., & Miller, P. (1989). Whole language and language experience approaches for beginning reading: A quantitative research synthesis. *Review of Educational Research, 59*(1), 87–116.

Stanovich, K. (1980). Toward an interactive-compensatory model of individual differences in the development of reading fluency. *Reading Research Quarterly, 16,* 32–71.

Stanovich, K. (1985). Explaining the variance in reading ability in terms of psychological processes: What have we learned? *Annals of Dyslexia, 35,* 67–96.

Stanovich, K. (1986). Matthew effects in reading: Some consequences of individual differences in the acquisition of literacy. *Reading Research Quarterly, 21,* 360–407.

Stanovich, K. (1991). Word recognition: Changing perspectives. In R. Barr, M. L. Kamil, P. Mosenthal, & D. Pearson (Eds.), *Handbook of reading research.* New York: Longman.

Stanovich, K., Cunningham, A., & Cramer, B. (1984). Assessing phonological awareness in kindergarten children: Issues of task comparability. *Journal of Experimental Child Psychology, 38,* 175–190.

Stanovich, K., Cunningham, A. E., & Feeman, D. J. (1984). Intelligence, cognitive skills, and early reading progress. *Reading Research Quarterly, 38,* 175–190.

Stanovich, K., & West, R. F. (1989). Exposure to print and orthographic processing. *Reading Research Quarterly, 24,* 402–433.

Stauffer, G. R. (1980). *Language experience approach to the teaching of reading.* New York: Harper & Row.

Stephenson, S. (1907). Six cases of congenital word-blindness affecting three generations of one family. *The Ophthalmoscope, 5,* 482–484.

Stern, C., & Gould, T. (1965). *Children discover reading.* New York: Random House.

Sternberg, R. J. (1985). *Beyond IQ: A triarchic theory of human intelligence.* New York: Cambridge University Press.

Stevens, R. J. (1987). Cooperative, integrated reading and composition: Two field experiments. *Reading Research Quarterly, 22,* 433–454.

Sticht, T. G. (1979). Applications of the "audread" model to reading evaluation and instruction. In L. B. Resnick & P. Weaver, (Eds.), *Theory and practice of early reading.* Hillsdale, NJ: Erlbaum.

Sticht, T. G., & James, J. H. (1984). Listening and reading in D. Pearson (Ed.), *Handbook of reading research* (Vol. 1), New York: Longman.

Stotsky, S. (1983). Research on reading–writing relationship: A synthesis and suggested directions. *Language Arts, 60*(5), 627–642.

Strickland, D. S., Feeley, J. T., & Wepner, S. B. (1987). *Using computers in the teaching of reading.* New York: Teachers College Press.

Szelezulski, P. A., & Manis, F. R. (1990). An examination of familial resemblance among subgroups of dyslexics. *Annals of Dyslexia, 40,* 180–191.

Taft, M. (1979). Lexical access via an orthographic code: The Basic Orthographic Syllabic Structure (BOSS). *Journal of Verbal Learning and Verbal Behavior, 18,* 21–39.

Tanner, N. (1988). Phonics. In J. E. Alexander (Ed.), *Teaching reading.* Glenview IL: Scott Foresman.

Thomas, C. J. (1905). Congenital word-blindness and its treatment. *Ophthalmoscope, 3,* 380–385.

Thorndike, E. L. (1910). *Handwriting Scale.* Teachers College Press.

Thorndike, E. L. (1921). *The teacher's word book.* Teachers College Press.

Thorndike, R. L. (1973). *Reading comprehension education in fifteen countries: An empirical study.* New York: Wiley.

Tierney, R. J. (1989). Review of the Gray Oral Reading Tests. In J. L. Conoley & J. J. Kramer (Eds.), *The tenth mental measurements yearbook,* Lincoln, NE: University of Nebraska Press.

Trabasso, T. (1981). Can we integrate research and instruction on reading comprehension? In C. M. Santa & B. L. Hayes (Ed.), *Children's prose comprehension.* Newark, DE: International Reading Association.

Treiman, R., & Chafetz, J. (1987). Are there onset and rime-like units in printed words? In M. Coltheart (Ed.), *The psychology of reading.* Hillsdale, NJ: Erlbaum.

Uhl, W. L. (1916). The use of the results of reading tests as bases for planning remedial work. *Elementary School Journal, 17,* 266–275.

Van den Bos, K. (1989). Relationship between cognitive development, decoding skill, and reading comprehension in learning-disabled Dutch children. In P. G. Aaron & R. M. Joshi, (Eds.), *Reading and writing disorders in different orthographic systems.* Boston, MA: Kluwer Academics.

Van Orden, G. C. (1987). A rows is a rose: Spelling, sound, and reading. *Memory and Cognition, 15*(3), 181–198.

Vellutino, F. R. (1979). Dyslexia: *Theory and research.* Cambridge, MA: MIT Press.

Venezky, R. (1976). *Theoretical and experimental base for teaching reading.* The Hague: Mouton.

Venezky, R. (1980). From Webster to Rice to Roosevelt: The formative years for spelling instruction and spelling reform in the U.S.A. In U. Frith (Ed.), *Cognitive processes in spelling.* London: Academic Press.

Vinsonhaler, J. F., Weinshank, A. B., Wagner, C. C., & Polin, R. M. (1987). Computers, simulated cases, and the training of reading diagnosticians. In D. Reinking (Ed.), *Reading and computers.* New York: Teachers College Press.

Walberg, H., & Tsai, S. (1983). Matthew effects in education. *American Educational Research Journal, 20,* 359–373.

Walcutt, C. C., & McCracken (1981). *Lippincott Basic Reading.* Philadelphia, PA: Lippincott, Division of Harper & Row.

Wallace, G. (1981). Teaching reading. In J. M. Kaufman & P. D. Hallahan (Eds.), *Handbook of special education.* Englewood Cliffs, NJ: Prentice Hall.

Wallin, J. E. (1920). Congenital word-blindness: Some analyses of cases. *The Training School Bulletin, 71,* 37–47.

Waterman, D. (1991). Whole language: Why not? *Contemporary Education, LXII*(2), 115–119.

Watson, D. J. (1989). Defining and describing whole language. *The Elementary School Journal, 90,* 129–141.

Weaver, C. A., & Kintsch, W. (1991). Expository text. In R. Barr, M. Kamil, P. Mosenthal, & D. Pearson (Eds.), *Handbook of reading research* (Vol. 2). New York: Longman.

Whalen, C., Henker, B., & Hinshaw, S. (1985). Cognitive behavioral therapies for hyperactive children: Premises, problems, and prospects. *Journal of Abnormal Child Psychology, 13*(3), 391–410.

Wiederholt, L., & Bryant, B. (1986). *Gray Oral Reading Test (Revised).* Austin, TX: Pro-Ed.

Wigfield, A., & Asher, S. (1984). Social and motivational influences on reading. In P. D. Pearson (Ed.), *Handbook of reading research* (Vol. 1). New York: Longman.

Wijk, A. (1966). *Rules of pronunciation for the English language: An account of the relationship between English spelling and pronunciation.* London: Oxford University Press.

Williams, F., & Williams, J. (1985). *Success with educational software.* New York: Praeger.

Williams, J. P. (1980). Teaching decoding with an emphasis on phoneme analysis and phoneme blending. *Journal of Educational Psychology, 72,* 1–15.

Williams, J. P. (1986). Teaching children to identify the main idea of expository texts. *Exceptional Children, 53*(2), 163–168.

Willig, A. C., Harnnisch, D. L., Hill, K., & Maehr, M. L. (1983). Sociocultural and educational correlates of success–failure attributions and evaluation anxiety in the school setting for black, hispanic, and anglo children. *American Educational Research Journal, 20*(3), 385–410.

Wilson, R. G., & Rudolph, M. (1986). *Merrill Linguistic Reading Program.* Columbus OH: Charles Merrill Pub Co.,

Wise, B., & Olson, R. (1992). How poor readers and spellers use interactive speech in a computerized spelling program. *Reading and Writing, 4* (in press).

Wijk, A. (1966). *Rules of pronunciation for the English language: An account of the relationship between English spelling and pronunciation.* London: Oxford University Press.

Witelson, S. (1977). Developmental dyslexia: Two right hemispheres and none left? *Science, 195,* 309–311.

Witelson, S. (1977). Developmental dyslexia: Two right hemispheres and none left? *Science, 195,* 309–311.

Witt, J. C., & Elliott, S. N. (1983). Assessment in behavioral consultation: The initial interview. *School Psychology Review, 12,* 42–49.

Wood, T. A., Buckhalt, J. A., & Tomlin, J. G. (1988). A comparison of listening and reading performance with children in three educational placements. *Journal of Learning Disabilities, 8,* 493–496.

Woodcock, R. W. (1987). *Woodcock Reading Mastery Tests* (rev. ed.). Circle Pines, MN: American Guidance Service.

Woods, M. L., & Moe, A. J. (1989). *Analytical Reading Inventory.* Columbus, OH: Merrill.

Ysseldyke, J. E., Algozzine, B., Shinn, M. R., & McGue, M. (1982). Similarities and differences between low achievers and students labeled as learning disabled. *Journal of Special Education, 16,* 73–85.

Zhang, G., & Simon, H. A. (1985). STM capacity for Chinese words and idioms: Chunking and acoustical loop hypothesis. *Memory and Cognition, 13,* 193–201.

Zola, D. (1984). Redundancy and word perception during reading. *Perception and Psychophysics, 36*(3), 277–284.

Index of Names

Subject Index

279